Midnight Assassinations and Other Evildoings

A Criminal History of Jasper County, Missouri

By

Larry E. Wood

Hickory Press
Joplin, Missouri

ISBN: 9781733471404

Library of Congress Control Number: 2019913102

Published by
    Hickory Press
    Joplin, MO

Table of Contents

Preface

Although the subtitle of this book is *A Criminal History of Jasper County*, I do not represent it to be a comprehensive history of crime in the county. The main title, *Midnight Assassinations and Other Evildoings*, is more indicative of the book's purpose: to chronicle a selected number of the more notorious incidents in Jasper County's history.

Some readers might wonder why certain episodes were included and other ones were omitted. I did have a few criteria in mind in deciding whether or not to include a particular incident in the book. To qualify as "notorious," an incident usually had to involve a heinous crime such as murder or rape. Any crime that resulted in a lynching or an execution was automatically selected for inclusion in the book. A crime was more likely to be included if it involved multiple victims. A crime with some element of intrigue, such as a love triangle, was more likely to be included than a spontaneous act of violence, like a barroom brawl.

Generally speaking, I excluded crimes during which no one got hurt. However, I did include a few such misadventures based solely on the notorious reputations of the criminals. For instance, I've chronicled Roy "Arkansas Tom" Daugherty's infamous escapades in Jasper County, even though he never killed or seriously injured anybody in the county.

In summary, the more notorious the crime or the criminal, the more likely the episode was to be included in the book. The other main criterion for inclusion was the time period in which an incident happened. Readers will notice that most of the events chronicled in this book happened a long time ago. Although I've included a few crimes that occurred within the past sixty years or so, those that happened before I was an adult were more likely to be included than recent ones for the simple reason that they seem more like history to me than those I can well recall.

Acknowledgements

Modern technology has made historical research a lot more convenient than it used to be. For one thing, it has greatly decreased the amount of travel one has to do, because a person can now access many historical databases online that were not available just a few years ago. So, I did a lot of the research for this book at home in front of my computer. There are still some things that have to be done the old-fashioned way, though, and I owe a debt of gratitude to several people for facilitating the tasks I could not or did not do online.

As with most of my previous projects, the Joplin Public Library served as the home base for my traditional research, and I want to thank the Reference Department, especially Jason Sullivan and Patty Crane, for fulfilling my numerous requests for interlibrary loans. The Local History Department was quite helpful as well during my several visits to that section of the library; I particularly want to mention Richard Porter. Also, Lydia Humphreys and Jill Sullivan of the Maker Space section of the Joplin Public Library were a big help with the cover design.

Benjamin Young guided my research at the Local History Department of the Carthage Public Library, and he also scanned and sent an image to me that I used in the book.

I thank the Local History Department of the Webb City Public Library and, in particular, Marilyn Clark, for help in procuring and providing a photo of Coyne Hatten.

I acquired the illustrations for this book from a number of sources, but I want to particularly thank the Missouri State Archives, which provided a large number of mug shots.

Chapter 1

An Awful Spectacle
The Burning of Two Slaves in Carthage

Perhaps the most atrocious incident ever in Jasper County is one many people may never have heard about, because it happened so early in the county history that few newspaper accounts or other contemporaneous records about it survive. What we know for sure, however, is that two slaves were burned at the stake in the streets of Carthage in July 1853 for the alleged triple crime of rape, murder, and arson.

About the first of July 1853, a slave named Colley belonging to area farmer John Dale met a runaway slave named Bart in Carthage. The two black men knew each other because both had been purchased earlier in the year from Cherokee Indians, and Colley asked a drastic favor of his old acquaintance. He wanted Bart to help him kill John Fisk, a local doctor. Colley, according to his later confession, held a grudge against Fisk because the doctor had recently scolded him on two separate occasions while visiting Dale's place a few miles south of Carthage. The first time, Fisk got mad because Colley didn't catch a horse quickly enough to suit him and told the slave he was so slow Fisk might as well have done it himself. The next time, Dr. Fisk again scolded Colley for not moving fast enough and told him he was "good for nothing." As an additional incentive for his proposed crime, Colley thought Dr. Fisk had a large sum of money resulting from a recent business transaction with Dale.[1]

Colley and Bart had received lax treatment from the Cherokee, and the two resented the stern taskmasters who greeted them in Jasper County. Bart ran away from his new owner, John Scott, not long after arriving, and now Colley was plotting to kill one of his owner's friends. Bart agreed to help Colley kill Fisk if Colley would, in turn, help him kill John Scott. They then planned to flee the area, using the money they took off Dr. Fisk to finance their getaway.[2]

On Saturday July 16, Bart called on Colley at Dale's farm and said he was ready to carry out their desperate plot. Late that night, Colley went to the neighboring Fisk home and called at the door, while Bart, traveling to the Fisk property by a different route, took up a hiding place nearby. Colley told the doctor that Dale's young child was sick and needed attention. Falling for the ruse, Dr. Fisk grabbed his medical bag and started on horseback for the Dale farm. He had gone but a short distance when Bart sprang up from his hiding place and knocked him from his horse with a club. Colley then rushed in from behind the doctor with an ax and "beat his brains out." The horse ran off in a panic as Colley and Bart rifled through the dead man's pockets, getting a small amount of booty.[3]

The two men then returned to the Fisk home and went inside. Mrs. Fisk demanded to know what they wanted and threatened them with punishment if they didn't leave. One of the men responded by knocking the woman down with his fist, and while the other man held her down, the first one outraged her. "In this way she was raped by both negroes," said a contemporaneous newspaper report.[4]

After the second man had his turn, he and his companion killed Mrs. Fisk with the same ax they'd used to bust open her husband's head. They also choked the Fisks' young child to death. Ransacking the house, they found a watch, about $200 in currency, and five pieces of silver or gold. They then set the house on fire with the dead bodies still inside and fled the scene. By now, it was after midnight; so none of the neighbors were awake to see the flames lighting up the night sky.[5]

The men hid their plunder in a corn crib and then went their separate ways, with Colley returning to his cabin at the Dale place and Bart taking off for parts unknown. Colley arose early the next morning and went out on the prairie to round up some horses. He returned after a short time and told the Dales that the Fisk home was on fire. Someone immediately started for the Fisk house but, before reaching it, came upon the doctor's dead body lying on the ground. Continuing to the Fisk home, the person also discovered the charred bodies of Mrs. Fisk and her child in the smoldering ruins.[6]

An alarm was given, and neighbors flocked to the scene of the crime. Suspicion quickly settled on Colley when some of Dale's other slaves revealed that he had been away from his cabin the previous night. As a test, Colley was assigned to watch over Dr. Fisk's body to see how he would react. "He exhibited unusual nervousness and soon became sick, and begged to be excused," according to a reminiscent account that appeared in the *Carthage Banner* a number of years later.[7]

Colley denied the heinous deeds, but he was arrested and taken back to Dale's farm, where he was held under guard. Mrs. Dale, who was a relative of Mrs. Fisk, suspected Colley had committed the crimes because she noticed that he had changed clothes. Searchers scoured his cabin and found the clothes he'd worn the previous day spattered with blood, but he still denied involvement in the crimes. The gathering mob took him to a nearby gate and drew him up with a rope to the high overhead beam, threatening to hang him if he did not confess what he knew.[8]

When he still refused to incriminate himself, a committee of three men was appointed to "guard him and talk with him." After being "talked with" for some time, he finally confessed "all the horrid details" of what he and Bart had done, including where the booty they'd taken was hidden, and it was found where he indicated. He was taken to Carthage and placed in the lockup.[9]

Excitement against Colley ran high, but it was decided to delay retribution until he and his partner could be punished at the same time. And Bart was still on the loose. Search parties went out looking for him every day for the next week and a half. They found traces of where he had been but did not spot the fugitive himself. Finally, on or about July 26, some children saw him hiding in the brush of northwest Jasper County near Georgia City. Bart had been on the run for ten days but had failed even to make it out of the county, because he was unfamiliar with the countryside and was forced to travel only at night for fear of being seen during the day.[10]

The children notified some adults in a nearby house of their discovery, and a squad of men quickly surrounded the brush and captured the runaway. He had a pistol and a shotgun in his possession but offered no resistance.[11]

Bart was taken back to Carthage, where he and Colley were given a drumhead trial before a committee of citizens on July 27. "When all the facts were brought to light," said one report, "popular indignation was almost without bounds." Everybody agreed that the two men deserved death, but there was some difference of opinion on the mode of execution. Some favored hanging, while a good many others, who thought hanging them would be too lenient, insisted on burning them at the stake. It was decided to put the question to a vote of the people, and former county judge James H. McPhatridge got up on a platform on the east side of the public square to take charge of the impromptu jury. He instructed two men to position themselves a few feet apart near the northeast corner of the square and told two other men to take similar positions not far away. Addressing the citizens who'd flocked into Carthage for the unofficial court, McPhatridge directed all those in favor of hanging to line up and walk between the first two men and all those who favored burning to march between the other two men. The number who marched through in favor of burning was about twice the number who favored hanging, although a good percentage of those present declined to participate in the spurious trial. The ex-judge announced that the sentence of burning would be carried out three days hence.[12]

On Saturday, July 30, the largest crowd ever assembled in Jasper County streamed into Carthage to witness the awful spectacle, some people traveling from as far away as fifty miles. About ten o'clock Colley and Bart were marched out to a hollow southeast of the square along present-day Macon Street with thousands of spectators following eagerly behind. Those in charge of the quasi-official proceedings had made a special effort to ensure the attendance of nearly all the slaves in the county, and they were given front row seats surrounding the execution site at the base of the natural amphitheater.[13]

Approximate spot on East Macon Street where burnings occurred, as it looks today. *Photo by the author.*

Three iron stakes had been driven into the ground far enough apart so that, when one man stood between the center bar and an outside bar and the other man stood between the center bar and the opposite outside bar, their arms would touch the bars. The two men were thus positioned and their arms chained to the stakes. Wood and kindling were piled around the men almost waist high. Two slaves were compelled to light the bonfire, according to one source, although Timothy Meador, eyewitness to the horrific scene, recalled years later that four or five people lit the blaze simultaneously.[14]

"The flames leaped up around the doomed men with a blast like a furnace," said Meador, "sucking their breath away, and they were dead in a quarter of a minute. One of the men gasped twice and the other cringed and cowered, but neither groaned, shrieked nor said a word, and there were none of the horrors one might imagine."[15]

A report that appeared in the *Carthage Banner* some years after the event but prior to Meador's reminiscent account claimed, on the other hand, that while Colley "stood the ordeal bravely and sang songs until the flames suffocated him," Bart, who had steadfastly denied his guilt from the time he was captured, "pleaded piteously for release" and offered to confess the whole story if they would take the fire away.[16]

The fire burned down after about an hour, and "little remained of the murderers," said the *Banner* account. It was a sultry morning, and a thunderstorm came up later in the day. Many of the people who'd turned out to watch the terrible event "got thoroughly drenched before they reached their homes," added the *Banner* as a footnote to its story, as though the inconvenience of the white spectators was almost as newsworthy as two black men being burned at the stake.[17]

The *Banner* concluded that although the extralegal punishment that had been meted out might seem "inhuman and awful," the case had its "extenuating features," because the "the crimes perpetuated by the negroes were almost without a parallel." Meador echoed the same sentiment, saying he was one of the last spectators to leave and that he didn't feel any sympathy for the men "considering the revolting nature of their crime."[18]

Chapter 2

The Disappearance of Mary Margaret Fullerton
A Tale of Bigamy, Murder, and Lynching

The disappearance and presumed murder of Mary Margaret Fullerton in early 1868 was one of the strangest and most sensational criminal cases in southwest Missouri history. Yet, it is also one that many people have probably never heard about because the woman's body was never found, because Judge Lynch meted out vigilante justice in secrecy, and because the affair was little reported in the immediate Jasper County area.

In 1866, a young man named Daniel Hosey met and wooed Mary Williams, a teenaged schoolgirl, in Butler County, Ohio, and they ran off to another part of Ohio to get married. Shortly afterward, according to Mary's story, the couple moved west to Kansas, where a child was born, but it died in infancy. Mary's husband proved to be a shyster and con man. He assumed several different aliases, including Daniel Springer, Joseph Lee, and A. G. "George" Hutton, and he often traveled away from home, sometimes compelling Mary to accompany him wearing male attire and disguised as a young boy. After staying in Kansas a short while, the couple moved to St. Louis.[1]

In the fall of 1867, Hosey came to Jasper County alone and settled in Sarcoxie. Going by the name Captain A. G. Hutton and representing himself as a single man, he made the acquaintance of Mary Margaret Fullerton, a thirty-six-year old widow with a pretty sixteen-year-old daughter named Mary. Devising a plan to bilk the well-to-do widow out of her money and property, "Hutton" sent for his wife in St. Louis, telling her to don her male attire before she arrived. Hutton then struck up a romance with Mary Fullerton, and when his wife got to Sarcoxie, she passed herself off as a poor, sickly lad named Tommy Turley whom Hutton had befriended and taken as his traveling companion. Feeling sorry for the "boy," Mrs. Fullerton took Tommy into her home. Then on December 15, 1867, Hutton and Mary Fullerton were married in the presence of his first wife, with "Tommy" helping the young bride-to-be prepare for her nuptials.[2]

Hutton tried to finagle Mrs. Fullerton into signing over her estate to the daughter he had recently married, but she refused. Resorting to a more desperate plan, he announced that he needed to move the ailing "Tommy" to the lad's relatives in Ohio, and he offered to give Mrs. Fullerton a hundred dollars and pay her expenses if she would accompany the sick boy and take care of him during the trip. Hutton also told Margaret, as Mrs. Fullerton was usually called, that if she would collect some money on checks he held on Ohio parties, he would give her part of those proceeds as well. In addition, Tommy's parents would surely pay her for her trouble. She balked at this proposition, too, but finally agreed after several weeks of urging from Hutton and Tommy. The plan called for Hutton to drive Margaret and Tommy in a wagon to Sedalia, where they would catch an eastbound train.[3]

Leaving the new bride at home, Hutton, his first wife in the persona of Tommy, and Mrs. Fullerton started for Sedalia about the middle of February 1868. After one day's drive, they stopped for the night, probably somewhere in Lawrence or Dade County. After supper, "Tommy" fell asleep, and when she awoke the next morning, Mrs. Fullerton was nowhere to be seen. When Hutton's first wife asked him where the older woman was, he said Mrs. Fullerton had gone back home and gruffly told Mary (i.e. Tommy) not to ask any more questions on the subject. From Hutton's manner and subsequent behavior, Mary became convinced that he had killed Mrs. Fullerton, but, according to her later story, she was afraid to try to do anything about it.[4]

Hutton and his wife continued on to Sedalia, and they remained there about a week. Why is not clear. Apparently, Hutton was either making arrangements to try to get his hands on Mrs. Fullerton's property through legal maneuvering, or else he simply wanted to stay away from Sarcoxie long enough to come up with a credible explanation for her disappearance. However, when he and his first wife returned to the Fullerton home in early March and Mary Fullerton asked Hutton where her mother was, he was still unable to offer a convincing answer. He gave contradictory explanations, claiming at one point that the widow had remarried and remained in St. Louis. Neither Mary nor her siblings found it plausible that their devoted mother would suddenly abandon them for a new husband without a word of farewell. "Tommy" was no help either. When Mary asked him about her mother, he said he didn't know where she was. Hutton now claimed that his so-called traveling companion was actually his younger half-brother, but Mary also began to have suspicions about "Tommy," especially after she saw him in possession of several articles of female clothing that belonged to her mother.[5]

After remaining at the Fullerton home for about two weeks, Hutton and Tommy once again struck out for Sedalia, going this time by way of Fort Scott. Before reaching Sedalia, Hutton told his first wife to change into her female attire and to assume the identity of Mrs. Fullerton so that she could sign the widow's name to a power of attorney. Hutton had the document drawn up at a lawyer's office in Sedalia, and his wife executed it on March 29, 1868, by signing the name "M. M. Fullerton." Mary then left for St. Louis, while Hutton returned to Sarcoxie in early April with his power of attorney in hand.[6]

Almost as soon as he got back, he started selling off parts of Mrs. Fullerton's estate, and when questioned about the propriety of his actions, he produced the power of attorney. In some cases, Hutton accepted considerably below-market value for the property, and his haste to liquidate the widow's assets only served to increase suspicion against him. By the middle of April, the excitement against Hutton reached such a pitch that some of his neighbors, including an older brother-in-law of Mary Fullerton, vowed to take matters into their own hands. On Friday, April 17, they tried to arrest Hutton near the Fullerton home a couple of miles east of Sarcoxie on suspicion in the disappearance of Mrs. Fullerton so they could take him into town for examination before a justice of the peace. When he attempted to flee, they fired a number of shots at him, wounding him in the shoulder and hip.[7]

The wounded Hutton was taken into Sarcoxie for treatment and guarded at a house there, pending a hearing scheduled for Tuesday, April 28. Found among the prisoner's effects after his arrest was a letter he'd received that was addressed to William Lee, postmarked St. Louis, and signed M. M. F., which were Mrs. Fullerton's initials. Investigators also found a trunk belonging to Hutton that contained a set of picklocks and other burglary instruments.[8]

These discoveries so incensed the friends and neighbors of Mrs. Fullerton that some of them decided not to wait for the preliminary hearing. On Monday night, April 27 or the wee hours of Tuesday morning, a mob of about twenty men with blackened faces took Hutton from his guard in Sarcoxie and carried him about three miles to the vicinity of Round Prairie School near the Lawrence County line, where they strung him up to a blackjack oak.[9]

In the wake of the vigilante hanging, the editor of the *Carthage Banner* said that he deplored "this rash act" and that it would "be better if horse-thieves and murderers, blacklegs and impostors generally, could be dealt with according to law, but in the eyes of some people, the law is sometimes slow and uncertain in its operations." Under such circumstances, it was understandable, suggested the newsman, that "a short shrift" might be resorted to. "Of course it is wrong, but it is very effectual."[10]

About the time of Hutton's lynching, Gilbert Schooling, Sarcoxie postmaster, set out for St. Louis under the supposition that the person who had written the letter to "William Lee" and signed it "M. M. F." might indeed be Mrs. Fullerton and that she, therefore, might be found in that city. Enlisting the aid of St. Louis law officers, he and a Detective Garlick went to the address on Mill Street mentioned in the mysterious letter as the place where Lee should send his reply. When they called at the home corresponding to the address and asked whether Mrs. Fullerton was there, the lady of the house said yes and brought a young woman to the door who said *she* was Mrs. Fullerton.

Schooling remarked that she was not the Mrs. Fullerton he was seeking and was about to leave when the detective noticed what he considered a strange and suspicion look on the girl's face. Garlick asked her to accompany him back to the police chief's office, and she readily agreed. As she and the two men started off together, though, Garlick saw her attempting to tear up a small photograph, and he took it from her before it could be destroyed. It proved to a be picture of George Hutton, the man who'd been hanged back in southwest Missouri.[11]

After the party reached the police chief's office and the young woman had been informed of George Hutton's fate, the officers showed her the letter that had been mailed to "William Lee" from St. Louis, and they accused her of having written it. She denied the charge and also denied that she'd ever been to Sarcoxie or Sedalia. The police chief finally told her she was free to go, but he instructed Garlick to keep an eye on her. The detective escorted her back home and then walked away as if to return to the police station. Instead he took up a position nearby with a full view of the young woman's premises. Presently, he noticed her leaving the house and, after following her a short distance, realized she was crying. When he approached, she recognized him, burst into tears, and said she'd been discharged from her job as a domestic at the house where she'd been staying. "I have no place to go," she sobbed. "I have no money. What shall I do?" Befriending her, Garlick helped her find lodging for the night.[12]

The next day, however, the girl was again taken before the police chief, who told her he was satisfied she was an accomplice of Hutton and that she had disguised herself as a boy and pretended to be "Tommy." She made no response at first but soon burst into tears again and made a partial confession. She admitted she was Hutton's first wife, but she said his name was really Daniel Springer. She also confessed that she had forged Mrs. Fullerton's name at Sedalia. Upon inspecting the contents of her trunk, officers found the hair she had cut off in order to disguise herself as a boy.[13]

A WIDOW MURDERED BY HER SON-IN-LAW.

THE MURDERER COMMITS BIGAMY WITH HIS FIRST WIFE'S CONSENT—THE MURDERER LYNCHED.

(From the St. Louis Times, May 12.)

ONE of the most revolting and heartless murders ever chronicled in the annals of crime has recently come to light in Jasper County, Mo., which shows to what desperate

The Fullerton tragedy made headlines internationally as well as nationally. *From the Sydney Morning Herald.*

The young woman was turned over to Schooling, who transported her back to Jasper County. During the trip she made a fuller confession, including a brief history of her married life with Hutton (aka Springer). She admitted that she had disguised herself as Tommy Turley, but she said everything she did was under duress from her husband. She was sure her husband had killed Mrs. Fullerton when the three of them had camped the first night after they left Sarcoxie, and she agreed to help try to locate the place. She said that her husband had made coffee that evening, that she drank some of it, and that she was convinced her husband had drugged her to ensure she did not awake during the night while he did his deadly work.[14]

Schooling reached Carthage with his prisoner on May 3 and continued on to Sarcoxie with her that evening. After arraignment before a local justice of the peace, she was brought back to Carthage the next day and placed in the Jasper County Jail in response to rumors of possible mob violence at Sarcoxie. Her preliminary hearing in Jasper County Circuit Court was scheduled for the first week of June, but she was granted a change of venue to Lawrence County. Sometime after she was brought back from St. Louis, the prisoner revealed that her real name was Mary Posey, not Mary Springer, and her lawyers filed a writ of habeas corpus for her under the former name seeking to have her released for lack of evidence.[15]

Despite the charges against Mary, some observers expressed a certain sympathy for her after her arrest. The *St.*

Louis Democrat said she appeared to be about twenty years old, "quite intelligent, with a remarkable command of her feelings and a determined will." The *St Louis Times* allowed that her history was "a sad one" that showed "how frequently women, in the madness of devotion, will cling to men even in the committal of the most revolting crimes."[16]

The ambiguity observers felt toward Mary was reflected in the remarks of the *Mount Vernon Spring River Fountain*. Although Mary was "handsome" and seemed to be "a refined and intelligent lady," the deeds she stood accused of branded her as "a most horrible fiend."[17]

The hearing on the motion to dismiss the charge against Mary Posey came up at Mount Vernon on June 1, 1868, before Judge John C. Price. The evidence against the defendant amounted to sworn statements from three witnesses taken during her initial arraignment before Jasper County justice of the peace T. J. Hammer. Mary Fullerton told of her marriage to George Hutton and his plot to get her mother's wealth, of the defendant's participation in the plot disguised as "Tommy," and of Tommy's urging her mother to make the trip to Ohio. Gilbert Schooling told of finding the defendant in St. Louis living under the identity of Mrs. Fullerton and of Mrs. Posey's confession during the return trip to Jasper County. Schooling admitted, however, that the defendant maintained from the beginning that she had nothing to do with murdering Mrs. Fullerton. W. A. Hager, Mary Fullerton's brother-in-law, swore that Mrs. Fullerton told him Hutton and the defendant had urged her for two months to escort "Tommy" to Ohio and had offered her considerable monetary inducements to do so. Hager said he advised Mrs. Fullerton not to make the trip. The evidence also included a statement from Justice Hammer verifying that "Mary Springer" had appeared before him and been charged with murder. After considering the evidence (or lack thereof), Judge Price dismissed the charge, largely on the grounds that Mrs. Fullerton's body had never been found and, therefore, it could not be definitely proved that a murder had even been committed.[18]

Mary Posey was set free, and she left on a stage the very next day. On the day following that, a posse of men from the

Sarcoxie area rode into Carthage, where Mary had originally been slated to appear for her preliminary hearing, and "the excitement seemed to run pretty high" when the men learned that she had already been tried in Lawrence County and released. The *Carthage Banner* concluded, "There is no doubt that there is a general desire, on the part of all, to have only justice done in this case, but there is a strong probability that the mystery will never be fully cleared up."[19]

And it never was.

Chapter 3

Will Never Whip a Wife Again
Dr. Taylor Gets His Neck Lengthened

Forty-year-old Dr. A. D. Taylor of Medoc in northwest Jasper County had been a surgeon in the Union Army during the Civil War and was a well-respected physician after the war. In addition, he had taken up preaching for the Christian Church and was a gifted orator. But he was also known as an abusive husband, beating and otherwise tormenting his wife on almost a daily basis. On several occasions he had threatened to kill her.[1]

On Friday, May 27, 1870, he "turned a fiend" and seemingly set out to carry through with the threat, beating his wife unmercifully. He hit her over the head with a gridiron, breaking it "to shivers." After she fell to the floor, he started kicking her and then began torturing her by stabbing her with a pair of scissors in different parts of her body and slicing her face and breasts with a butcher knife. He also used the knife to cut her hair off. "He seemed to kill her by degrees," said a correspondent to the *Kansas City Journal*. "By the time his fury had abated, he had inflicted such horrible wounds that life was almost extinct."[2]

When some neighbors heard the woman's screams and started toward the Taylor house to investigate, Dr. Taylor, apparently realizing he'd gone too far this time, fled to the woods and hid out. On Sunday morning he appeared at a neighbor's door asking for breakfast, but instead of feeding the hungry doctor, the man, who knew there was a warrant out for Taylor's arrest, apprehended him and took him to the local constable, who held him pending charges.[3]

The people of the Medoc community, having heard of Taylor's horrid treatment of his wife and of his arrest, gathered throughout the day on Sunday, and by that evening "began to show signs of violence." Several citizens were enlisted to assist the constable in guarding his prisoner.[4]

About 9:30 Sunday night, the constable decided to move the prisoner to a justice's residence about two miles away for safekeeping. Halfway to his destination, the constable was intercepted by a posse of about thirty armed men, who took Taylor from the lawman and strung him up to a nearby tree.[5]

A Missouri Fiend—A Man in Kansas City Kills his Wife Inch by Inch—He is Hanged to the Nearest Tree by his Indignant Neighbors.

We learn the particulars of a savage and brutal affair which occurred at Medoc, a small town in Jasper county, Mo., from a

The headline writer for this Virginia newspaper apparently didn't bother to read the first sentence of the story to see where the incident occurred. *From the Richmond Dispatch.*

He remained hanging until after daylight on Monday morning, when his body was cut down, taken back to Medoc, and laid out in the doctor's own office. At last report, Mrs. Taylor was clinging to life, but it was uncertain whether she would survive.[6]

In pondering the vigilante action that had cost Dr. Taylor his life, the *Kansas City Journal* correspondent opined, "It is doubtless the best policy, in most cases, to punish crime by law, but who will say that any man ought to be allowed to live one hour after torturing his wife (whom he has voluntarily sworn to love and protect) as this man did!"[7]

Another report summarized the incident like this: Taylor's neighbors, upon hearing about the beating of Mrs. Taylor and "believing that the crime was caused by Dr. Taylor's neck being too short, lengthened it about an inch by hanging him to a tree. The remedy was effectual. He will never whip a wife again."[8]

And that, apparently, is how wife beaters were dealt with in the old days.

Chapter 4

I Am Shot Through the Paunch
Murder at a Joplin Bawdy House

Joplin, which sprang up as a wild and wooly mining camp (actually two separate camps) in the early 1870s, witnessed more than its share of fighting, hell-raising, and general lawlessness during the "reign of terror" of 1871-1872, but the town's first homicide didn't occur until early 1873. On Sunday morning, February 16, 1873, Edward Daugherty was loitering and drinking at Mrs. Elizabeth "Lizzie" Greenma's house just east of Joplin on the Granby road when two other young men, Edward Adkins and Mike Davis, came in about 10:00 a.m.[1]

Sometimes called "Irish Liz's," the Greenma place was known as a "house of ill fame," and it was a resort for hard characters like the thirty-five-year-old Daugherty. A native of Ireland, he'd previously been a railroad hand in Greene County, but he'd come to Joplin from Seneca during the summer of 1872 and opened a saloon. Since closing his saloon later the same year, he had "not been engaged in any particular business." He'd spent Saturday night with Lizzie and had, in fact, been making Lizzie's place his home for the past several months. However, according to Lizzie, he did not "live with" her. Adkins was also about thirty-five, and he, too, had come to Joplin from Newton County, although he was originally from Texas. Since coming to Joplin in the spring of 1872, he'd been engaged in mining in the bottoms along Joplin Creek. According to at least one report, he was considered a "quiet, inoffensive and industrious man," although Lizzie said that was only true when he had not been drinking.[2]

And on this particular Sunday morning Adkins and Davis, who'd spent the previous night carousing together, were already drinking again by the time they reached Lizzie's. About the time they came in, Lizzie and Daugherty got into an argument, and Adkins, who was acquainted with both parties, tried to intercede on Lizzie's behalf, telling Daugherty he shouldn't "act that way." Daugherty told Adkins to quit pestering him and to mind his own business, and he and Lizzie kept quarrelling off and on for the next couple of hours. Adkins kept trying to intervene, though, and finally, in the early afternoon, he and Daugherty got into a heated argument, swearing at each other. Now Lizzie tried to assume the role of peacemaker. She begged Adkins to leave, but instead he grabbed Daugherty by the collar, shoved him down against a chair, and, according to Lizzie, threatened to kill him. While the two men were still struggling, Daugherty reached into his coat pocket and fired one shot from a Derringer pistol that struck Adkins in the side.[3]

Despite being seriously wounded, Adkins attacked Daugherty, knocking him down, and collapsed on top of him. Daugherty got up and started hitting Adkins until another patron of Lizzie's place, W. A. McKee, came over and pulled him off. Adkins rose to his feet and exclaimed, "I am shot! I am shot through the paunch." As he quickly sank back down, Daugherty took the gun out of his pocket, tossed it under a table, and fled.[4]

Daugherty ran north from Lizzie's place with several men in pursuit. After "considerable of a chase," they captured the fugitive and turned him over to authorities.[5]

Mike Davis left to summon a doctor, but by the time the doctor arrived about a half hour later, Adkins was already dead. An inquest held Sunday afternoon concluded that Adkins had come to his death as the result of a pistol bullet fired by Edward Daugherty. On Monday morning, February 17, Daugherty waived his preliminary hearing, and he was taken to Carthage and turned over to the sheriff. Adkins was "decently buried" the same day.[6]

Daugherty was subsequently charged with first degree murder, and Lizzie was indicted as an accessory after the fact for allegedly advising him to flee and aiding his escape.[7]

Daugherty's trial began in Jasper County Circuit Court on November 13, 1873. In his opening statement, prosecuting attorney H. H. Woodmansee seemed to lament the fact that there had never been a legal hanging in Jasper County, and he suggested that Daugherty was a proper candidate to be the first man to suffer such punishment. When testimony began, Mike Davis took the stand as the state's star witness. He said Adkins interfered between Daugherty and Lizzie only because he was trying to keep Daugherty from hurting the woman. He suggested that Adkins was unarmed and that his most aggressive act toward Daugherty was to take him by the collar and shake him. On cross examination, Davis admitted that he had his back to the two men when the fatal shot was fired. He also admitted that Adkins did have a revolver at one point on the morning of the killing, but he said he took the weapon from Adkins prior to his deadly encounter with Daugherty.[8]

W. A. McKee and Lizzie Greenma told a different story, both painting Adkins as the aggressor. McKee said Adkins threatened to drive Daugherty's head through the wall and took a position as though he was going to hit him. McKee intervened, but as soon as he stepped away, the two men started arguing again and Adkins slapped Daugherty. Adkins also boasted about his manhood, according to McKee, proclaiming that he was "a man amongst men." McKee's only damning testimony to the defendant's case was that he saw smoke coming from Daugherty's coat pocket after the fatal shot was fired. Lizzie said Adkins was "awful rough" when he'd been drinking, and she testified that she saw him shoving Daugherty around and driving him down onto a chair. Adkins seemed angry, as he was cursing Daugherty, and when she asked Adkins to leave, he replied that he wouldn't leave until he killed Daugherty. Lizzie also claimed to have seen Mike Davis hand Adkins a gun just before the deadly shot was fired. Furthermore, she added that she did not see Daugherty with a weapon.[9]

Recalled to the stand to refute Lizzie's testimony, Davis denied that he handed Adkins a weapon before his deadly encounter with Daugherty, and he also said that he did not hear Adkins refuse to leave until after he killed Daugherty or to make any such threat. Apparently, the jury gave more weight to Mike

Davis's word than to that of W. A. McKee and Lizzie Greenma. After deliberating about three hours, they returned with a verdict finding Daugherty guilty of second degree murder and assessing a punishment of fifteen years in the state penitentiary. Meanwhile, the case against Lizzie was dropped during the same term of court.[10]

Offender Information	Name	Edward Daugherty - Offender
	Sex	Male
	Race	White
	Age/Approx. Year of Birth	35/1838
	Nativity	Ireland
	Trade	Laborer
Offense Information	Offense	Murder, 2nd degree
	Location of Court	Jasper
	Sentence	15 years from Nov 15, 1873
	Term of Court	November
	When Received	12/8/1873
	Full Time Sentence Expiration	11/15/1888
	Date of Discharge	7/4/1882
	Discharge Notes	Full Pardon by Gov T T Crittenden

Summary of Daugherty's Missouri State Penitentiary record. *From the Missouri State Archives website.*

Daugherty's request for a new trial was turned down, and the state supreme court refused to consider his appeal. He was received at the Missouri State Penitentiary in Jefferson City on December 8, 1873. He was pardoned by Governor Thomas T. Crittenden and released on July 4, 1882, after serving less than nine years of his fifteen-year sentence.[11]

Chapter 5

Hard Times
A Robber Hung Near Minersville

About 8:30 p.m. on the evening of November 10, 1873, two men burst into the home of James A. Hunter four miles north of Minersville (now Oronogo) with revolvers drawn. They found twenty-six-year-old Catherine Hunter still up but had to roust her husband from his bed. Putting their pistols to Hunter's head, they demanded his money. The thirty-five-year-old Hunter handed over his pocketbook, which contained only about seventy-five cents.[1]

One of the intruders then stood guard over Hunter and his wife while the other commenced ransacking the house in search of valuables. Hunter recognized the man guarding them as a fellow he'd seen in Minersville earlier that very day, but he kept mum. Meanwhile, the other robber broke open two or three trunks, a washstand, and a table drawer. "Is robbing your business?" Mrs. Hunter asked as the plundering went on.

"Yes, in hard times," one of the men replied.[2]

The search, however, proved almost fruitless, turning up only a pair of gold bracelets belonging to Mrs. Hunter. The desperadoes carried off their ill-gotten booty without further molesting the couple.

The next morning, Hunter trekked into Minersville to report the crime. He swore out a warrant before Justice Isaac Fountain by describing the robbers. Hunter and Fountain began scouring the town for any sign of the crooks. They soon spotted the man who had stood guard over Hunter and his wife the night before. As they placed him under arrest, Hunter remarked, "Last night you had me; now I have you."[3]

The culprit identified himself as Alfred T. Onan. He and four companions were all taken into custody and guarded overnight at Minersville. The next morning, November 12, the five prisoners appeared before Justice Fountain, and all were discharged expect Onan, who was held in lieu of $1,000 bond to appear at the circuit court in Carthage on a robbery charge.[4]

Onan lived on Shoal Creek in Newton County, but he was also known around Minersville, where he sometimes worked in the mines. He was about thirty years old, was stoutly built, weighed about 180 pounds, and had red complexion and a light mustache. He was supposedly a desperate man who had been through many "hard scrapes and close contests," and, according to at least one report, he claimed to have ridden with notorious Confederate guerrilla leader William Quantrill during the Civil War. He might have been a desperate man, but he was not, in fact, a Quantrill man. Instead, he was a native of Boone County, Missouri, and served during the war under Confederate captain George W. Bryson of that county.[5]

The plan was for Onan to be escorted to Carthage later the same day after he was indicted by Justice Fountain, but the guards, who had been up all night watching the prisoners, fell asleep and let the train go by. Resorting to a back-up plan, they loaded Onan into a buggy about sundown and started for Carthage with him. The posse had proceeded only about a mile when they were waylaid by a party of about fifteen disguised and armed men. The mob demanded that Onan be turned over to them, and the guards offered no resistance, because the vigilantes "had the drop on them" before they could draw their pistols. While part of the gang continued to cover the guards, the others took Onan a short distance into the woods and hanged him from a blackjack oak tree.

As soon as the lynching had been accomplished, the vigilantes released the guards, who returned to Minersville to report what had happened. The next day, November 13, Fountain headed to Carthage to report the travesty of justice. On his way, he rode by the scene of the lynching and saw Onan's dead body still "dangling between heaven and earth."[6]

LYNCHED!

A Robber Hung Near Minersville

One of Quantrell's Gang Swung to a Black-jack !

Full Particulars of the Robbery. Capture and Hanging !

A Stain Upon the Fair Name of our County !

Headline from the *Carthage Banner* tells the story of Onan's lynching.

In reporting the extralegal hanging, the editor of the *Carthage Banner* opined that, while he had no sympathy for men such as Onan, "we cannot indorse mob law." The newsman continued,

> The common practice in some states and some counties of Missouri of hanging men without lawful trial is reprehensible and cannot be too severely condemned. True, justice is not cheated when the right man is disposed of, but what man is safe in a country or community where lynch law is resorted to? Spite, prejudice and over-zealousness to punish robbers, murderers and thieves leads men to commit rash acts upon innocent men, oftentimes. The fame of our county has received an irreparable injury in the case we have recorded. We hope it may never fall to our lot, as a journalist, to again record an act of mobbing in Jasper County no matter how great the crime committed or how mean the criminal that did it. Let all good citizens reflect upon this matter and it will be readily seen that innocent citizens—desirous of doing good—have committed a greater crime than robbery by the hanging of Onan.
>
> So much stealing has been going on in and around Minersville lately—for we are told that eight or ten horses have been taken within

two weeks—accounts in part for the incensed feeling against robbers and thieves.[7]

As it turned out, it was less than a year before journalists would be called upon to report another lynching in Jasper County.

Chapter 6

Another Outrage
The Lynching of Daniel Reed

As most of us know, lynching was fairly common in America during the 1800s and early 1900s. In fact, it was probably more common than many people realize. Only the most sensational lynchings were widely reported. Many others occurred that received only passing mention in newspapers of the time. A case in point is the lynching of Daniel Reed (aka George Reed) in Joplin on Thursday, October 1, 1874. This event was so obscure that I failed to run across any mention of it during my fairly extensive research for *Wicked Joplin*. I only became aware of this shadowy episode in Joplin's notorious history a year or two after that book was published.

Reed was arrested in late September 1874 near Kansas City for allegedly having stolen two mules from John Depriest of Joplin. He was taken to the Vernon County Jail in Nevada to be held there in safekeeping until his case came up in Jasper County. On Monday, September 28, a Jasper County deputy, accompanied by Depriest and one or two other men, called at the Nevada jail demanding that the prisoner be turned over to them. Vernon County authorities were reluctant to give him up, their suspicion being aroused when it was reported to them that one of the Jasper County men had purchased a rope from a Nevada merchant. After several hours of wrangling between the two sides, the Vernon County officers, receiving assurances that Reed would not be foully dealt with, finally released him into the custody of the Depriest party, and the prisoner was, in fact, delivered to Joplin without incident and placed under guard at the city hall.[1]

But his safety was only temporary.

Reed claimed he was innocent because he had won the mules from Depriest in a game of cards, and he said he'd be able to prove his case at his examination, which was scheduled for Monday October 5. But Reed never got a chance to present his evidence. In the wee hours of Thursday morning, October 1, a mob of about thirty armed and disguised men took him from his guards and hauled him to the "most thickly settled part of the city," where they strung him up to a tree.[2]

A local newspaper, the *Joplin Bulletin*, regretted the fact that "our city has received another blot on her name." At this time (1874), Joplin had recently incorporated and was striving, somewhat vainly, to emerge from the lawlessness that had characterized the place during the early 70s when it was still just an unincorporated mining camp. The *Bulletin* further admitted that the mob was guilty of murder and that lynching Reed was a greater crime than the crime of theft with which he had been charged. At the same time, the local paper tried to justify the lynching to a certain degree by painting Reed as "a desperate character" who had no friends in Jasper County, despite the fact that he had lived there for some time. The paper also reported that Reed supposedly confessed to stealing the mules before he was hanged.[3]

ANOTHER OUTRAGE.

Daniel Reed Hung by a Vigilance Committee.

Headline in the *Fort Scott Monitor* announcing the lynching of Daniel Reed.

The *Fort Scott Monitor*, on the other hand, opined that the circumstances surrounding the whole affair "looked suspicious, to say the least." The *Monitor* implied that there were already whisperings of vigilante justice when Reed was handed over to Jasper County officials in Vernon County, that the Jasper County officials knew of these rumors but failed to take any action to prevent the lynching, and that some of the deputies were even in on the lynching. The *Monitor* said there was at least a fair chance that Reed was innocent as he claimed, and the paper also reported that the hanging was badly handled and that Reed's body ended up being bruised and butchered because of the botched execution. In contrast to the *Bulletin* editor, the Fort Scott newsman thought it was Depriest, not Reed, who was "a pretty hard case."[4]

In a follow-up report, the *Monitor* openly asserted that Reed was innocent of stealing the mules and that the real reason for his lynching was that he knew too much about the burning of the Hannibal Smelting Works in Joplin a couple of months earlier. The arsonists wanted to get him out of the way so he couldn't testify against them.[5]

The Fort Scott newsman wasn't the only person who proclaimed Reed's innocence. A correspondent from Granby wrote to a Lexington, Missouri, newspaper asserting that Reed had, indeed, won the mules and that he had five witnesses ready to testify to the fact. The letter writer said that Reed's innocence was shown by the fact that he loaded up his wagon, to which the supposedly stolen mules were hitched, in broad daylight and left Joplin without trying to conceal his actions.[6]

Three or four of the men suspected of being among the mob that lynched Reed were overhauled and arrested as they passed through Granby on the night after the hanging, and they were taken back to Joplin for examination. John Depriest was apparently among the men arrested in Granby, because, shortly afterward, the *Monitor* crowed that Depriest was now "in limbo, and his little game did not work as he expected. He has succeeded in having an innocent man hung, but he did not cover his tracks sufficiently well to keep himself out of difficulty."[7]

The Fort Scott newsman concluded, "The prospect is now that every one connected with this disgraceful affair will be made to answer for the crime, and a stop put to the outrages in that locality."[8]

Alas, it was not to be. Only two men, John A. Depriest and J. L. Horton, were ever indicted for the murder of Daniel Reed. When their cases came up in Jasper County Circuit Court in September of 1875, the charges against Horton were dropped, and Depriest was granted a change of venue to neighboring Dade County. He was acquitted the following month upon trial at Greenfield.[9]

And the "outrages" in Jasper County went on.

Chapter 7

"The Firing Became General"
The Webb City Riot or the Blunt Raid

George Hudson had been implicated in one Newton County murder and was still under indictment for another, and Allen "Bud" Blount had already earned a notorious reputation as well when they and several of their Granby sidekicks set up operations in late 1876 at the booming mining camp of Carterville in neighboring Jasper County. The young men sporadically engaged in mining, but, at least for Hudson and Blount (often spelled Blunt), digging for ore was little more than a sideline. Their real specialty was raising hell, and that's exactly what they did when they invaded the adjacent mining town of Webb City in January of 1877.[1]

On Tuesday, January 16, one of the desperadoes, Jim Messick, got tanked up in Webb City and got himself thrown in the calaboose on a disorderly conduct charge for firing off his revolver in the streets. His pals came over from Carterville later that day or the next day and tried to get him released, attempting to batter down the jailhouse at one point, but they failed in their mission. On Thursday morning the 18th, Messick paid a fine and was released, but when he got back to Carterville, he and his comrades decided to go back to Webb City and teach the town a lesson.[2]

Early that afternoon, Messick, Hudson, Blount, Jim Powell, Todd Starks, and Blount's brother John rode into Webb City "whooping and hallooing" and full of "forty-yard whisky." They rode up and down the main street yelling, brandishing their arms, and threatening to shoot anybody who dared to confront them. The streets were quickly cleared as "no person wanted to come into contact with these ruffians," and the gang took entire possession of the town.[3]

George Hudson was on a spree and "perambulating around the city" when a man dared to appear on the street. Hudson struck him across the face and leveled his pistol at the man's head. About that time, the boisterous Hudson noticed some ladies watching him from the door of the Scott home, a boarding house on the other side of the street. Imagining that they were talking about him, he started in their direction to "make their acquaintance." Speaking of one of the young women in particular, he said, "I am going to have that gal." When the women saw him coming, they withdrew into the house, but Hudson jumped inside through an open window.[4]

George Hudson, one of the leaders of the "Webb City Riot," pictured on the right standing in front of a Granby saloon with his brother Jack. *Courtesy of the Granby Mining Museum.*

The women screamed, and when a young lad came to their aid, Hudson struck the boy with his hand. Hearing the commotion inside the house, Bud Blount and the rest of Hudson's gang came in to check out the action. Mr. Scott, who had been sick in an upstairs bed, was also roused by the disturbance and came downstairs to see what the matter was. "For God's sake, don't kill that boy," he exclaimed when he saw Hudson still scuffling with the lad. Hudson promptly conked the man with his pistol, knocking him down and putting a gash in his head. At this point, Bud Blount took upon himself the unlikely role of peacemaker and herded Hudson out of the house before his partner could do any more damage. The gang mounted up and again galloped up and down the street "yelling like a band of Comanche Indians" before departing for "the classic shades of Carterville."[5]

As the *Webb City New Century* observed, this was just "the start of the trouble."

After the desperadoes left, the Webb City marshal, L. P. Marks, finally appeared on the scene and started organizing the citizens to defend the town if the gang should make another appearance. Marks and a man named William McCulloch went out to the edge of town about 3:30 p.m. to see if they could spot any sign of the gang, and they met John Blount, who'd apparently roamed back toward Webb City alone to do a little scouting of his own. They ordered him to throw up his hands. When he didn't obey but instead started to flee or draw his revolver, they opened fire on him with shotguns. Blount managed to get off two shots of his own before he was wounded in the hip and shoulder, causing him to drop his revolver and lose his hat. Wounded and bareheaded, Blount turned and galloped back to Carterville. This ended "Chapter Two" of what came to be called the "Blunt raid" or the "Webb City riot."[6]

Chapter Three started after just a brief intermission, and it would prove to be the exciting climax.

After John Blount reached Carterville, his brother and the rest of the gang set out about 5:00 p.m. to avenge the attack on one of their own. Leaving John in camp to nurse his wounds, they rode back into Webb City armed with pistols and carbines, while the citizens mainly had only shotguns. The five desperadoes took up strategic positions under the cover of buildings and "opened a promiscuous fire on those they thought the most interested." The gunfire was returned by the citizens from various parts of the downtown area, but mostly from the post office and the upper floor of the Webb City Hall, a large two-story frame building. "The firing became general and lasted until quite dark," said one observer. In total, about two hundred shots were exchanged during the melee. Of the seven Webb City citizens who sustained injuries, only one, whose arm bone was shattered by a shot to the elbow, was thought to have been badly hurt. One other man's wounds later proved to be more serious than first thought. A horse belonging to the gang was shot, but the desperadoes themselves, including the rider who had to abandon his horse, escaped unscathed.[7]

Fearful of another attack, Webb City citizens kept a vigil while Marshal Marks went to Oronogo to wire the sheriff for help. The sheriff and his posse reached Webb City in the wee hours of the next morning, but the gang had not returned. Instead, they had been spotted headed toward Granby driving a wagon. After daylight, the sheriff's posse went out in pursuit of the villains but failed to find them. Meanwhile, several men, including John and Bud Blount's brother Jake, were arrested as suspected accomplices of the gang of six, but the cases against all of them were eventually dropped.[8]

Warrants were issued, as well, for the principals in the Webb City raid, but only one or two of the suspects were ever apprehended, and none were ever successfully prosecuted for the raid. At least in the case of George Hudson and Bud Blount, law enforcement had more serious crimes to worry about.[9]

In early April, just a couple of months after the Webb City affair, Hudson was turned over by his bondsman to a Newton County deputy on the prior murder charge, but he promptly escaped with the aid of Bud Blount. In June of the same year, Hudson was implicated in the murder of a man named "Tiger Bill" at the fledgling mining camp of Galena, Kansas. Shortly afterward, Hudson and Bud Blount absconded to Colorado, where they resumed their criminal careers by shooting a man, robbing him, and leaving him for dead. Returning to the Ozarks in late November of 1879, Hudson, along with Bob Layton, who'd also been implicated in the Tiger Bill killing at Galena, got into a gun battle at Batesville, Arkansas, leaving Layton dead. Released on bond, Hudson fled again to Colorado but came back to Granby in time to kill another man there in 1884. In 1886, he graduated to murder for hire when he gunned down Dr. L. G. Houard, a dentist who was strolling down Main Street in Joplin. Despite damning evidence against him, Hudson was found not guilty, but he was eventually killed in Granby in 1892 by a lawmen sent to arrest him for the Colorado assault thirteen years earlier.[10]

Meanwhile, after his misadventure with Hudson in Colorado, Bud Blount made his way to Arizona Territory, where he was sent to prison for killing a man at the Tip Top mining camp in 1881. Pardoned and released in 1883, he came back to Missouri and engaged in a number of criminal pastimes, culminating with the murder of a railroad brakeman near Ritchey in 1890. Blount was convicted of murder and sentenced to hang, but he got the sentence commuted. Eventually paroled and then pardoned altogether, he later worked in Joplin as a bartender and then spent his latter years in the state hospital at Nevada.[11]

In the meantime the "Webb City riot" (aka the Blunt Raid) had been consigned to the annals of local lore as a mere footnote in the history of Jasper County.

Chapter 8

A Tale of Betrayal, Jealousy, and Murder
The First Legal Hanging in Jasper County

John Able's killing of John "Wick" Lane occurred in McDonald County in 1874, but, after a change of venue, the crime ultimately led to the first legal hanging in Jasper County in February of 1878. Able's execution was also the only truly public hanging ever held in Jasper County.

Able had married a pretty young girl named Martha Dewitt in Indiana in 1867 when he was a forty-nine-year-old widower and she was just sixteen. They came to Missouri shortly after the marriage and settled in western McDonald County about 1872. Described by one observer as "a fascinating, buxom, plump little creature," Martha "did not lean to 'virtue's side' but ran off in the opposite direction." She soon tired of the old man and sought the embrace of younger suitors. Indeed, she seemingly "lavished her affections with an unsparing hand upon the sterner sex, and transferred them from one paramour to another with 'a lightness of heart.'"[1]

Able was scarcely aware of his wife's roving eye until, in the spring of 1874, she ran away with a married man from the neighborhood named Neil Dodson, who deserted his wife and young children in favor of Martha. Able suspected that another young man, twenty-four-year-old John "Wick" Lane, was in on the scheme and knew the whereabouts of the runaways. Lane denied it and offered to help the old man track the pair down, if Able would pay him. Able had no horse of his own; so, he and Lane set off together taking turns riding Lane's horse. They went northeast into Newton County and perhaps one or two other neighboring counties but turned up no sign of the missing couple. Upon their return to McDonald County, Able again grew suspicious of Lane, thinking he had led him on a wild goose chase in order to give Dodson and Martha more time to escape. Able and Lane were seen together in the vicinity of Big Sugar Creek in eastern McDonald County on April 16, and a couple hours later Able was spotted going toward Pineville alone on horseback. The next day, Lane's dead body was found near a spring on Granny's Branch, not far from where Able and Lane had been seen together. The dead man had been shot twice, and his revolver was missing from its holster. The position of the body suggested that the killing had been done execution style, in cold blood. At least that was the theory pursued by the state in subsequent legal proceedings.[2]

Suspicion toward Able mounted when he sold a horse and tried to sell a pistol that were identified as belonging to Lane. Able fled to Indian Territory but was soon captured there by the McDonald County sheriff and brought back to Missouri.[3]

Able was indicted in McDonald County in early June 1874, but in October he received a change of venue to Jasper County. Although Able insisted he did not kill Lane, he scarcely cooperated with his court-appointed attorneys, thus hampering his own defense, and he was found guilty of first-degree murder when his trial came up at Carthage in March of 1875. In April, circuit judge Joseph Cravens sentenced him to hang on June 11, but the verdict was immediately appealed to the Missouri Supreme Court, automatically staying the execution. In April of 1877, the high court overturned the verdict, remanding the case for a new trial.[4]

Able's attorneys asked for another change of venue, and although the motion was denied, a new judge, Samuel G. Williams, was brought in from a neighboring circuit for the trial, which took place at Carthage in October 1877. Able was again convicted, and Judge Williams sentenced Able to hang on December 7. Again, the prisoner's lawyers appealed to the state supreme court, which stayed the execution until December 28. However, on December 20, the high court affirmed the decision of the lower court. The defense's last hope was an appeal to Missouri governor John S. Phelps for clemency, although Able himself said he would just as soon hang. Phelps stayed the execution until January 18, 1878, to give Able's lawyers time to prepare and submit their petition. [5]

JOHN ABLES.

John Able on the eve of his hanging. *From the Mount Vernon Lawrence Chieftain.*

On the evening of January 17, with no word from the governor, Able, thinking he would die the next day, made a full confession at the Jasper County Jail before Deputy Sheriff J. V. Wheelhouse and W. C. Robinson, one of his attorneys. He admitted killing Lane but said he did so in self-defense. According to Able, he had given Lane a revolver when they started off looking for his runaway wife with the understanding that he would also pay the young man cash if and when they found the wife. On the day of the killing, though, Lane announced that he wanted the cash right then, struck the old man across the face, and started to draw his revolver. Able rammed into the younger man, knocking him off balance long enough to make a break for it. Able ran toward a big tree as Lane fired three shots at him. Able said he didn't know he'd been hit until he started to draw his own revolver and realized he'd been shot in the arm below the elbow. He got the weapon out, though, and the two men chased each other around the tree, each trying to get a clear shot at the other. When Able fired, Lane jumped back and lost his balance, dropping his pistol as he fell.[6]

Lane's robbery attempt convinced Able that the young man was, indeed, in on his wife's elopement and knew where she was. As the old man covered Lane with his pistol, he demanded to know what the younger man knew about Martha's whereabouts. Lane first said that Andy Fleming had taken her to Texas, but Able knew that was a lie, because Fleming was still at home when the two men had left in search of Martha. Lane then admitted that Neil Dodson had taken her to Arkansas and that Fleming was planning to meet her down there. About that time, Lane reared up and made a lunge for his pistol, but Able shot him in the head, killing him almost instantly.[7]

Able then told of how he tended his wounded arm, and he showed off a scar on his arm as proof that he'd been shot. He said that, after the shooting and when he was captured, he hid the fact that he'd been wounded because he didn't want anyone to know he'd even been in a fight with Lane. He said that, when he was taken into custody, a mob quickly formed and he feared he'd be lynched if he admitted to killing Lane, even if it was in self-defense. Able claimed he told the whole story to his first attorney in McDonald County. However, the lawyer told him not to tell anyone else, and nothing more was said about it. So, when his case was transferred to Jasper County, he kept quiet, thinking he might have made a mistake by confessing to his first lawyer.[8]

Able said he realized that Robinson and his other lawyers might have done more for him if he'd told them the whole story at the beginning, but he said it made no difference now. He was ready to hang, and he had no hard feelings against anybody. He said he'd always gotten along well with the sheriff and other county officials. Prior to the supreme court ruling against him, he'd been given the run of the jail and had helped out as a janitor in the sheriff's office. He'd even been allowed to run errands throughout the town of Carthage.[9]

Later the same evening, January 17, just hours before Lane's scheduled execution, Governor Phelps granted another reprieve until February 15 to give himself more time to study the case. Lane's confession was not immediately made public, but Robinson used it in support of his plea to the governor for clemency. Despite the new evidence, though, Phelps declined to interfere a third time.[10]

On the night of February 14, as his date with death again approached, Able broke down and cried bitterly, repeating the story he'd told in his confession and bemoaning his fate. "There was none of the braggadocio and profanity which made him so disgusting four weeks ago," said a *Carthage Banner* reporter. Sheriff J. C. Beamer wired a last-minute plea to Jefferson City, informing Governor Phelps that Able was sticking to his story of self-defense and that he, the sheriff, believed it to be true, but the governor promptly replied that he had made his final decision. Later that evening, a minister visited the condemned man in his cell. Able had previously eschewed spiritual advice, but he finally joined the minister in prayer.[11]

After spending an anguished night, Able was offered brandy the next morning, and "very soon his courage began to return." During the rest of the morning, he sipped from a flask that he was allowed to keep handy. As the hour for the execution drew near, a crowd estimated between seven and eight thousand people gathered around the scaffold, which had been erected west of the jail on the courthouse grounds, to witness the spectacle. About 1:30 p.m. the prisoner dressed himself in a suit of black, and the final preparations for the hanging began. The minister who'd visited Able the night before once again offered spiritual solace, but the condemned man declined to talk on religious matters, saying it would do no good. Shortly after 2:00 p.m., Able was brought out of his cell into the sheriff's office.[12]

After having his arms pinioned, the doomed man stepped out of the sheriff's office and walked around the jail to the west side, where the scaffold was. The eager spectators crowding around had to be kept back by the Carthage Light Guards. Escorted by the sheriff and two deputies, Able mounted the steps to the platform. He sat down while the sheriff read the death warrant and then rose and stepped onto the trap at the sheriff's instruction. Able's feet and legs were bound, and a black cap placed over his head. After the noose was looped around Able's neck, Sheriff Beamer sprung the trap at 2:20 p.m., and Able fell six feet. No pulse was detected after ten minutes, and the body was cut down another nine minutes later. A post-mortem examination revealed that the fall had broken the condemned man's neck and that unconsciousness was instantaneous. The body was placed in a casket and taken to a potter's field south of town, where it was buried.[13]

"Thus ends the life of old John Ables;" opined a *Banner* reporter, "a life fraught with many trials and tribulations; a life perhaps decreed by fate to be one of torment in this world; a life, in our opinion, equally as much sinned against as sinning." The newsman explained that four men had now lost their lives on account of one woman, Martha Able. In addition to the killing of Lane and the hanging of Able, Dodson, the man who carried Martha away from her husband, had been shot in Arkansas by his brother-in-law just a month or so after Lane was killed, and another man implicated in the elopement had committed suicide in McDonald County a few months later. The woman herself was now living in Indian Territory in an adulterous relationship with Andy Fleming, who had induced Dodson to steal Martha away from Able and who was the real instigator of the tragic chain of events.[14]

Chapter 9

Bloody Britton
AKA Britton the Bold

Twenty-five-year-old Lane Britton had already earned a reputation as a "hard character" when he and his wife moved to the new mining community of Blende City at the southwest edge of present-day Carl Junction near the beginning of 1883. Britton had killed a man at a bawdy house in Neosho during the Christmas season of 1875 when he was just seventeen. The case was moved on a change of venue to Greene County, where Britton was eventually acquitted by reason of justifiable homicide in 1878. Returning to his native Newton County, he got into a scrape at Granby with a miner named Bishop in the summer of 1879. When Jack Hudson, a Granby deputy marshal, went to arrest him on an assault charge, Britton fled, and Hudson fired several shots at him. At least one of the shots struck Britton in the leg, but he managed to escape.[1]

After getting married and living in Kansas at Empire City (now part of Galena) for a few years, Britton was now back in Missouri, and it didn't take him long to get in trouble again. Britton somehow got himself appointed marshal of Blende, but he became a "terror to the place," disturbing the peace at least as much as he kept it. In the late spring of 1883, he grew irate with the town's mayor, ripped off his badge, threw it to the ground, and stomped it. Mounting his horse, he rode up and down the street with his revolver in hand and proceeded to "run the town" for several hours before he was finally arrested and fined.[2]

Bishop, the man whom Britton had assaulted in 1879, did not press charges against him at the time, but in the spring of 1883, Jack Hudson, perhaps learning of the disturbance Britton had caused at Blende City, got Bishop to revive the case and swear out a warrant. Now a Newton County sheriff's deputy, Hudson, accompanied by Granby constable Aaron Davis, trekked to Jasper County on June 28 intent on serving the warrant. A Joplin justice of the peace endorsed the writ, and Joplin constable G. G. "Gid" Davis joined the posse.[3]

The three lawmen found Britton at Carl Junction, where he was unloading mineral from his wagon. Arrested without incident, Britton asked permission to take his team and wagon back home before accompanying the officers to Newton County, and the request was granted. Hudson left to get a team ready for the trip to Neosho, while the two constables escorted the prisoner to Blende.[4]

At home, Britton stabled his horses and then asked to go inside his house and get some clothes. Agreeing to the proposition, Davis and Davis stayed outside while Britton went inside. Moments later, the desperado suddenly emerged from the house and leveled a navy revolver at Aaron Davis. "Drop your pistol, you son of a bitch!" Britton ordered.[5]

When the constable complied, Britton stepped up and struck him across the face with his revolver, knocking him down. At this point, Gid Davis, who had retreated behind a corner of the house, stepped out and fired an errant shot at Britton. Turning his attention to the second Davis, Britton wheeled and shot the lawman in the side of the head just above the ear. Gid Davis fell gravely wounded, and Britton turned back to Aaron Davis, who still lay outstretched on the ground. Britton shot him through the body, killing him instantly.[6]

After surveying his "bloody work" for a moment, Britton went to the stable and brought out two horses. He mounted one and took the other one by the reins to follow. He rode to the door of the house, where his wife handed him another pistol and a belt of cartridges, which he strapped around his waist. Bidding his wife goodbye, he rode off on the first horse with the second one trotting behind.[7]

The first people to reach the scene of the shooting found Aaron Davis already dead and G. G. Davis unconscious with blood and brains oozing from his head wound. Aaron Davis's body was removed for burial, and Gid Davis was transported to Joplin, where he died later the same evening. Meanwhile, Jack Hudson returned to Newton County empty-handed.[8]

A couple of days after the murders, the Jasper County Court offered a hundred-dollar reward for Britton's arrest, but apparently little effort to capture the fugitive was made in the immediate wake of the double murder. He reportedly returned to Blende on the night after the crime and spent a good while at his house visiting his twenty-two-year-old wife, Mary. The same night, Mary was supposedly seen "skipping around as gleeful as a school girl out for a recess," and the *Joplin Daily Herald* opined that she "must be a woman of the class out of whom John the Baptist cast seven devils."[9]

Lane Britton and his wife, Mary. *Photo courtesy Linda Childers and Judy Sire.*

The day after the murders, Britton ran onto an acquaintance near Joplin and told him the reason he had resisted arrest was because he feared Jack Hudson. He thought Hudson was just trying to get him out on the road to Newton County, where he would find some pretext to shoot him. Britton's concern was not without some foundation, since Hudson, brother of the notorious George Hudson of Webb City riot fame, was a tough character in his own right and had been involved in more than one shooting scrape.[10]

On July 2, a man came into Joplin from the Jackson Diggings southwest of town just across the Newton County line and told the *Daily Herald* that he'd seen Britton every day since the killings, including earlier that very morning. Britton's brother-in-law worked at the diggings, and Britton had been hanging out there as well. "Britton the Bold," the *Herald* said, "makes no attempt at seclusion but walks around with the air of a conquerer."[11]

Britton was seen near Neosho on Sunday, July 8. "Mr. Britton of late is somewhat retired in his habits," the *Herald* reported tongue in cheek, "confining his society to a secret circle of intimate friends."[12]

Mary Britton left Blende about July 10 and sold a wagon and team at Webb City a day or two later. It was thought she was making preparations to rendezvous and take flight with her fugitive husband.[13]

And that's exactly what happened. Britton and his wife fled to Texas, then New Mexico, and finally Phoenix, Arizona, where Britton was recaptured in the summer of 1885. He broke jail, however, before he could be extradited to Missouri, and he was never heard from again.

Until about ten years ago, that is—when it was learned through genealogical inquiries that he had lived out his life under an assumed name, settling down and rearing a family and finally dying in Hollywood, California, about 1920.[14]

Chapter 10

An Infuriated Human Tiger
Joe Thornton and the Killing of Officer Sheehan

Late Saturday afternoon, July 18, 1885, Joe Thornton, who operated a saloon and gambling parlor on the Kansas state line near Galena, drove into Joplin in a buggy, accompanied by a lady companion whom the *Joplin News* described as "the woman who claims to be his wife." Alighting from the buggy, Thornton, who'd had several scrapes with the law and was known as a tough character, took a revolver from his pocket and placed it under the seat to give the impression that he was disarming himself. As he and the woman strolled north on Main Street, they were spotted by Joplin police officer Daniel Sheehan, who'd been instructed to keep an eye out for Thornton.[1]

The thirty-three-year-old Thornton had come to the Galena area with his parents and siblings prior to 1880, and for some time, Joe, like the rest of the family, enjoyed a good reputation. After a few years, though, he "took to drink and associating with lewd women" and started getting into all kinds of trouble.[2]

In early 1884, Thornton got into a scrape with Galena police and paid a fine for carrying concealed weapons. During the same time period, he took over an "amusement parlor" on the state line at Dubuque, a mile east of Galena. Dubuque, or Budgetown as it was more commonly known, got its start in 1881 shortly after Kansas's newly enacted prohibition law went into effect. To circumvent the new law, a large "double building" was constructed with the eastern half lying in Missouri, where liquor was legal, and the western half sitting in Kansas, where gambling was legal. The Missouri half was used as a saloon and the western half as a casino, with a dance hall also on the same premises. The place burned down in May of 1884, but Thornton quickly rebuilt.[3]

On September 29, 1884, Thornton displayed a pistol in a threatening manner toward a citizen in Joplin. When city marshal Cass Hamilton went to arrest him, Thornton shoved the barrel of the weapon against the marshal's side and snapped it twice, but it misfired. Thornton was arrested for flourishing a deadly weapon and assaulting a law officer. He paid a $200 fine on the former charge, while the latter one was later dropped. In early December, Thornton beat up a man named Ginn at his saloon on the state line, supposedly because Ginn was paying too much attention to Thornton's woman. Thornton rode to Galena and announced in a boisterous tone that he had just killed a man at Budgetown, but when a doctor went to attend to the man, he found that Ginn was not seriously injured.[4]

In mid-May 1885, a report again reached Galena that Thornton had killed a man at his "notorious resort" on the state line. Investigation revealed that Thornton and a man named Roberts had, indeed, gotten into a drunken brawl and Thornton had struck the man on the head with a rock, but the blow did not kill Roberts. He was seriously injured, but Thornton, declaring that he and Roberts were good friends who'd both been drinking too much, was not arrested. About this same time, Thornton was also charged in Galena with assaulting a man named Ulrey, but, since Thornton lived on the Missouri side of the line, the case against him was postponed.[5]

During the fall of 1884 and spring of 1885, Thornton was charged in Missouri with several counts of selling liquor without a county license. Rather than lying low, though, Thornton seemed to enjoy flouting the law, and now he was doing so again, driving boldly into Joplin and ambling up Main Street with his so-called wife. Marshal Hamilton had told Officer Sheehan not to approach Thornton alone but to let him know if the desperado showed up. However, Hamilton was visiting the mines on the outskirts of town, and Sheehan determined just to shadow Thornton and see what he was up to. Near the corner of Second and Main, Sheehan ran onto Jasper

County deputy Julius Miller, who was carrying one of the outstanding warrants against Thornton. They were joined by George McMurtry of the Joplin Police, and Miller volunteered to serve the warrant with the help of the other two officers.[6]

The three lawmen went to Swartz's nearby dry goods store, where Thornton and his wife were shopping. McMurtry stayed at the door as Sheehan and Miller walked inside. Miller approached Thornton, who was standing near the middle of the store with his back to the door, and tapped him on the shoulder. When the suspect turned around, Miller asked whether his name was Thornton, and the desperado replied that it was. "I've got a warrant for you," the deputy said as he gripped Thornton by the right arm and Sheehan took hold of his left.[7]

Thornton started off with the two officers as though not to resist, but after taking a couple of steps, he suddenly jerked his right arm free and whipped out a .45 caliber revolver from beneath his belt. Before he could fire the pistol, Miller threw his arms around him from behind and grabbed the weapon with both hands. Sheehan went to work trying to loosen Thornton's grip on the pistol, but the desperado managed to get off a shot just as McMurtry came up and struck the muzzle downward hoping to deflect the path of the bullet into the floor.[8]

Too late! The ball ripped into Sheehan's gut, but the seriously wounded officer kept his grip on Thornton's arm. As Sheehan and Miller continued struggling to disarm Thornton, McMurtry, who was unarmed, struck the culprit a powerful blow on the side of the head, sending all three men sprawling to the floor in a narrow space between a counter and a showcase, with Sheehan on the bottom, Thornton in the middle, and Miller on top. The deputy was still gripping the pistol with both hands, and Thornton began savagely biting the lawman's hands. "Miller held on while his flesh was being mutilated by the teeth of the infuriated human tiger," said the *Joplin News*, "realizing that to let go meant death.[9]

"In the meantime," continued the *News*, "the show case had been removed and McMurtry was trying to get his work in. Sheehan's club was beneath the human heap and in reaching for it, McMurtry's hand got within range of Thornton's teeth and received a bite...but he got the club and commenced belaboring the criminal's head."[10]

The space McMurtry had to work in was limited, though, and Thornton and Miller's heads were so close together that the officer was afraid of hitting the wrong man. He did give Miller a glancing blow that almost caused the deputy to lose his grip, but "whenever McMurtry was able to get in a blow on the right head, he made it count. Blood spurted and the victim would cry out," but the desperate Thornton kept gnawing Miller's hands. By now, spectators had gathered round, and Miller called on them to help out. One of the bystanders jerked the counter out of the way to make more room, and another stepped in and was able to wrest the pistol from Thornton's hands. Seeing that further resistance was futile, Thornton quit fighting and was dragged from the store and off to jail.[11]

Afterward, Sheehan rose to his feet and leaned against a counter, and a bystander asked him if he was hurt. "Yes, I'm shot," he replied as he began sinking back down. He was taken to Dr. Robert Kelso's office, where an examination revealed he'd been shot near the navel with the bullet ranging downward through the abdomen and lodging near the spine. The wound was pronounced fatal, and the patient was removed to his home where his family could be at his side.[12]

But the vigilantes of Joplin didn't wait for him to die.

Throughout the evening, knots of men lingered in the vicinity of the jail, located on Second Street between Main and Joplin. Thornton talked freely to his guards and the other people who were allowed to get a glimpse of him, and he seemed unconcerned about the prospect of death. Announcing at one point that he was "too lazy to work" and "too ornery to live," he said that, if the people wanted to "send (him) over the road," he was ready. "I deserve to die, and if they bring on the rope I'll march out and die game." He added that he'd rather die now than go to the penitentiary. His speech, according to the *Joplin Daily Herald*, was "thickly set with oaths."[13]

About two o'clock Sunday morning, July 19, the crowd began to thin out, and three special officers assigned to help guard the prisoner left the jail to go check on Sheehan's condition. Suddenly a band of about fifteen to twenty masked men reappeared at the jail and began battering the outer iron door with a heavy piece of lumber. The commotion quickly drew curious bystanders to the scene, but the mob kept them at a distance with "a reckless flourish of revolvers."[14]

The masked men took but a moment to break the outer door down. Bursting into the jail, they covered the guards with their pistols and quickly overpowered them. The vigilantes used a pick to break the lock off Thornton's cell door, went in, and dragged the prisoner out. Placing a rope around his neck, they led him to the corner of Second and Joplin a half block away, where several maple trees stood in a residential lawn. The rope was looped over a limb of one of the trees, and Thornton was told that, if he had anything to say, to say it fast. Displaying the same boisterous courage he'd shown earlier in the night, the prisoner replied that he didn't think he'd been treated fairly but that he would "die game." The leader of the mob then gave an order to pull, "a dozen strong arms instantly obeyed the order, and Joe Thornton was suspended between heaven and earth."[15]

Daniel Sheehan's gravestone at Fairview Cemetery. *Photo by the author.*

The "midnight executioners" slipped away, and the gaping crowd surged up to the tree but quickly departed after taking a gander at the dangling corpse. The sheriff and a justice of the peace soon appeared and cut the body down. A coroner's jury convened and concluded that Thornton had come to an untimely death by hanging "at the hands of parties whom the jury did not have the honor to know." Meanwhile, Officer Sheehan died at ten o'clock Sunday morning after lingering for about fifteen hours. He was later interred at Fairview Cemetery in Joplin, while Thornton's body was taken back for burial in Galena, where his brother was a well-respected grocery store owner.[16]

Chapter 11

A Midnight Assassination
The Murder of Eben Brewer and the Hanging of James McAfee

Saturday, July 31, 1897, was a busy night in Joplin. It was payday for the miners, and the downtown area swarmed with people. Thirty-one-year-old James McAfee was among those roaming the streets. A "tough character" who'd been in "numerous scrapes," McAfee had been a miner himself until he strained his back the previous Tuesday and "took a layoff." Perhaps his lack of work prompted, at least in part, the desperate plan he devised that night. Sometime during the evening, McAfee proposed to an acquaintance, Ben Shoemaker, that they team up and rob Joplin storekeeper Eben Brewer when Brewer started home later that night.[1]

Shoemaker ostensibly agreed to the idea, but instead of carrying through with the crime, he promptly reported McAfee's plan to Joplin deputy constable Frank English. The constable, in turn, revealed the scheme to Brewer, who suggested that he and the police lay a trap for McAfee. Brewer would close up and start home as normal, but, unbeknown to McAfee, he would be armed and the officers would also be lying in wait for the robber. English advised against the plan, telling the storekeeper that the police force was short-handed. The city marshal and a deputy were out of town, and most of the rest of officers were busy monitoring the Saturday night crowd. However, the twenty-four-year-old Brewer insisted, explaining that he would enlist the help of his father-in-law, Joe Shelver, and English finally agreed to the proposition.[2]

Constable English went back out on the streets and stayed busy keeping the peace in the rowdy "North End" until late in the evening. He'd promised Brewer to take up his position near the rear of the store by eleven o'clock, but it was a quarter after by the time he arrived at the business, located at 1213 Main Street, and stepped inside. Another man, whom English didn't recognize, came in about the same time he did, purchased a pack of chewing gum, and then went to the water pail to get a drink. While the young man was drinking, English asked Brewer in a hushed tone whether McAfee had made an appearance. The storekeeper winked and motioned toward the man at the water pail. About that time, McAfee left through the back door.[3]

English offered to escort Brewer home and again tried to talk him out of carrying through with his scheme to catch McAfee red-handed. The constable pointed out that, since McAfee was already nearby, it was too late for him (English) to take up a strategic hiding position as he'd planned. Brewer nonetheless insisted that the "matinee should come off at once" and that he could "take care of himself." Explaining his plan of action, he said he would leave the store accompanied by his father-in-law. Brewer would have a revolver concealed in a paper sack, and Shelver would have a double handful of red pepper to throw in the robber's eyes. If McAfee ordered Brewer to throw up his hands, he would raise them with the sack in his hand and shoot through the sack while his father-in-law threw the pepper in the crook's eyes.[4]

English thought it was a dangerous plan, but Brewer still insisted. Agreeing to take up the best position he could to help nab the robber, English left the store and hid at the south end of the alley behind the store. Meanwhile, officer Ben May and the police informant, Ben Shoemaker, stationed themselves at the north end of the alley. As soon as Brewer and Shelver closed the store, they left by the front entrance, walked to the south side of the building, and turned east across a vacant lot toward the alley. Brewer's home was located on the west side of Virginia Avenue adjoining the alley and almost directly behind the store, but just as he and Shelver reached the alley, McAfee stepped out from behind an outhouse blocking Shelver's path. Shelver tried to throw the pepper in his assailant's eyes, but a gust of wind caught it and blew it back in Shelver's own eyes. He took off running, and McAfee fired a shot at him that went through the brim of his hat. The robber then turned and fired at Brewer, hitting him under his arm on the left side. Brewer staggered across the alley to the turnstile leading into his backyard, where he opened fired on McAfee but missed.[5]

Immediately after the first shots rang out, Constable English saw a shadowy figure racing toward him in the alley. English called "halt," and when the man obeyed, the constable quickly recognized him as Shelver. Looking down the alley toward the scene of the crime, English saw McAfee fleeing north about eighty feet away. He fired two shots at the suspect but missed. Upon reaching the north end of the alley, McAfee encountered Shoemaker and Officer May, who fired a hail of bullets at him, but he managed to "run the gauntlet" and make his escape.[6]

Very soon afterwards, however, Officer Ogburn of the Joplin Police spotted McAfee at the corner of Ninth and Main and halted him for questioning. McAfee denied involvement in the shooting, but he fit the description Ogburn had been given, he was breathing hard, and his shirt front was speckled with blood. McAfee was taken to the city jail on suspicion. Constable English identified him as the man who'd come into Brewer's store and bought chewing gun shortly before the shooting, and Ben Shoemaker said he was the man who tried to enlist him as a partner in crime. McAfee, though, continued to deny his guilt. He said that he had not been to Brewer's store on Saturday night, and he claimed he didn't even know Ben Shoemaker. McAfee said he'd been downtown most of the evening and had already gone to his home on Wall Street between Second and Third and was in bed when he heard the gunshots and got up to investigate. He said he went south on Main, where he was arrested by Officer Ogburn, but nobody believed his incredible story. Not only were the circumstances and the testimony of English and Shoemaker against him, but his alibi seemed implausible. Folks in the vicinity of Fourth and Main had not heard the gunshots from eight blocks away; yet, McAfee claimed the sound of the shots roused him from his slumber two and half blocks farther away.[7]

Medical help was summoned for Eben Brewer immediately after the shooting, but the doctors who treated him held out little hope for his recovery. As word of the deadly assault spread, a mob formed and talked of lynching McAfee; so City Marshal W. E. Morgan decided the next day, August 1, to take the prisoner to Carthage for safekeeping. In preparing McAfee for the trip, the marshal discovered a hole in the left shoulder of the prisoner's coat and asked what caused it. McAfee replied that a crowbar fell on the garment while it was lying on the ground at the mines, but upon investigation, Morgan found a wound on the prisoner's arm corresponding to where the hole in the coat was. Officers had thought at first that McAfee escaped the gun battle unscathed, but it now appeared he'd been wounded by one of the officers. The shot had gone completely through his arm, and McAfee had plugged up both the entry and the exit wound with tobacco and ravelings from his coat. Upon further questioning, McAfee admitted that he had another wound that was causing him more pain than the one in his arm. An examination revealed a second wound in the prisoner's thigh that had also been plugged up with tobacco and ravelings. McAfee had borne the pain of both wounds rather then reveal that he'd been shot.[8]

Headline from the *Springfield Republican* tells the story of Eben Brewer's killing.

McAfee was escorted later that day to the Jasper County Jail at Carthage, where he received medical attention for his wounds. His attempt to conceal his wounds having been discovered, the prisoner broke down and confessed the robbery attempt and shooting of Brewer. He told where he had ditched his weapon after the crime, and the next day, Monday, August 2, a .44 revolver was found near a mine shaft at the corner of Tenth and Pennsylvania. Brewer died a couple of days later, and a grand jury subsequently charged McAfee with first-degree murder.[9]

McAfee's case came up in the Jasper County Circuit Court at Carthage in late April 1898. Constable English was one of several damning witnesses for the prosecution, but McAfee's lawyers also put up a stiff defense, nearly "building a stone wall around their client out of tissue paper," according to one source. At the end of a week-long trial, the jury was initially split eight to four for conviction, but after a night of deliberation, the jury came back on May 4 with a verdict finding McAfee guilty of first-degree murder. Judge Joseph D. Perkins overruled a defense motion for a new trial and sentenced McAfee to hang on July 15, 1898. The execution was automatically stayed when the defense appealed to the Missouri Supreme Court.[10]

The high court affirmed the decision of the lower court in early March 1899, and the execution date was reset for April 8, 1899. McAfee's attorneys then turned to Missouri governor Lon V. Stephens, who stayed the execution until July 6, 1899.[11]

On the night before he was to be hanged, McAfee dozed in peaceful slumber, according to the *Joplin Daily News*, sleeping until 5:20 a.m., but he "ate sparingly of a tempting breakfast." After breakfast, he paced restlessly about his cell, casting occasional glances at the scaffold and surrounding stockade outside his window just west of the jail. He was then left alone for about an hour with his spiritual advisor, who prayed with him and read the Bible.[12]

Outside the jail, curiosity-seekers milled around. Many tried to gain entrance to the stockade, but the sheriff had issued passes only to a select few individuals to be allowed inside the structure. Counting deputies and other officials, only about fifty people would be allowed inside the stockade as witnesses.

About 9:30 Sheriff W. H. Warren entered McAfee's cell and read the death warrant. A deputy bound the condemned man hands and arms. The procession to the scaffold then began.

Escorted by his attorney, his spiritual advisor, several county officials, and a couple of other men, McAfee marched down the stairs to the lower floor of the jail and from there walked straight onto the scaffold by means of a stairway through a window. His legs were bound, and he was positioned directly over the center of the trap door. Asked whether he had anything to say, McAfee didn't utter a word, and a minister finally broke the silence with a public prayer. The rope was placed around the doomed man's neck, and a black cap was adjusted over his head. Sheriff Warren then swung the trap at 9:52 a.m.[13]

The condemned man fell several feet, and his neck broke with an audible snap. McAfee was pronounced dead after about fifteen minutes, but his body was left hanging for another hour so that those who'd been denied the pleasure of watching a man die could at least take a gander at his dead body after he had been hanged. Among those who availed themselves of this opportunity were Eben Brewer's young widow, Emma, and the couple's little boy, who had been born after his father was killed. "If ever a man met a just death, it is that man there," Mrs. Brewer reportedly remarked as she pointed at the corpse. McAfee's body was cut down shortly after 11:00 a.m. and taken to a local undertaker, who later turned it over to the McAfee family for burial.[14]

Chapter 12

The Fate of a Defamer
Shot Dead for "Circulating Bad Stories" About a Young Woman

Immediately after William DeAtley shot and killed Fred Robertson in Joplin in December of 1899, stories circulated that the twenty-two-year-old DeAtley committed the crime because of an alleged wrong done to his younger sister. But at the coroner's inquest the next day, no extenuating circumstances were introduced to justify the shooting except that the two men had gotten into a fight and the thirty-two-year-old Robertson had beaten DeAtley up. Even at DeAtley's trial in February 1900, his lawyers pursued a self-defense argument rather than risk exposing the sister to public humiliation. Not until after the February trial ended in a hung jury and DeAtley went on trial again in July 1900 did the whole truth come out.

DeAtley worked at the Pennsylvania Mine in Leadville Hollow on the northwest edge of Joplin. He was on his way home after work on the late afternoon of December 20, 1899, when he ran onto Robertson and a friend of Robertson's named Reece Reeves, both of whom worked in the nearby Chitwood mines. Angry words were exchanged, and Robertson, with the help of Reeves, attacked the smaller DeAtley and gave him "a good pounding."[1]

When Robertson and Reeves finally let DeAtley up, he ran toward town and retrieved a pistol from his home on Empire Street in west Joplin. DeAtley hurried back out to meet Robertson and Reeves, who had followed DeAtley toward his home, and fired several shots at Robertson, none of which took effect. DeAtley then went back home.[2]

Nervous with excitement, he told his mother what had happened. He got some money from her and started downtown to buy more ammunition. Immediately afterward, his mother set off carrying a large butcher knife toward Mrs. Butler's house in the 800 block of Locust Street (now Picher), where Robertson and Reeves boarded. Young DeAtley bought more ammunition for his pistol and raced back home. When he found his mother gone, he headed for Mrs. Butler's house looking for her. She wasn't there, but when DeAtley knocked on the door, Robertson appeared with a revolver in his hand. DeAtley shot him through the glass in the upper part of the door, as he reached to open it.[3]

DeAtley fled, and medical help was summoned for Robertson. Arrested at his home a short time later, DeAtley was taken to the circuit court jail in Joplin.[4]

Reeves was also taken into custody for questioning. He swore out a warrant against DeAtley's mother, Sarah, for coming to the Butler house with the butcher knife before her son shot Robertson. Reeves claimed she displayed the knife in a threatening manner. The police interviewed Mrs. DeAtley, but they either did not arrest her or quickly released her. She told officers her son was not to blame for what happened and that, if the case came to trial, "Robertson's villainy would all be exposed." To even the score with Reeves for swearing out the warrant against Mrs. DeAtley, William DeAtley swore one out against Reeves for assault.[5]

On the evening of his arrest, reporters from the *Joplin Globe* and the *Joplin Daily News* called at the jail and spoke to DeAtley. The young man acknowledged that Robertson had been "circulating bad stories" about his sister, fifteen-year-old Della Belle, but he "begged like a good fellow not to have his sister's name mixed up with the tragedy." The prisoner said Robertson had formerly boarded with the DeAtleys and had shown some attention to Belle. After Belle married another young man, Prentice Hedrick, Robertson continued trying to "make himself familiar" with her and began telling vile stories about her. Belle told her brother and her mother about Robertson's mistreatment of her, and Mrs. DeAtley ordered Robertson out of her boarding house, with her son delivering the message. Robertson left in anger, but "instead of persecuting" Belle or her mother, William DeAtley "came in for the lion's share" of Robertson's wrath.[6]

FATE OF DEFAMER.

Wm. DeAtley Killed Fred Robertson at Byersville Last Night.

SCENE OF THE CRIME NEAR JOPLIN

The Victim Had Defamed DeAtley's Sister's Good Name.

Galena Evening Times headline tells the story of Fred Robertson's killing.

DeAtley said that, when he met Robertson and Reeves as the three young men were heading home after work earlier that day, Robertson first asked him whether he was carrying a gun. When DeAtley replied that he was not, both Robertson and Reeves jumped him, knocking him down and beating him up. "DeAtley's face and head bore all the evidences of a good beating," said the *Globe* reporter, "his lips and cheek being swollen with scratches innumerable upon his face." When DeAtley's attackers released him, Robertson threatened to kill him if he reported them to the police. Instead of going to the law, DeAtley decided to take matters into his own hands and "went for his gun."[7]

DeAtley, according to the reporter, was "nothing but a large, smooth-faced boy," while Robertson was older and "much larger than DeAtley."[8]

The *Globe* reporter also sought an interview with Reeves. He was "rather reticent concerning the whole affair, but when pumped right hard, acknowledged that the trouble originated from remarks made by Robertson concerning DeAtley's sister." His story of the fight earlier that day was very similar to DeAtley's except that he claimed he and Robertson did not beat DeAtley up after they jumped him but instead only threw him down and held him.[9]

Two doctors attended Robertson, but he died later that night about 10:30 p.m. The pistol ball had entered his diaphragm and ranged downward, but the doctors were unable to locate and extract the bullet.[10]

Despite DeAtley's statements to the reporters the previous evening, "nothing sensational" was brought out at the coroner's inquest held on December 21, and "no testimony was offered in justification" of the shooting. The most noteworthy evidence was a deathbed statement the coroner had taken from Robertson in which he described the circumstances of his fatal encounter with DeAtley. He said merely that he and DeAtley met and "came to blows" as they were leaving work and that DeAtley shortly afterward came to his boarding house with a pistol. Robertson admitted that he also had a gun in his hand as he approached the door, but he said he did not display it in a threatening manner. He said DeAtley held a grudge against him because of a woman he ran around with, but Robertson claimed he did not even know the woman's name and did not know whether he'd "made any statements about her or not." He made no mention of DeAtley's sister.[11]

The coroner's jury concluded that Robertson died from a gunshot wound and that the gun was fired by William DeAtley. The alleged killer was bound over for trial on a charge of first-degree murder.[12]

The same day as the coroner's jury, Reeves pleaded guilty to the charge of assaulting DeAtley, paid a one-dollar fine, and left town.[13]

DeAtley's trial got underway in Joplin in early February 1900. The highlight of the proceeding came on February 8 when DeAtley took the stand in his own defense. His statement was similar to what he'd told the reporters on the evening of his arrest, but he added a few details. He said Robertson had threatened to "fix" him on the day that he had, at his mother's direction, kicked Robertson out of his mom's boarding house, which occurred about a month before the shooting. He said there was a girl who worked for his mother while Robertson was staying with the DeAtleys but that he and Robertson never argued about her. He added that, when he went to the Butler home, Robertson not only had a revolver in his hand but also pointed it at him.[14]

Several character witnesses testified as to DeAtley's good reputation. A young married couple said they'd both known DeAtley since he was nine years old and that he was a peaceful, law-abiding citizen.[15]

DeAtley's lawyers did not dispute the prosecution's story of the shooting, which was basically what all parties had conceded from the beginning: that DeAtley had fired his pistol at Robertson and Reeves after they'd beaten him up and that he'd then retrieved more ammunition, gone to the Butler home, and shot Robertson. DeAtley's attorneys wanted to put Belle DeAtley on the stand to testify about Robertson's mistreatment of her in order to save her brother from the penitentiary. Her husband was also ready to testify for the defense. However, DeAtley and his parents refused to drag Belle's name into the proceedings. When the judge issued instructions precluding a verdict of not guilty by reason of self-defense, DeAtley's attorneys had to resort to citing mitigating circumstances and arguing for the lowest possible punishment, which was a verdict of manslaughter in the fourth degree, a $100 fine, and three months in the county jail. The prosecution, on the other hand, said DeAtley had plenty of time to contemplate his act before he did it and that it was, therefore, willful murder.[16]

The case was given to the jury on the late afternoon of February 9. After being out three days and nights, they came back on February 12 and announced that they were hopelessly deadlocked. They agreed that DeAtley should not go scot-free but were unable to reach a verdict on the defendant's degree of guilt. One-half argued for fourth-degree manslaughter, while the other half held out for a higher degree of manslaughter. The judge declared a mistrial and dismissed the jury.[17]

At DeAtley's second trial, which began on July 17, 1900, both the prosecution and the defense pursued more aggressive arguments than they had at the first one. During its opening statement, the prosecution said it would show that Robertson and DeAtley were vying for the affections of the same young woman, a Miss Kennedy, and that DeAtley was angry because Robertson was more successful in his courtship of the girl. DeAtley had even threatened to kill Robertson. The defense, on the other hand, said the dispute between the two men involved DeAtley's sister. While boarding with Mrs. DeAtley, Robertson had "accomplished the ruin" of her fifteen-year-old daughter and afterward, to save himself trouble, had induced another young man, Hedrick, to marry the girl. Shortly after the hasty marriage, Hedrick deserted his teenage bride and joined the military. Robertson then began once again paying unwanted attention to Belle, making insulting statements about her, and boasting that he could "do as he pleased" where she was concerned, using words "that cannot be printed."[18]

Despite the opening statements, the state did not attempt to introduce evidence concerning Miss Kennedy, and early in the defense phase of the trial, each time DeAtley's lawyers tried to introduce testimony about Belle DeAtley, the judge sustained the prosecutors' objections. Finally, though, such testimony was allowed in when Belle's father, Henry

DeAtley, took the stand on the second day of the trial and announced that his daughter had given birth the night before. A deposition the girl had given was allowed into evidence over the state's objection. In her statement, Belle said she was still fifteen and would not turn sixteen until later in July. She said that on September 30, 1899, Fred Robertson raped her while they were alone at the DeAtley home, forcing her to "do things she did not want to." Two days later, she married Prentice Hedrick to hide her shame, and she did not know which man was the father of her baby. Hedrick left her, she said, the day after her brother's first trial concluded.[19]

Prosecutors located Reeves in McDonald County and brought him back to Joplin for the second trial. After DeAtley testified in his own defense, they put Reeves on the stand to try to rebut the defendant's story of the confrontation that led up to the shooting. Reeves said DeAtley started the fight just as much as he and Robertson did, and he claimed the only reason he'd pleaded guilty to assaulting DeAtley was because he had no one to go his bail and he wanted to leave for McDonald County, where he had a young woman waiting to marry him.[20]

Henry DeAtley's testimony and his daughter's deposition, however, had already put a big dent in the prosecution's case. In fact, July 18, the second day of the trial, was a "field day for the defense," as one newspaper called it. At the first trial, DeAtley's lawyers had tried to argue self-defense, but this time they had thrown that argument "to the winds and stood first, last and all the time on the fact that the defendant did commit the crime, but that the circumstances palliated and even excused his crime."[21]

Apparently the jury agreed that the circumstances palliated the crime but did not quite agree that they excused the deed. Although the state clung to the idea that the real cause of the trouble between DeAtley and Robertson revolved around Miss Kennedy and argued for a second-degree murder conviction, the jury came back on the evening of July 19 after being out less than three hours with a verdict of manslaughter in the fourth degree and assessed a sentence of two years in the state penitentiary. According to the *Joplin Globe*, the verdict showed the jury "attached great weight to the evidence proving the commendable motives of the boy, but at the same time they wished to put a stop to the cheapening of human life, and allowing every man to carry in his own mind the tribunal of justice...."[22]

Interviewed after the verdict was announced. DeAtley said, "It is not as good as I expected, but I am very well satisfied."[23]

DeAtley was transported to Jefferson City on August 12, 1900, and was processed into the penitentiary the next day. He was discharged on January 1, 1902, under the three-fourths time good behavior rule. After his release, DeAtley got married, moved to Idaho and later Oregon, and raised a family.[24]

Chapter 13

I Came Out Here to Die Like a Man
The Murder of Gertie Reid and the
Hanging of Ernest Reid

On Sunday, June 17, 1900, Ernest Reid visited his estranged wife, Amanda Gertrude "Gertie" Reid, at the Frank Wyatt residence in Carthage, Missouri, where she had been boarding for the past month. Reid took dinner with the family, and sometime during the visit he and his wife got into an argument, as they were wont to do of late. The quarrel escalated to the point that Reid threatened to kill Gertie if she did not come back to him.[1]

Ernest and Gertie Reid had come to Carthage from Kansas about a year earlier and had seemingly gotten along okay at first. But during the early spring of 1900, they had a serious dispute. Declaring she could no longer live with her husband, Gertie left him and went to work for a white family in Carthage as a live-in housekeeper. Reid "took this state of affairs to heart" and tried to commit suicide on the Carthage square by eating a dose of Rough on Rats; however, the police found him and summoned doctors, who saved his life.[2]

Ernest started coming around to where Gertie was staying to bum money from her when she was paid at the end of each week. At first, she agreed to help him out, but, seeing that he was just gambling the money away, she cut him off about the time she came to live with the Wyatts, who were black like she and Ernest. He soon started making threats against her life, saying he was going to kill her if she didn't give him more money.[3]

Now, he'd renewed the threat, and this time he meant to carry it out. On Tuesday, June 19, two days after taking dinner at the Wyatts, Reid went to a second-hand store in Carthage and paid twenty-five cents to rent a pistol until the next day, pawning some clothing as a guarantee to return the weapon. That evening he asked his younger brother, Ben, to tell Gertie that the Reids' brother and cousin were in Carthage and wanted to see Gertie before they left. They would be at the train depot about 8:30 p.m. on their way out of town, and Ernest wanted his brother to take Gertie to the depot at the designated time. He promised to meet them there after he got off work and changed his clothes.[4]

When Ben Reid called at the Wyatt home near the corner of Locust and Vine in the northeast part of town, Mrs. Wyatt balked at the idea of Gertie leaving to meet her estranged husband and tried to talk her out of it. Gertie, though, assured Mrs. Wyatt that she would be all right.[5]

Gertie walked with Ben about a half mile to the depot near Main and Limestone (i.e. Claxton) streets. After waiting until about 8:45 with no sign of either Ernest Reid or his relatives, Gertie and Ben started to leave. Just as they were walking out the door of the depot, Ernest showed up and announced that the brother and cousin must have decided to stay over until morning. He proposed that he, Gertie, and Ben go to Tiger Hill (at the north end of Garrison) and pay a visit at the home where the relatives were staying. Gertie and Ben both objected, but Ernest talked them into making the trek.[6]

They crossed Main and started west on Limestone. Ernest seemed to be in a good mood and showed affection toward his wife. As they came alongside the Stout-Parke foundry at the corner of Limestone and North Maple, however, Ernest and Gertie stopped and began exchanging heated words, as Ben ambled on several steps ahead. Ernest had a photo of Gertie that she had asked him to return to her, and he demanded to know why she wanted it back. He accused her of "being too thick" with a man named Sims, who was also boarding with the Wyatt family, and Ernest thought she wanted to give the photo to Sims.[7]

Reid took hold of his wife's arm with one hand and berated her for not wanting to go to church with him or go up town with him. He said she was ashamed to be seen with him. He admitted that he'd lied to her about his brother and cousin, because tricking her was the only way he could get her away from the Wyatts' house so he could see her. Gertie started sobbing and begging Ernest to turn her loose. Instead of letting her go, he tightened his grip on her arm while reaching with the other hand for the revolver he'd brought along. Flourishing the weapon, he shot Gertie in the leg, and she fell to her knees. When he released his grip, she sprang up and started running, and he fired three more shots as she retreated. The first shot missed, but the next two struck Gertie in the back.[8]

Despite being gravely wounded, Gertie continued down the street, and Ben helped her back to the Wyatt home. Meanwhile, Ernest fled the scene, heading back to downtown Carthage. As he passed a hotel, he told a group of people gathered there, "A man has just shot a woman down there," indicating the direction he'd come from. He made similar remarks to others gathered on the streets during his walk and after he reached the public square. To one group, he said a black man had just shot a woman down in the bottoms, and he told another that someone had just shot his wife.[9]

Learning of the affray, two policemen went immediately to the Wyatt home, where Gertie and Ben told them what had happened. As the officers were leaving, they encountered Ernest Reid approaching the house and took him into custody. He was still carrying the pistol with which he'd done the shooting, and an inspection of the weapon revealed four empty cartridge shells. On the way to jail, Reid admitted shooting his wife. Asked why he had done it, he said he had "made up his mind to kill her rather than have her live with someone else."[10]

Gertie lingered in pain throughout the night, and doctors announced the next day that her chances of recovery were slim. A representative of the county prosecutor's office, accompanied by the Carthage city marshal, went to the Wyatt home and transcribed in ink a statement from the dying woman in which she described the shooting and the events leading up to it.[11]

The officials left the statement with Gertie with instructions for her to sign it when death approached if she still wanted to attest to the facts in the statement. Gertie continued lingering throughout the night and into the very early morning of June 21. Between 1:00 and 2:00 a.m., she called for the paper and signed it in pencil. Below her signature, she added in her own handwriting, "This is my testimony. He shot me on purpose." Gertie died barely over an hour later.[12]

A quarrel over this photo of Gertie Reid led to her death. *From the Carthage Evening Press.*

Ernest Reid went on trial at Carthage for first-degree murder in November 1900. Among the prosecution witnesses were several people the defendant had talked to in the immediate aftermath of the shooting, including one who testified that Reid admitted doing the shooting. Also testifying for the state were the two officers who arrested him and the two men who took Gertie's dying statement. "The evidence introduced by the prosecution," opined the *Carthage Evening Press*, "made a wonderfully strong case."[13]

Reid took the stand in his own defense. He admitted shooting his wife, but he claimed it was done in the heat of passion. He said that when he demanded to know why his wife wanted him to return her picture, she admitted it was for Mr. Sims and snatched the picture from him. In the heat of the moment, Reid drew his revolver and opened fire.[14]

The only other defense witness was the man who rented Reid the pistol with which he'd shot Gertie. The defense wanted to show that Reid had obtained the revolver for a reason other than harming Gertie, but this testimony was disallowed.[15]

On the afternoon of November 16, the jury returned a verdict of murder in the first degree after deliberating almost three hours. It took three ballots to secure a unanimous verdict, as one or two jurors voted for acquittal on the first two ballots.[16]

A defense motion for a new trial was denied in early December 1900, and Reid was sentenced to hang the following January. His attorneys, however, appealed to the Missouri Supreme Court, primarily on the grounds that the jury should have been given the option of finding Reid guilty of second-degree murder. The execution was automatically postponed pending the high court's decision.[17]

In early May 1901, the supreme court affirmed the lower court's decision, ruling that Reid's purchase of the pistol on the day of the shooting and his later admissions to the arresting officers showed clear premeditation. The execution was rescheduled for June 7, but Missouri governor Alexander M. Dockery granted a respite until June 21. He later stayed the execution a second time, until July 5.[18]

As the fateful day approached, preparations for the hanging began. On the Fourth of July, a scaffold was erected on the courthouse grounds just outside the jail. "The building of the scaffold right under Reid's window must have been a trying ordeal for him," observed the *Carthage Evening Press*. "He did not seem to notice it, however."[19]

The only time he gave way to his emotions was when a band participating in the Fourth of July parade came down to the jail at his request and played "Old Kentucky Home" for him. Reid was allowed to come out of his cell and stand at the front window, and "the tears ran down his cheeks while it was being played."[20]

Reid's extraordinary fortitude continued throughout the evening of the fourth and into the next morning. "Reid's cool nerve, yet quiet demeanor with absence of all braggadocio, was certainly remarkable and won the admiration of all who witnessed it," said the *Evening Press*. "It is the same spirit he has shown all along."[21]

The condemned man had professed religion and been baptized several months earlier, and he spent the early morning hours of July 5 in song and prayer with one of his spiritual advisors. The death warrant was read to the prisoner shortly before ten a.m. A few minutes later, Reid's hands were tied in front of him and his arms strapped to his body at the elbows. Marched to the scaffold shortly after ten o'clock, Reid was allowed to make a statement to the small crowd gathered inside the stockade surrounding the platform. "I came out here this morning to die like a man," he announced in a low but firm voice. "Why do I say I came out here to die like a man? Because God stands with me here on this scaffold." Reid went on to thank his friends, his spiritual advisors, and others who'd treated him well since his incarceration.[22]

Reid had already positioned himself on the trap door as soon as he stepped onto the scaffold, and after he finished his speech, his legs were bound, a black cap placed over his head, and the noose adjusted around his neck. "He was cool and brave to the last," said the *Evening Press*.[23]

The trap was sprung at 10:19 a.m., and Reid dropped into eternity, which, in this case, was a distance of seven feet. He was pronounced dead seven minutes later. The body was promptly taken down, transported to Knell's Undertaking, and buried later that evening in Park Cemetery. Throughout his incarceration, Reid had remained devoted to the wife he killed, and, in a bit of tragic irony, he requested that the only picture he had of her, the same photo that instigated the fight resulting in her death, be buried with him.?[24]

Chapter 14

The Killing of Officer Theodore Leslie, the Lynching of Thomas Gilyard, and the Joplin Race Riot

In the early evening of April 14, 1903, Joplin hardware merchant Sam Bullock reported to police that two black men had stolen two revolvers from him. Another young black man told Bullock he knew where the two men who'd stolen the guns were hiding, and Bullock and the lad, accompanied by Officer Ben May, set off to look for the culprits. Meanwhile, Officer Theodore Leslie reported to the night captain that he'd been informed there were two black men with guns in the yards of the Kansas City Southern Railroad, located in the Joplin Creek valley just east of downtown. Dispatched to join the other three searchers, Leslie set out to overtake them but was unable to locate them. His failure to do so probably cost him his life.[1]

Working alone, Leslie approached a string of boxcars parked on a siding in the bottoms about a hundred yards north of Broadway. He spotted a black man standing on the east side of the northern-most car and ordered him to halt and be searched. Leslie had just finished searching the man when a shot rang out, apparently coming from inside the nearby boxcar. The officer returned the fire, completely emptying his revolver. Just as Leslie fired his last shot, a bullet struck him in the head, and he collapsed and died almost instantly.[2]

A number of people who'd trailed behind the officer witnessed the exchange from over a hundred yards away, and they saw a young black man leap from the boxcar and head north just after Leslie fell dead. "It was growing quite dusk at that time," observed the *Joplin Globe* the next day, "and it was almost impossible to tell exactly all that transpired."[3]

As the suspect started north, nineteen-year-old Ike Clark and three other young white men gave chase. Clark got within about fifty yards of the fleeing man and fired two shots at him. At this point, the suspect, who'd reloaded his revolver as he fled, wheeled and returned fire at his pursuers. Clark fired two more shots, but none of the shots seemed to take effect. The four pursuers then called off the chase and returned to where Officer Leslie had fallen. Although none of the shots fired at the fleeing man slowed him down, some of his pursuers later reported that they thought he might have been wounded.[4]

The black man whom Leslie had just finished searching broke and ran when the shooting started, but he ran right into another officer and was placed under arrest. The young black man who'd acted as a guide for Bullock and Officer May was also taken into custody, but both men denied any complicity in the shooting. The man who'd been searched said he'd just met the man in the boxcar less than five minutes before the shooting, and the police were inclined to believe him.[5]

As word of the of the shooting spread, hundreds of men congregated near the scene, and excitement ran high. Bloodhounds arrived from Webb City and were put on the trail of "the assassin," as the *Globe* dubbed the shooter. The dogs followed the scent of the fugitive to a point about three miles north of Joplin between Turkey Creek and Center Creek before their handlers called off the chase about 11:00 p.m., giving as their reason the fact that they had not been provided with rides and having to walk was slowing them down. Reward money totaling $1,650 was offered for the capture of the shooter, and dozens of officers and citizens continued scouring the countryside throughout the night.[6]

About three o'clock the next day, April 15, a black man who had been wounded and who was armed with a pistol sought refuge at the Bauer Brothers slaughterhouse near Midway Park on the northeast outskirts of Joplin. An employee of the slaughterhouse and a nearby resident, concluding that the man was the wanted fugitive, managed to disarm and capture him by edging close to him and presenting a knife at his throat. They brought him to Joplin, where he was promptly lodged in the city jail on the south side of Second Street between Main and Joplin.

He admitted he'd been in the boxcar when Officer Leslie was shot and that he'd been wounded by one of Leslie's bullets, but he said that three other black men were in the car with him and that he had not done the shooting.[7]

Word spread rapidly after the young black man was captured, and thousands of people quickly thronged the streets outside the jail. Cries of "Get a rope!" and "Hang the Negro!" went up. Mayor-elect Thomas Cunningham and other officials addressed the crowd urging them to let the law take its course. Their pleas seemed to have some calming effect but only for a moment. The prisoner had been locked up only about fifteen minutes when "an angry mob attacked the weather-beaten old jail." It was not quite 5:00 o'clock in the afternoon.[8]

The police tried to stymie the mob, but each time a battering ram was taken from one group of vigilantes, another group stepped up to the task. Within a few minutes an iron door that faced an alley on the jail's east side was battered down, and a number of men trooped inside and began work on the lock where the black man was held. "The breaking of the lock was but the work of a minute," said the *Globe*, "and then a rush was made for the victim."[9]

The prisoner fought fiercely but was quickly overpowered and dragged from the jail. A mob estimated at no less than 3,000 people surged west on Second Street with the prisoner, surrounding him on all sides. "Men shouted and women and children screamed," said the *Globe*. "The mob went on a run and the street was filled from curb to curb for a distance of more than a block." The captive still tried to resist as he was dragged along, but the heartless mob beat, choked, and trampled him unmercifully.[10]

At the southeast corner of Second and Wall, the mob paused, and men and boys scampered up trees and climbed onto the roofs of nearby buildings to get a better view of the anticipated lynching. The man with the rope was bringing up the rear of the mob, which gave Mayor Cunningham and other officials a last chance to talk the horde out of carrying through with the extralegal hanging. Joplin attorney Perl Decker rode into the mob on horseback and pleaded with the crowd to take the prisoner back to jail. Decker placed Ike Clark on his horse, and Ike, the lad who had followed and shot at the fugitive, told the crowd that the man they were about to hang was not the one who had killed Officer Leslie.[11]

AT THE SCENE OF THE LYNCHING.
(Sketched From the East Side of Wall Street Looking to the Northwest.)

Scene of the lynching, sketched by a *Joplin Globe* artist.

The testimony of Clark and the pleadings of the other men caused the crowd to hesitate, but suddenly another outburst of shouts and shrieks went up and the mob surged across the street to the northwest corner of Second and Wall. The prisoner was positioned beneath a telephone pole and one end of the rope looped around his neck. A man scampered up the pole and placed the other end of the rope over a crossbeam of the pole.[12]

A number of men took hold of the loose end of the rope and began trying to hoist the prisoner up, but several others took hold of the other end, where the black man was tied, in an effort to prevent the lynching. A regular tug of war lasted for some time, before the men determined to hang the prisoner finally succeeded in lifting him into the air. The man was nearly dead from the beating and cuffing he'd received at the hands of the mob, even before he was hoisted up, and his body was almost naked. After he was lifted up, someone fired a shot into his dangling body, putting him out of his misery. It was 5:50 in the afternoon.[13]

"There was a stifling stillness just after the gruesome task," according to the *Globe*. The quiet lasted an hour or two. Then, after the saloons, which the sheriff had ordered closed, were opened back up and people began to discuss the lynching, excitement flared back up, directed this time at the entire black community. Shortly before 8:00 p.m., a band of two or three dozen men marched down Main Street yelling, "Down with the Negroes!" and "Hang the coons!"[14]

The small cluster quickly grew to "an animated and highly inflamed horde" that "pushed and shoved one another and ran pell mell over everything in their path." Again prominent citizens tried to calm the frenzied mob that congregated near the corner of Fifth and Main but to no avail. The angry crowd surged north down Main Street with over a hundred boys from age seven and up trailing behind and yelling "like young demons."[15]

The throng descended on a black neighborhood in the North End, where they set fire to a half dozen "negro shanties." The mob, numbering over a thousand, then marched to another black district on East Seventh and torched several "negro cabins." Many black residents of Joplin fled the city to escape the wrath of the seething mob, and some never returned.[16]

The body of the lynching victim was taken down about an hour after he'd been hanged, removed to a local undertaker, and then, when the mob began to reform, spirited away in secrecy to prevent the vigilantes from burning the corpse. The young black man had given his name to an officer when he was first brought to the Joplin City Jail, but the officer had forgotten the name. The young man was finally identified late that night as twenty-year-old Thomas Gilyard, although the identification was still tentative.[17]

A coroner's inquest into Officer Leslie's death had begun on the night of the 14th, and it continued on the 15th, the day of the lynching. Although Ike Clark had told the mob that the man they were about to hang was not the man who'd jumped from the boxcar after Leslie was shot, he sang a different tune when he appeared before the coroner's jury. Clark positively identified the lynching victim as the man he'd chased and added that he'd seen the man fire two shots at Leslie after he jumped from the boxcar and after Leslie was already on the ground. The jury accordingly concluded that Leslie had come to his death at the hands of the man who'd been lynched.[18]

The next day, April 16, an inquest was also held over the body of Thomas Gilyard, although he was still referred to as "a negro whose name is unknown." The jury concluded that Gilyard had come to his death by hanging, and Sam Mitchell, "Hickory Bill" Field, and B. H. Barnes were named as the leaders of the lynch party. All three men were indicted for murder, and Mitchell, who was identified as the man who looped the rope around Gilyard's neck, was convicted in June and sentenced to ten years in the state prison. However, he was acquitted on retrial later in the year.[19]

Considering that instigators of lynchings in late nineteenth and early twentieth century America were rarely identified and even more rarely indicted, the only real surprise is that Mitchell was brought to trial and convicted in the first place.

Chapter 15

Foot and a Half Butler and His Sidekicks
The Killing of Joplin Policeman Claude Brice

In the wee hours of December 31, 1904, shots rang out near the corner of Broadway and Main in Joplin, and those who rushed to the scene found city police officer Claude Brice lying dead in the middle of the intersection with two or three bullets to his body. Police quickly rounded up about forty people for questioning, but "the whole affair (was) shrouded in mystery," according to the *Webb City Register*.[1]

Brice had gone to the scene to investigate a possible burglary in progress, but little else was known about the circumstances of the crime. A coroner's jury held on January 4, 1905, developed "nothing of importance" in the case, but a web was "being weaved slowly but surely around Ted Daly," a Joplin man who was one of those confined in jail on suspicion. Also in custody was Jennie Quinlan, "a Joplin police court character" known familiarly as "Big Jim," because Daly and some of the others suspected in the crime had frequented Jennie's house of ill fame near the scene of the crime on the night in question.[2]

A bartender, carpenter, and sometimes prizefighter, the thirty-year-old Daly was arraigned on a first-degree murder charge before Jasper County Circuit Court judge Hugh Dabbs in Joplin on January 20. He entered a plea of not guilty and was returned without bond to the county jail in Carthage, where he'd been held since shortly after his arrest.[3]

One report claimed Daly was uncooperative in the wake of his arrest, but he or one of the other people questioned must have done some singing, because authorities soon identified Estel Butler, John Franklin, and George Rogers as primary suspects, in addition to Daly, in the killing of Officer Brice. Daly, as a Joplin resident, had hung around long enough after the crime to get himself arrested, but the other three absconded to parts unknown.[4]

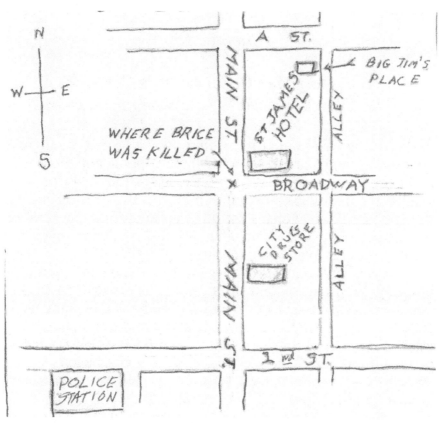

Replica of sketch from *Joplin Globe* showing where Officer Brice was killed.

Butler was located and captured in Shreveport, Louisiana, in late February and brought back to Joplin. Known as "Foot and a Half" because the front part of his right foot was split in two, the twenty-four-year-old Butler said he didn't kill Brice but he knew who did. Still, he dreaded going back to Joplin for fear of mob violence. Despite Butler's protestation of innocence, the police were convinced of his involvement in the shooting, because he was "regarded as one of the worst criminals in the country." Originally from the Kansas City area, he'd previously served a term in the Kansas State Penitentiary for grand larceny and a term in the Missouri State Penitentiary on a Federal charge of robbing a post office.[5]

In March, Franklin was captured at Cedar Rapids, Iowa, and also brought back to Joplin. However, George Rogers, the fourth suspect, could not be located.[6]

Teddy Daly was the first of the suspects to go on trial. When the proceeding got underway in Joplin on or about May 18, Foot and a Half Butler was the star state witness. He admitted he was with Daly and Franklin at the intersection of Broadway and Main on the night in question but claimed he had crossed to the other side of the street before Officer Brice approached Daly and Franklin and was shot dead.[7]

Sketch of Daly and his wife at his trial. *From the Joplin Globe.*

Daly's wife, Christine, testified for the defense that Butler had come to the Daly residence on the evening before Brice was killed and borrowed a pistol from her husband. Teddy himself took the stand to deny that he'd killed the officer. He admitted being in the vicinity, explaining that he'd gone to Jennie Quinlan's place because she'd been a good customer of the Broadway Bar, which he'd previously run, and that he wanted to solicit her business for a new saloon he was opening up. Citing Estel Butler's criminal record, Daly's lawyers attacked the state's star witness as untrustworthy. To impeach his testimony, they called to the stand a Jasper County Jail prisoner who said that Butler had told him on more than one occasion that Daly was not guilty of the crime.[8]

The prosecution countered that they had enough evidence against Daly to convict him even without Butler's testimony. Especially incriminating was the fact that he'd originally denied even being in the area of the crime when it happened and had only changed his statement after witnesses came forward to place him at the scene.[9]

Arguments in the case were completed on May 19, and the jurors retired to deliberate. After two hours they reached agreement on a verdict of second-degree murder and sentenced Daly to fifty years in the peniteniary.[10]

Jury selection for Franklin's trial began the next day, May 20, and testimony got underway on Monday the 22nd. Although Daly had previously discussed the crime only with reluctance, he freely took the stand to testify against Franklin now that he'd already been convicted himself. "I am going to the penitentiary for fifty long, dreary years," he announced, "and I'll not go alone. I shall take some with me to keep me company."[11]

Daly claimed that Franklin had told him he was at the scene of the shooting but that Butler was the one who pulled the trigger. Butler, on the other hand, had told him Franklin did the shooting. Daly admitted that he, Franklin, Butler, and George Rogers were planning to rob the City Drug Store on Main Street the night Brice was killed but that, when the shooting occurred, he himself was three blocks away hiding some nitroglycerin they planned to use in the holdup. On cross-examination, Franklin's lawyers pointed out that Daly's testimony differed substantially from what he'd said at his own trial. He explained that he'd determined to tell the whole truth only after being convicted of a crime he didn't commit.[12]

Estel Butler again turned state's evidence in the Franklin case and took the stand for the prosecution. His testimony essentially mirrored what he'd said at Daly's trial—that he'd left Daly and Franklin in the intersection of Broadway and Main and walked to the east side of Main Street when Officer Brice approached the other two men and was shot dead.[13]

Franklin took the stand in his own defense, but the general opinion was that he did not help his case because he seemed confused and was unable to answer basic questions. For instance, he said he was from Pittsburgh, Pennsylvania, but he didn't know where in Pittsburgh he'd lived and was unable to name any of the city's main streets.[14]

According to the *Joplin Globe*, Franklin was about twenty-eight years old and was sometimes known as "Frenchy." He had a "robust appearance," but he apparently was "not the equal in intelligence" with either Daly or Butler, who was "the brightest intellectually of the trio."[15]

Franklin might have lived in Pittsburgh for a while, but the reason he was known as "Frenchy" was that he was a native of France, and he was only twenty-four years old. He, like Butler, was an ex-convict, having served a term in prison at Fort Leavenworth under the alias Frank Jones for receiving stolen property.[16]

One of Franklin's lawyers elicited a chuckle from the packed courtroom when he insisted during closing arguments that his client couldn't be guilty of killing Brice because, at the very moment of the shooting, he was engaged in breaking into the City Drug Store a half block away.[17]

After deliberating overnight, the jury in the Franklin case came back on the morning of May 23 with a verdict finding the defendant guilty of murder in the second degree and sentencing him to ninety-nine years in prison. Despite the long sentence, Franklin was in a good humor upon learning he'd avoided the death penalty. "The verdict might have been worse," he said, "a good deal worse." He added that Franklin was an alias and he was not going to reveal his real name because his family was respectable and well-off and he didn't want to bring disgrace to them.[18]

When Estel Butler went on trial in October, both Daly and Franklin were brought back to Joplin from the penitentiary to testify for the state. Butler had ratted them out, and now they planned to return the favor. Daly's most damning testimony against Butler was that he heard the shots that killed Officer Brice while he was a couple of blocks away hiding the nitroglycerin and as he started south toward the sound of the shots he met Butler coming the other direction carrying a revolver. Daly also said that Butler had at first admitted killing Brice but had later denied it and tried to blame it on Franklin.[19]

Franklin's testimony was even more damning, because, unlike Daly, he admitted being near the scene, about seventy-five feet away. Brice, he said, halted Rogers and Butler in the intersection and was in the process of arresting them when Rogers whipped out a pistol and fired two or three shots that either missed their mark or only wounded the officer. As Brice started to draw his weapon, Butler, who was even closer to the officer than Rogers, fired a couple of more shots that brought Brice down.[20]

The defense strategy was mainly to impugn the testimony of the state's star witnesses. Butler's lawyers introduced a letter that Franklin had written to their client from the state prison two months earlier in which he said Butler was innocent; Franklin, however, claimed the letter was partly forged. He and Daly both admitted their testimony during Butler's trial was different from the statements they'd given at their own trials, but they insisted they were now telling the truth, since they now had nothing to lose. They'd only lied, they said, to try to save their own skins.[21]

Many observers thought the strategy of attacking the state's witnesses might work and that Butler might be acquitted or get off with a light sentence. Not only might the jury not give much credence to the testimony of two convicted killers, but Butler, despite his reputation as an habitual criminal, had a winning personality. Women, in particular, seemed drawn to him. "Butler exercises a weird influence over the fair sex...," said the *Joplin Globe*. "His friends of the gentler sex constantly seek his side to offer encouraging words, and to press his hand. Butler has a flashing smile that is enslaving, and one likes him despite themselves."[22]

Sketch of Estel "Foot and a Half" Butler. *From the Joplin Globe.*

On the evening of October 21, the jury returned a verdict of second-degree murder after two hours of deliberation. The trial was the shortest murder trial in the history of Jasper County at the time. Another thing marking it as out of the ordinary, said the *Globe*, was the personality of the defendant, who had "the manner of a courtier, the confidence of an invincible champion..., and the atmosphere of the innocent."[23]

But the jury wasn't buying his act and they assessed him a term of forty years in the penitentiary. Heretofore considered an accessory to the crime, Butler was now marked as a principal.[24]

After Butler's trial, county prosecutor William Andrews announced that Daly and Franklin refused to testify against George Rogers. Andrews said he would, therefore, not pursue a conviction against the remaining suspect. Daly and Franklin were returned to Jefferson City, but Butler was granted a new trial in mid-November before he could join them.[25]

Butler's second trial took place in January 1906. Throughout the proceeding, the defendant was "still cool," according to the *Joplin News Herald*, but lacked "the supreme confidence" he'd shown during his first trial. Once again, Daly and Franklin were brought from the state prison to testify against the defendant. On January 15, near the end of the trial's second day, Butler caused a near riot in the courtroom when he attacked his jailer, Ed Hansford, after Hansford testified as to incriminating statements Butler had made at the county jail. The officers had some difficulty in restraining the bystanders from lynching Butler on the spot and in restoring order.[26]

Late on the night of January 16, after the jury had retired to deliberate Butler's fate, Butler, Daly, and Franklin were placed in an interurban car for transport to Carthage, because the Joplin City Jail was considered insecure. The prisoners were accompanied by Sheriff John Marrs and Deputy Sheriff Ellsworth Marquis. During the trip, Butler got into a fight with the other two men, and he had to be separated from Daly and Franklin. When the group reached Carthage, Sheriff Marrs deemed it prudent to keep the men separated, and he started toward the jail with Butler, while Deputy Marquis escorted Daly and Franklin by a different route. When Marquis reached the jail door, his prisoners suddenly made a break for freedom. Although Daly and Franklin were handcuffed together, the shackles, having apparently already been filed, broke as soon as they started scuffling with the deputy. The two men broke away and started running, and Marquis fired several shots at them.

Although Franklin fell twice, apparently wounded, he hopped back up both times and kept running. Neither fugitive was ever recaptured, and George Rogers was also never apprehended.[27]

The jury brought in a guilty verdict against Butler the next day, though, and he was sentenced to fifty-five years in prison, fifteen more than he'd been assessed at his first trial. Transferred to Jefferson City in early February 1906, he had his sentence commuted by Governor Elliott Major in November 1916. The commutation was revoked in June of the following year, and he was returned to prison from Kansas City. He again had his sentence commuted in February 1919, this time by Governor Frederick Gardner, on the grounds that "he had been 'cured' of his criminal ways." But it didn't take him long to return to his old ways. Taking up residence in Nebraska City, Nebraska, he faced an illegal liquor charge there in 1920, and early the next year he got into a fight with his wife and was arrested for domestic abuse.[28]

Later in 1921, Butler got into more serious trouble. Charged with auto theft, he was convicted in early 1922 and sentenced to two years in federal prison at Leavenworth. When he was released in January 1924, he was arrested at the prison gate and charged with stealing a pouch of mail back in 1920. He was acquitted of that charge in May 1924, but he got into a fight in Kansas City a month later and was seriously wounded. Another month later, he was arrested in Kansas City on multiple charges, including wife beating, carrying concealed weapons, and destruction of property. In 1928, Butler was jailed again in Kansas City on a contempt of court charge. Suffice it to say that, when Estel Butler was released from prison in 1919 after serving about twelve years of his fifty-five-year sentence for killing Joplin policeman Claude Brice, he was far from "cured" of his criminal ways.[29]

Chapter 16

The Green-Eyed Monster Rears Its Head
Joplin Night Watchman Killed in a
"Disagreement Over a Woman"

Joplin night watchman and special policeman Ben Collier had an eye for younger women. After his first wife died, he remarried in Jasper County to a girl named Birdie in 1898, when she was still a teenager and he was almost fifty years old. Birdie left the old codger after a few years, though, and absconded to Hot Springs, Arkansas.[1]

Not to worry. It wasn't long before Collier set his sights on another young woman, thirty-year-old Rose Proctor. Rose, "a small and pretty blonde," had married Edward Morrison in 1892, when she was sixteen, but she divorced him after a few years. She married Ben Proctor in 1902, but her second marriage didn't take either, and she separated from Proctor in late 1905. Afterward, she and an unmarried sister took rooms at 1216 Main Street in Joplin. Collier had known Rose since she was a girl, and his job working for businessmen along Main guarding their stores at night gave him an opportunity to see her on a regular basis. In the spring and summer of 1906, he started spending time with her and soon became lovestruck.[2]

But Ben Collier wasn't the only man attracted to Rose. Twenty-three-year-old Will "Rabbit" Cofer had known Rose since he was a boy growing up in Joplin, where his father, Tom Cofer, served as chief of police. His folks moved away in 1905, but Rabbit stayed in Joplin and was hired as a policeman himself. He spent most of his first year as a beat cop along Main Street, where he renewed his acquaintance with Rose Proctor. Rabbit was married with a five-year-old son at home, but that didn't stop him from spending time with Rose. In fact, the rooms at 1216 Main where Rose and several other young women lived became somewhat notorious as "a rendezvous for policemen."3

Will "Rabbit" Cofer. *From the Joplin Globe.*

Recently Rabbit had been promoted to day captain, but he still found time for Rose. In mid-August 1906, Rose attempted suicide, reportedly because she was despondent over her separation from her husband. Rabbit took a special interest in his old friend after that, consoling her and assisting in her recovery. But Ben Collier suspected there was more than just friendship between the two. He was jealous of the attention Cofer was paying to Rose and protested to Rose against her relationship with the young police captain.4

In early to mid-August, about the time of Rose's attempt on her life, Collier had a conversation with Joplin Police night captain Frank Ogburn in which he was "very bitter against

Cofer." But Collier's jealousy didn't faze Rose Proctor and Will Cofer. Rabbit often took Rose to the wine room of the Mascot Saloon at 926 Main, and on Wednesday, August 29, he even escorted her to a fair at Carthage.[5]

Rose Proctor, object of a lethal love triangle. *Sketch from the Joplin News Herald.*

Collier saw Rose and Rabbit together as they were leaving for Carthage, and the next morning he showed up at Rose's rooms and threatened to kill both her and Cofer if she didn't stop seeing Rabbit. Drawing his revolver, Collier pointed it at Rose and said, "I have half a notion to pull the trigger."[6]

The following Wednesday, September 5, Cofer was standing at the corner of Fifth and Main in Joplin with a *Joplin Globe* reporter when he saw Collier standing across the street at the same intersection. Gesturing toward Collier, Rabbit remarked, "There stands a fellow who has sworn to kill me and I am afraid that he will try to do it before long. If he would only come to me and tell me about it, it would be a different matter and we might get things straightened up, but he always talks behind my back."[7]

Early Friday morning, September 7, Collier met Joplin police officer Henry Burns on the street and renewed his threats toward Cofer. He said he planned to get Cofer before night, adding that he was going to "hit him on the jaw."[8]

Apparently Rabbit didn't get the warning, or if he did, it didn't scare him. He spent most of Friday afternoon with Rose in the sitting room of Washington Flats, a rooming house at 905 Main. From there, he and Rose went across the street to the Mascot, arriving about 7:30.[9]

Meanwhile, Ben Collier was on the prowl. He showed up about 8:00 p.m. at Rose's rooming house in the 1200 block of Main looking for Rose. Not finding her at home, he went next door to May Stout's apartment and stayed for over an hour. As he was leaving, he demanded to know where Rose was, and May told him she was out with Cofer. "I'll kill him if I can find him tonight," Collier swore.[10]

About 9:30, Collier approached the Mascot Saloon walking rapidly. He brushed past a patrolman named Johnson, who was standing outside the saloon, and hurried inside. Rose had already risen to leave, and Rabbit had stepped outside the saloon through a rear door when Collier strode in and walked toward the rear of the room. Collier, with his hand near his pistol, called to Rose, demanding that she come to him. "What do I want to come to you for?" she asked but started in his direction for fear he might shoot her.[11]

Hearing the commotion, Cofer came back inside and saw the cause of it. "Come on, Rose, I'll take you home," he said.

Collier immediately turned his ire toward Rabbit. "I have been looking for you, and I have got you now," he said as he drew his pistol.

Cofer made a rush toward Collier and grabbed his arm before he could shoot. Fred Palmer, the bartender, also grabbed Collier's arm. While holding Collier with one hand, Cofer drew his own pistol and began shooting. Two shots were misfires, but three bullets slammed into Collier's body. Collier toppled into a nearby slop bucket and died almost instantly.[12]

Patrolman Johnson hurried inside, disarmed Rabbit Cofer, and placed him under arrest. On the way to the police station, Johnson met assistant police chief Jake Cofer, Rabbit's uncle, and turned the suspect over to him. Assistant Chief Cofer took his nephew to the station and then went back to the scene of the shooting to investigate. Rose Proctor was still there, and the elder Cofer escorted her home. Joplin police chief Joe Myers later ordered her arrested, but when he and the sheriff went to her place, she was not home. They sent Jake Cofer back to arrest her, and he finally located her about 3:00 a.m. Saturday morning in another building near the rooming house where she lived and brought her to the station.[13]

Rose was the star witness at a coroner's inquest held later that day, September 8. She admitted that both Collier and Cofer had been paying her attention lately and that she knew bad blood existed between the two men, but she denied knowing she was the cause of the ill will. She said she had heard Collier make threats against Cofer but that she had never heard Rabbit say anything about Collier except that he wanted to avoid trouble. Other witnesses confirmed that they had heard Collier threaten Cofer, and they also largely corroborated Rose's account of the shooting.[14]

Thus, the jury came back late Saturday afternoon with a verdict declaring that Ben Collier had died from gunshots fired from a revolver in the hands of Will Cofer and that the shots were fired in self-defense. Both Cofer and Rose Proctor were immediately released, but later the same day, Cofer left the Joplin police force, turning in his badge to the police chief.[15]

The *Joplin Globe* and the *Joplin News Herald* differed markedly in their take on the Collier shooting, including their interpretation of Cofer's leaving the police force. While the *Globe* implied that it was a voluntary resignation, the *News Herald* reported that Cofer had been fired by the police chief. The *News Herald* considered it a disgrace that police officers like Will Cofer regularly associated with women of questionable virtue like Rose Proctor, and the editors decried the fact that Assistant Chief Cofer had escorted Rose home rather than arresting her on the spot. "It is common knowledge that many members of the force are controlled absolutely by women of the town," said the *News Herald*. "The women boast of their immunity."[16]

The *Globe*, meanwhile, refrained from such editorializing and generally seemed less annoyed by the shooting affray and the outcome of the coroner's jury than its rival. Instead of rebuking Will Cofer and his uncle, the *Globe* thought it more newsworthy to mention that many of Will's friends greeted him at the police station with congratulations when he was released.[17]

Not long after leaving the Joplin Police, Will Cofer and his wife, Amelia, moved to Oregon, where Will's family had previously taken up residence. By 1920, Amelia had either died or gotten a divorce, and Will, ironically, had remarried a woman named Rose, although she was not the same Rose he had killed a man over back in Joplin, Missouri.[18]

Chapter 17

"God Don't Love a Liar"
The Murder of Millie Plum and the
Hanging of Willie Wilson

After fifteen-year-old Millie Atwood married Roy Plum at Cherokee, Kansas, in 1907, "domestic troubles" came quickly, and by the summer of 1908, the couple had already split. Millie's mother and father, who bitterly opposed her marriage to Plum, had practically disowned her after the wedding and had moved to Oklahoma. Cast adrift by a faithless husband and unrelenting parents, Millie needed a lifeline. When J. G. Miller's traveling carnival came to neighboring Weir about the first of July 1908 for a week-long stay, Millie saw it as an opportunity to strike out and make her own way. Traveling the five miles to Weir, she hooked on with the carnival as a cook for the other employees.[1]

As it turned out, joining the carnival proved to be the farthest thing from a lifeline for Millie Plum.

Among the carnival's other employees was twenty-four-year-old William "Willie" Wilson. The young black man had left his Louisiana home in early 1908 to join Miller's carnival. He worked as a roustabout, running the merry-go-round and doing other odd jobs. Wilson stayed with the carnival as it worked its way north, but traveling from town to town and never staying in one place long enough to get to know anybody was a lonely job. So, he couldn't help but take notice when the pretty sixteen-year-old "girl-woman" joined the circus at Weir.[2]

About the 5th of July, the carnival moved from Weir to Carl Junction, Missouri, for another week-long run. The engagement ended on Saturday, July 11, and late that night or just past midnight on Sunday morning, after all the equipment had been loaded aboard the railroad car preparatory to moving again the next day, Wilson, according to later evidence, slipped into the car where Millie slept with the intent of "doing business with her." When she refused his proposal and sprang up in bed, he slugged her or choked her into unconsciousness. Presuming she was dead, he looped a rope around her neck, and dragged her to the side door of the car. He then carried her toward an empty Frisco box car that sat on the tracks about two hundred yards away. Halfway there, he grew tired, and when he laid her down, he noticed that she was still breathing faintly. Using the rope around her neck, he dragged her the rest of the way to the box car. If she wasn't dead at first, she was by the time he got through dragging her.[3]

Wilson intended to put Millie's body in the box car to hide it, hoping it wouldn't be discovered until both the carnival and the Frisco box car were long gone. He also thought to string the body up inside the box car to make the incident look like suicide, but exhausted from carrying and pulling the body two hundred yards, he couldn't lift it into the car. He also heard stirring inside the box car and realized it wasn't vacant. Abandoning his plan to hide the body, he quickly retreated to the carnival equipment car, where he had his sleeping quarters.[4]

Millie's body was discovered about 1:45 a.m. on Sunday morning, July 12, just an hour and a half after the attack, with the rope still around her neck. Fresh tracks of a man in sock feet were found leading back to the equipment car, and the size and shape of the footprints fit Wilson's feet. Wilson denied any knowledge of the crime, but he was arrested and taken to the calaboose in Carl Junction for interrogation by city marshal H. O. Barnard, carnival manager Miller, and another man. Under grilling and prodding from the three men, Wilson broke down and gave what was later described as a half confession-half denial. He admitted going into Millie's car, but he said that she so resented his proposition that she came at him with a butcher knife. He knocked her down in self-defense and ran out of the car, but she sprang up, chased after him, and came at him with the knife again. He then knocked her unconscious and, thinking she was dead, carried and dragged her to the Frisco box car.[5]

After his quasi-confession, Wilson was taken after daylight Sunday to the Jasper County Jail at Carthage on a murder charge. Here he was again interrogated, this time by the jailer, a deputy sheriff, and the assistant county prosecutor. Late Sunday afternoon, he finally gave a fuller confession, which the assistant county prosecutor transcribed and the suspect signed as a sworn statement. Wilson repeated much the same story he'd told at first, explaining that he took off his shoes to slip into Millie's quarters. He admitted that Millie did not come at him with a butcher knife and did not strike or cut him. Authorities felt Wilson was now largely telling the truth, although some believed Millie had been choked to death in the car rather than knocked down, because they thought Mrs. Miller, sleeping in an adjoining car, would have been aroused by the sound of Millie being knocked down.[6]

After Wilson's preliminary hearing in late August 1908, Justice Warren Woodard ordered him held in the Jasper County Jail on a first-degree murder charge. Large crowds attended Wilson's two-day trial in mid-December, and "sentiment was very strong against the Negro," according to the *Webb City Register*. Arguing for the death penalty, the state relied on the officers to whom Wilson had allegedly confessed his crime as its primary witnesses. Meanwhile, Wilson, who was the only defense witness, took the stand to deny that he killed Millie Plum or that he had ever confessed to the crime.[7]

Unconvinced by Wilson's denial, the jury came back on December 18 with a guilty verdict and a sentence of death by hanging. A defense appeal to the Missouri Supreme Court, however, automatically stayed the execution. The defense bill of exceptions included a contention that Wilson's confession had been given under duress, but the high court, in its November 1909 ruling, allowed the confession and upheld the lower court's verdict. The new execution date was set for January 12, 1910. At the time of the supreme court ruling, the *Register* observed that Wilson, who had been held at Carthage for over a year, had "shown very little interest in his fate" and had "lived his life in jail in a careless, jovial manner as though he was incarcerated for a crap shooting deal." The *Joplin Globe* added that Wilson's "constant smile" had "won him many friends among the other prisoners, and they were more affected by the news of the court's decision than he was."[8]

Willie Wilson, from the *Joplin News Herald.*

After the supreme court ruling, a number of individuals and organizations, especially the black citizens of Carthage and their churches, began lobbying for leniency on behalf of the condemned prisoner, and on or about January 1, 1910, Missouri governor Herbert Hadley granted a reprieve, staying the execution until February 18 to give Wilson's lawyer more time to prepare a request for a commutation of sentence. Hadley later declined to commute the sentence, but again on February 17, just one day before Wilson's new date with death, the governor granted another reprieve until March 4 to give the defense time to present new evidence that had supposedly turned up. A report circulated that a Carl Junction woman had come forward saying that a young woman matching Millie Plum's description and suffering from obvious wounds had come to her house on the night of Millie's murder and stated that she'd been attacked by an ice cream cone vendor. When the prospective witness was located, however, she denied that she'd made such a statement.[9]

Sentiment against the governor's action in granting the second reprieve ran high throughout Jasper County, and after the episode of the dubious witness, the governor declined to interfere again. Thus, the death watch began anew. The condemned man spent his last evening chatting with his jail mates, praying, and singing until 2:00 a.m. on the morning of March 4, 1910. Sometime during the evening or night, Wilson reportedly made a final confession to the two ministers who had been serving as his spiritual advisors. "The real facts of the case," he said, "are that I am perfectly guilty." He said he wanted to go to heaven and he knew "God don't love a liar." He asked that a copy of his confession be sent to his mother in Louisiana because he wanted her to know that he told the whole truth.[10]

According the *Joplin News Herald*, Wilson slept well after he finally retired in the wee hours of the morning, and he ate a hearty breakfast when he arose two or three hours later. Shortly after 5:30 a.m., he was led to the scaffold, which had been erected inside a stockade just outside the Jasper County Jail. He made a "dramatic talk" to the small audience who'd been allowed inside the palisade, declaring that he was going to heaven and asking his listeners whether they were, too. Wilson was "courageous to the last," bidding the county officials and his spiritual advisors farewell even as his legs were bound and the cap was pulled over his head. Sheriff Arch McDonald pulled the lever that dropped the condemned man through the chute at 5:55 a.m., and he was pronounced dead eleven minutes later. After his body was cut down, it was taken to Knell Undertaking, where many curiosity-seekers came by to view it, and it was later buried in a potter's field at the county poor farm south of Carthage.[11]

Chapter 18

A Webb City Murder and The "Unwritten Law"
Will Costley's Killing of Benjamin Newman

After J. W. "Will" Costley was arrested for killing Benjamin Newman in October 1909 at a boarding house run by Costley's wife in Webb City, the defense invoked the so-called "unwritten law," a principle widely cited to justify homicide arising from affairs in which the victim had offended a man's honor, a woman's virtue, or the sanctity of marriage. Costley claimed he'd caught Newman sleeping with his wife, but Costley and his wife were separated. Would the "unwritten law" still apply in his case and be enough to get him acquitted?[1]

In 1909, forty-six-year-old Will Costley and his wife, Mary, ran a boarding house on North Webb Street in the booming mining town of Webb City. Sometime in early October, the couple got into a big fight that led to a separation. Costley was charged with assaulting his wife, but after he was released on bond, he still wouldn't leave her alone. He was especially upset by the attention thirty-year-old Benjamin Newman was paying to his wife, and he made threats against both of them.[2]

After the separation, Mary remained at the boarding house and still ran it. One of her roomers was miner Ralph Page, and late Saturday night, October 23, Newman, who was a fellow miner, accompanied Page home. About midnight Page fell asleep on the lounge where Mary normally slept, leaving Newman and Mary still awake. About three hours later, Costley slipped into the house through a window and found Newman and Mary in bed asleep together in a room adjoining the one where Page was. Retrieving a heavy gas pipe with a nut on one end, Costley roused Newman and Mary and attacked Newman with the pipe when he sprang up in bed.[3]

Mary fled upstairs screaming for the two young women who roomed there to help her because Costley was "killing the men." The two women started down the stairs but were met by Costley, still carrying the pipe, and he ordered them back upstairs "where they belonged." Meanwhile, Newman staggered from the house with a broken nose and several severe gashes in his head. The commotion also aroused Page, and either he or the severely wounded Newman alerted authorities.[4]

Costley surrendered peacefully to the two officers who arrived on the scene, declaring, "I caught that fellow with my wife." Charged with felonious assault, he was taken to the county jail at Carthage to await a preliminary hearing. Ralph Page was also arrested and held as a material witness. It was suspected that he might have been in cahoots with Costley and might have alerted him ahead of time that Newman would be at the boarding house on Saturday night.[5]

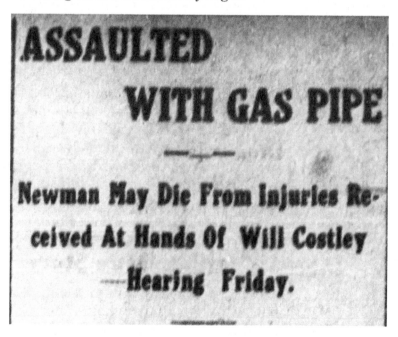

Headline from the *Webb City Register* tells the story of assault on Newman.

On Monday, October 25, Costley was taken before a justice on the prior charge of assaulting his wife, and he was sentenced to ten to twenty days in jail on a reduced charge of disturbing the peace. Three days later, Newman died at the Salvation Army Hospital in Webb City, and the second assault charge against Costley was promptly upgraded. In early November, as soon as his sentence for disturbing the peace of his wife expired, he was re-arrested and officially arraigned on a second-degree murder charge.[6]

Costley's preliminary examination was held before a Webb City justice of the peace on November 19, 1909. At the hearing's conclusion, the justice ordered Costley held for trial in lieu of $3,500 bond, and he was returned to the Carthage jail. Ralph Page was discharged but was ordered to appear as a witness at the trial. Arraigned in the circuit court at Joplin in early January 1910, Costley pleaded not guilty, and Judge David Blair ordered him held without bond, revoking the chance for him to be released on bail.[7]

While Will Costley was awaiting trial for murder, his estranged wife's residence was earning a reputation as a "disorderly house." Around the first of the new year 1910, a man was arrested for causing a disturbance at the boarding house on North Webb Street. Shortly thereafter, Mary Costley moved to Neck City, where the same man fled from officers and escaped when they went out to arrest him in late January. During the same time period, a Webb City landlord was charged with renting Mrs. Costley a house "for immoral purposes."[8]

Costley's trial began in Joplin in mid-February, and the *Joplin News Herald* reported that, during jury selection on the 17th, the defendant was "an eager listener to every detail of the case." His face bore very little expression, and his appearance was described as "tall and gaunt, with a grim and bony face and bright, deep-set eyes."[9]

Arguments and testimony in the trial got underway later the same day. Mary Costley did not appear either as a witness or as a spectator. Costley's children were also kept away from the courtroom. The *Joplin Globe* reported that Costley faced his murder trial alone with no loved ones at his side as defendants often had in similar proceedings.[10]

The main state witnesses were other occupants of the Costley boarding house, including Ralph Page. He testified that Mary Costley was still up when he went to sleep, that he was awakened in the middle of the night by a disturbance, and that he saw Newman after he had sustained his wounds. However, he said he did not witness the attack on Newman and had no knowledge of the events directly leading up to it. Others in the house, such as the two young women on the second floor, also said they had not actually witnessed the assault. The two officers who had arrested Costley testified, however, that he had confessed the attack to them, and the defense did not try to deny this fact.[11]

Instead, Costley's lawyers, in addition to invoking the "unwritten law," claimed self-defense. Costley took the stand himself and declared that, upon discovering his wife in bed with Newman, he retrieved the metal pipe because he was afraid to approach the man unarmed. Then, when he approached and roused Newman from his sleep to demand an explanation, Newman reached beneath a pillow for a revolver. As he started to pull the revolver from its hiding place, Costley struck him with the gas pipe.[12]

The jury received the case late Friday afternoon, February 18, and reported back on Sunday morning, after deliberating throughout the day on Saturday, that they could not reach an agreement. The judge declared a mistrial. One report said the jurors agreed on conviction but were deadlocked on what the length of the prison sentence should be, with ten agreeing on two years and two holding out for ten years. Another report said ten jurors stood for conviction while the remaining two wanted an acquittal. "In any event," observed the *Webb City Register*, "it is felt that the unwritten law saved William Costley from serving a term in the state prison for killing Ben Newman."[13]

When Costley's second trial got underway in Joplin at the May 1910 term of Jasper County Circuit Court, "little interest" was shown in the proceedings, and testimony in the case, as in the first trial, consumed only a few hours. On the afternoon of May 19, the state called eleven witnesses to outline the circumstances surrounding Newman's killing and to establish the case against the defendant, while Costley himself again took the stand as the only witness for the defense.[14]

Closing arguments the next morning were well attended and featured a contentious debate during which the prosecution and defense "vied with each other in bitterness of attack." Judge Blair had to reprimand both sides for straying from the facts of the case at hand. Despite the court's admonition against invoking the so-called "unwritten law" as a defense, Costley's lawyers wove it "surreptitiously into evidence and addresses to the jury." And contrary to Blair's instructions, the state introduced evidence concerning Costley's alleged assault on his wife a few weeks prior to Newman's killing to undercut the "unwritten law" defense, suggesting that the Costley marriage had already been defiled before Newman came on the scene. Referring to the Costley boarding house, the prosecuting attorney thundered, "It is not right to dignify that 4-room house by the name of 'home.'"[15]

The jury got the case at 11:00 o'clock Friday morning, May 20, and, after thirty-three hours of deliberation, came back on Saturday evening with a not guilty verdict. The acquittal surprised many observers, who felt confident that the outcome of the trial would be another hung jury. The jury was reportedly split seven for acquittal and five for conviction at the outset, and it took numerous votes and much deliberation "to swing the refractory five jurors into line." Mrs. Costley, who had not previously appeared during the trial and had also not attended most of the proceedings of the first trial, was in the courtroom beside her husband when the verdict was announced.[16]

Chapter 19

Burning Man
Herman Barker's Jasper County Antics

Throughout the Prohibition years of the 1920s and the Depression era of the 1930s, a number of notorious outlaw gangs, like Bonnie and Clyde, crisscrossed the Midwest, inspiring terror in the heartland, but none of them had closer ties to southwest Missouri and the Ozarks than the Ma Barker gang. Although Kate "Ma" Barker was the titular head of the gang, her incorrigible sons were the real villains, and none of the boys was more incorrigible or villainous than the eldest one, Herman. Born in Aurora in 1893, Herman Barker moved with his family about 1903 to Webb City, where he got his start down the criminal path.[1]

In Webb City, the Barkers made their home on South Hall Street, where Herman entertained a number of his friends on the evening of October 30, 1906, in celebration of his thirteenth birthday. It wouldn't be long, though, before the boy would graduate to more mischievous undertakings than birthday merrymaking. On September 19, 1908, two of Herman's pals, Tom Patrum and Floyd Porter, sat up a hamburger stand beside a shoe shop on South Allen Street (now Main Street). Herman, a lad named Roy Dejarnette, and some other boys were playing near a red hot plate Patrum and Porter were using to fry the hamburgers. Someone knocked over a jug of gasoline spilling some of its contents onto the hot plate, which burst into flames. Dejarnette and the fourteen-year-old Barker started trying to put the fire out, and one of the boys picked up the overturned jug of gasoline to get it out of the way. When he gave it a fling, some of its contents spilled onto

Dejarnette's hair and clothing, and flames instantly covered the boy's body.[2]

Several men, attracted by Dejarnette's screams, raced to the scene and helped put out the flames. The burned boy was taken to a nearby drugstore to have his wounds dressed. He said he wasn't sure which one of the other boys had spilled the gasoline on him.[3]

Barker, Patrum, and Porter said that Dejarnette was the one who picked up the jug to get it away from the fire and that he had inadvertently spilled some of the gasoline on himself. At least a couple of bystanders claimed, to the contrary, that Barker, Patrum, and Porter had deliberately poured gasoline on Dejarnette and set him on fire. The three juveniles were arrested and taken to police headquarters for questioning but were soon released.[4]

Not long after this incident, the Barker family moved to Stone County, Missouri, but in June of the following year, when Herman was fifteen, he made his way back to Webb City on his own and promptly got into trouble. About the middle of the month he was arrested for receiving stolen property and was sentenced to ninety days in jail by an Oronogo justice of the peace. After spending about a week behind bars, the recalcitrant lad was paroled by the circuit court on the condition that he "behave himself and go home to his parents on a farm in Stone County."[5]

But Herman Barker couldn't stay away from Webb City and couldn't seem to "behave himself" either. On the evening of Friday, October 25, 1912, Barker, now eighteen, and nineteen-year-old Ed Cardell, who was out on parole from a two-year sentence in the state reformatory, stole four automobile tires from an unlocked garage on North Roane in Webb City. The young men were promptly apprehended with the help of the garage's owner, and they were arraigned the next day before a Webb City justice on charges of grand larceny. After their preliminary hearing on the 29th, they were bound over to the circuit court and taken to the county jail at Carthage in lieu of $500 bond each. On November 16, Cardell received a two-year prison sentence for larceny, and, having violated his previous parole, he was sent to Jefferson City to serve the sentence out.

Barker also pleaded guilty to larceny, but he received a two-year suspended sentence and was released on parole.[6]

Less than a year later, though, Barker was back to his larcenous ways. On the morning of October 28, 1913, Webb City police raided "a den of a gang of young thieves" in the 200 block of North Webb Street and placed Barker and three other occupants of the house under arrest. Suspected of having stolen pork chops and other food from the kitchen of a boarding house on North Hall the night before, the young men, ranging in age from seventeen to nineteen, were caught in the act of cooking some of the food and were charged with burglary. When "the boys," as newspaper reports called them, had their preliminary hearings in early November, the cases against them were dismissed.[7]

In early 1915, the arc of Barker's criminal path spiked upward when he participated in an armed robbery of a Webb City grocer. In the wee hours of Sunday morning, March 7, James Vance was playing cards with some other men in the back of his store at 211 W. Daugherty Street, when two masked men barged in through a side door and demanded Vance's money. Despite the disguises, the storekeeper recognized the holdup men as Herman Barker and Jim Lewis. At least one of the robbers, Lewis, was armed, and Vance forked over $230 without putting up a fight.[8]

On Monday evening, the twenty-one-year-old Barker and two of the men with whom Vance had been playing cards were located in Joplin at a rooming house in the 1200 block of Main Street with over a $100 in cash in their possession. Barker was arrested on suspicion of robbery, and the other two men were taken into custody as suspected accomplices. Lewis was arrested the next morning in Webb City. All the suspects denied any involvement in the robbery.[9]

On Tuesday the 9th, Barker pleaded guilty to a reduced charge of vagrancy and was sentenced by Joplin authorities to ninety days in the county jail. The two suspects arrested with Barker faced charges of vagrancy and gambling, while Lewis was arraigned on a charge of carrying a concealed weapon.[10]

How much of his ninety-day jail sentence Barker actually served is unclear, but in any case, it didn't take him long after getting released before he was back in trouble again.

On November 6, 1915, Barker was found hiding in the basement of the Jackson Drugstore in Joplin shortly before closing time with burglary tools in his possession. A store clerk notified police, who took the wannabe burglar into custody. Barker, who gave his name at first as H. H. Scott, was also carrying a recommendation from Kansas governor Arthur Capper authorizing him to solicit subscriptions to Capper's publications. The police speculated that Barker used the governor's recommendation as a ruse to gain entry to people's homes so that he could scout them out before burglarizing them. The *Joplin News Herald* reported at the time of Barker's arrest that he had previously been "arrested and 'mugged' by police in several cities."[11]

At his preliminary hearing on November 15, Barker was bound over to district court and returned to jail when he was unable to give bond. His case was continued in December, but its ultimate outcome has not been determined. Based on what happened next, Barker was apparently released, either on bond or outright.[12]

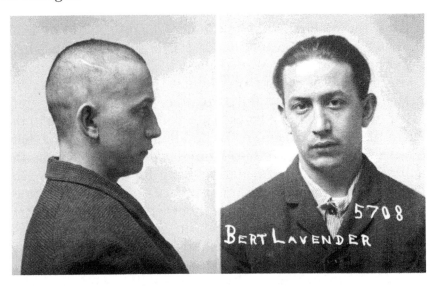

Herman Barker mug shot, 1916. *Montana State Historical Society.*

Sometime toward the end of 1915 or beginning of 1916, the Barker family moved to Tulsa, Oklahoma, where Herman's brothers joined a gang of hoodlums in the Central Park district and set out on criminal careers of their own. Herman later spent some time with the gang, too, but in early 1916 he was still busy with his criminal endeavors back in Missouri. About the tenth of January, he robbed a jewelry stand on the Springfield square. In August, he was convicted of burglary and larceny and sentenced to four years in prison, but he escaped from the Greene County Jail before he could be transported to Jefferson City. He was arrested in Montana later the same year on another burglary charge under the name Bert Lavender and sentenced to from six to twelve years in the Montana state pen.[13]

Released from the Montana prison after a few years, Barker returned to Oklahoma, where he was arrested and convicted of grand larceny in early 1925. After spending less than a year in the Oklahoma State Penitentiary, Barker was released again and quickly hooked up with Ray Terrill, an old acquaintance from the Central Park Gang. In November 1926, Barker helped Terrill break Matt Kimes, another career criminal, out of jail at Sallisaw, and in January of 1927, the three set out on a multi-state bank robbing spree. After pulling jobs at Sapulpa, Oklahoma, and Rogersville, Missouri, the gang set its sights on the First National Bank of Jasper, operating from a hideout house in Carterville, just a long throw from where Barker had grown up in Webb City.[14]

In the wee hours of Monday morning, January 17, Barker, Terrill, Kimes, and two other sidekicks rolled into Jasper in two cars and a truck. They backed the truck up to the rear of the bank, broke into the building by cutting some bars across a rear window, and used burglar tools to force open the vault. About 3:00 a.m. a man arriving for work at a nearby bakery noticed the commotion at the rear of the bank, slipped home, and called the local telephone operator, who notified authorities and gave a general alarm. A hastily formed posse arrived and was setting up an ambush at the rear of the bank when the robbers realized they'd been spotted. They had just wheeled a safe from the vault and were getting ready to load it onto the truck, but they abandoned both truck and safe and fled through the front of the bank, which was unguarded. The gang piled into the two cars, which they'd parked in front of the bank, and sped away. Barker and Terrill occupied one vehicle, while the other car carried Kimes and the two unknown bandits, one of whom was a woman.[15]

Barker and Terrill retreated to the Carterville hideout at 602 Main Street, while Kimes and other two accomplices took off toward Kansas. Officers had received a tip that the Carterville house was the headquarters of an outlaw gang, and they'd been watching it since noon on Sunday. They had seen Barker and Terrill leave the house Sunday night and had followed them, but "unable to keep pace with the fast bandit car," they returned to the house and staked it out. Notified of the holdup attempt at Jasper, the officers realized one of the cars used there matched the description of the vehicle they'd followed from the Carterville house a few hours earlier. Now, as the two robbers came back to the house driving the same car and went inside, the officers took up strategic positions outside and ordered them to surrender.[16]

Barker ran out the back door. When he ignored an order to halt and throw up his hands, Detective Alec Brown of the Joplin Police shot him with a sawed-off shotgun, and he fell to the ground filled with buckshot but not gravely wounded. Terrill fired four shots from the house, keeping the officers pinned down for several minutes, before he emerged with his hands up and surrendered.[17]

Terrill was taken to the Joplin City Jail, while Barker, giving his name as R. L. Douglas, was transported to St. John's Hospital and guarded there. Interviewed at the hospital, the patient admitted his real identity as Herman Barker, but he added that he also had seven aliases. The *Joplin Globe* reported that Barker was wanted for a jewelry store robbery in Ardmore, Oklahoma, a diamond robbery in McAlester, and several other crimes in Oklahoma and Kansas. Terrill was under a twenty-year prison sentence for a bank robbery at Pawnee, Oklahoma, and was wanted for numerous other crimes. He had broken jail in Oklahoma three different times and had escaped once from the Arkansas State Prison.[18]

Terrill was turned over to Oklahoma authorities to be taken back to serve his prison term there, but he escaped during the return trip. Barker, as soon as he was sufficiently well, was handed over to Arkansas authorities, charged with a bank robbery at West Fork.[19]

In late March, Barker also regained his liberty, escaping from the Fayetteville City Jail, but his freedom was short lived. On the morning of August 29, Barker and two companions engaged in a gun battle with two Wichita policemen who suspected them of a robbery at nearby Newton the night before. Barker was seriously wounded in the battle, and he turned his gun on himself rather than be taken alive.[20]

Herman Barker headstone at Williams Timberhill Cemetery, Welch, Oklahoma. *Photo by the author.*

His body was brought back to Oklahoma and buried at Williams Timberhill Cemetery near Welch. Separated from Herman's father, Ma and her other sons carried on the family's criminal name for several years after Herman was killed, but they too eventually met ignominious ends.[21]

Chapter 20

Joplin and Jasper County
Training Ground for the Underhill Brothers

Henry Underhill had a tough life. Born in Illinois and orphaned at a young age, he had to make his own way from the time he was an early teenager. Then, as an adult living in the Newton-Jasper County area, he worked hard to support his wife and seven kids and was, from all indications, a law-abiding citizen. But Henry Underhill's industry and good citizenship didn't transfer to his four sons, and when he died in May of 1912 at the age of forty-six, the only good thing about his premature demise was that he didn't have to endure the disgrace his boys were destined to bring to the family name.[1]

The oldest boy, Earl, and the youngest, George, would spend time in prison for burglary and larceny. The next-oldest, Charles Earnest, killed a man when he was only eighteen and spent virtually his entire adult life behind bars. But even Earnest wasn't the worst of the lot. That dubious distinction fell to the father's namesake, Henry Wilbur. The next-youngest boy in the family, Wilbur Underhill grew up to become the "Tri-State Terror," briefly topping the list of America's most wanted men. And like his brothers, the "mad dog of the underworld," as Wilbur was also known, got his criminal education on the mean streets of Joplin.[2]

Earl Underhill was the first of the Underhill brothers to run afoul of the law. In 1912, the Underhill family lived in the 1200 block of South Sergeant, and in January of that year, when Earl was twenty-two, he was arrested for stealing a hatchet from his neighbor's property.[3]

After the father died in May of the same year, the pace of his sons' criminal activities picked up. Less than two months later, eighteen-year-old Earnest spent the night of July 4th in jail for stealing fireworks earlier that day from some younger boys who were "industriously celebrating their nation's birthday."[4]

And Earnest would quickly graduate to more serious crime than Fourth of July hijinks.

In the wee hours of Sunday morning, January 19, 1913, Philip Burton, a peanut and hot tamale vendor in downtown Joplin, was shot to death by one of two young men who waylaid him in an alley south of Seventh Street between Joplin and Wall as he was pulling his cart home after a night's work. The other young man fired a shot at Burton's companion, F. H. States, but missed, and the two highwaymen fled the scene.[5]

Earnest Underhill came under suspicion during the intense investigation into the murder that followed, and he was arrested on the night of February 10 and taken to the police station for questioning. A pistol believed to be the murder weapon had been found discarded near Tenth and Byers, and a young man identified it as one he'd loaned to Underhill. In addition, a sixteen-year-old alumnus of the state reform school told police Underhill had tried to recruit him to help rob Burton. Confronted with the evidence, Underhill confessed the murder and implicated a seventeen-year-old lad named Earl Louck as the accomplice who fired the errant shot at States. Underhill said he killed Burton because the vendor did not throw up his hands when ordered to do so but instead reached for the tongue of his wagon as if to retrieve a weapon. The young murderer also confessed to a previous robbery of Joplin assistant postmaster V. L. Vawter and a couple of other attempted holdups.[6]

At their trials in late October 1913, both Underhill and Louck pleaded guilty to first degree murder and were given life sentences in the Missouri State Penitentiary. Louck was paroled after only seven years, while Underhill remained at Jeff City until 1936, when he was finally paroled, just a year before he died.[7]

After Earnest Underhill got sent up the river, there was a lull in the lawless exploits of the Underhill family that lasted six years. Then in early 1919, Wilbur, the baddest of the bad seed, made his entrance onto the criminal stage at the age of seventeen. On the night of February 9, he broke into the Sanitary Creamery Company at 1510 South Main Street in Joplin and was caught red-handed by two policemen. He confessed to the crime the next day and was arraigned on February 11.[8]

At his trial in Carthage on March 13, he pleaded guilty, was given a two-year suspended sentence, and was paroled to the custody of his mother, Almira Underhill, who now made her home on South Picher Avenue. Unappreciative of the second chance he'd been given, Wilbur took all of three days before getting into trouble again. On the night of March 16, he and a twenty-year-old ex-con named Dewey Webb were arrested on suspicion of stealing some silverware from the home of a neighbor who also lived on Picher.[9]

At his preliminary hearing in the Jasper County Circuit Court at Joplin in April, young Underhill pleaded not guilty. When his trial came up in May, he admitted stealing the silverware, but his lawyer pleaded insanity. As a boy a few years earlier, Underhill had been hit on the head by a case of bottles dropped from an upstairs window of Alcott School, and he was supposedly "never the same" afterward. Claiming he was not responsible for his actions because of the injury to his head, he threw himself on the mercy of the court. Judge Grant Emerson took the case under advisement and, after deliberating a few days, let the young hoodlum off with another suspended sentence.[10]

But Wilbur Underhill just couldn't seem to stay out of trouble. Less than five months later, on the night of October 18, a masked bandit accosted a man and a woman near Schifferdecker and West 20th Street. Flourishing a pistol, the robber demanded the couple's money but got only fifty cents for his trouble. Underhill was arrested on suspicion, but apparently the charges were dropped, although the exact disposition of the case is unknown.[11]

In the late spring of 1920, someone started pulling off robberies in Tanyard Hollow (present-day Crane Road), an isolated area on the southwest outskirts of Joplin that was used by "spooning couples" as a parking spot. Joplin Police decided to lay a trap for the bandit by recruiting a young couple to act as decoys. On Friday night, June 4, the couple, "posing as pleasure seekers," parked at Tanyard Hollow, while detectives hid in the backseat of the automobile. Presently a masked man approached carrying two revolvers and was about to rob the decoys when the detectives sprang up and opened fire. The bandit escaped to the woods through a hail of bullets, although the officers felt confident at least one of the shots had struck the would-be robber.[12]

Two days later, Wilbur Underhill was arrested on suspicion of being the lover's lane bandit. A bloody shirt and pants were found in his home in the 2000 block of South Connor, and he was suffering from a bullet wound in his left leg. He claimed he'd gotten the injury when he fell against a hot stove, but a doctor who examined him swore it was a bullet wound.[13]

Underhill was taken to jail in Neosho, since Tanyard Hollow lay just across the Newton County line. At his preliminary hearing in mid-June, he was committed to jail in lieu of bond on a charge of highway robbery. At his trial in October, Underhill testified in his own defense that the evidence against him was "framed," but he was nonetheless convicted and sentenced to two years in the sate prison.[14]

During Wilbur Underhill's trial at Neosho, his seventeen-year-old brother, George, was among those who trekked from Joplin to witness the proceedings. While George was at the courthouse, a Neosho businessman spotted him and openly accused him of being the person who recently held him up near Witmer Park (now Wildcat Park) south of Joplin. Young Underhill denied the charge, then turned and walked away, but he did not reappear on the final day of his brother's trial. The next day, Joplin officers arrested George at his home in Joplin and escorted him back to Neosho to answer the robbery charge. However, he was either paroled or released for lack of evidence.[15]

Wilbur Underhill was discharged from the state pen under Missouri's merit-time rule in mid-December of 1921 after serving a little over a year of his two-year sentence. He might have behaved well enough during his incarceration to earn an early release, but whatever efforts were made toward rehabilitating the inmate didn't take on the now-twenty-year-old Underhill. By April 1922, four months after his release, he was back behind bars in Joplin, charged with grand larceny and unable to make bond. In June, he pleaded guilty to a reduced charge of petit larceny and was sentenced to four months in the county jail at Carthage.[16]

After his release from the Jasper County Jail, it took him even less time to get in trouble again than it had after his discharge from the big house. On the night of December 14, Underhill robbed a filling station at the corner of 19th and Main in Joplin of $25 and marched the attendant several blocks at the point of a gun. On the evening of December 26, Wilbur and his brother George were arrested on suspicion, and the next day the service station attendant identified Wilbur as the man who'd held him up.[17]

On the 27th, Underhill sawed out two bars from a window of his cell at the city jail but was arraigned on an armed robbery charge and taken to the county lockup at Carthage before he could effect his escape. At his preliminary hearing on December 30, he testified in his own defense, claiming he was nowhere near the 19th and Main Street intersection on the night of the filling station robbery. Several defense witnesses took the stand to verify that the defendant was in the places he said he was on the night in question, but none of them were able to recall whether the time they saw Underhill coincided with the time of the robbery. The service station attendant, on the other hand, was sure Underhill was the man who'd robbed him, and the defendant was bound over for trial in lieu of $2,500 bond.[18]

On the morning of January 9, 1923, officers at the county jail interrupted another jailbreak attempt by Underhill and two other prisoners when they discovered several bars on a cell window sawed out. The prisoners had begun digging through a thick wall that still blocked their escape when the plot was uncovered. Wilbur Underhill's mother and his brother George, who had visited him two days earlier, were suspected of aiding the escape attempt by supplying two saws. Both Almira and George were arrested, but only Almira was charged with a crime. George was released for lack of evidence, and Almira was let out on bond.[19]

At his trial in February, Wilbur pleaded guilty to robbing the gas station and was sentenced to five years in the state penitentiary. After Wilbur was sent back up the river for another stint at Jefferson City, the case against his mother was not pursued.[20]

Earnest Underhill was still serving his life sentence when Wilbur arrived at the big house in mid-February for his second go-around, and both of them were still there when their older brother, Earl, was sentenced in December of 1925 to a year inside the walls at Jeff City on a burglary charge from Newton County. Youngest brother George joined the family reunion at the state prison in March of 1926, also on a burglary charge from Newton County.[21]

Earl Underhill was discharged in late July 1926 and became a relatively law-abiding citizen the rest of his long life. George was paroled from the Missouri state prison in March 1929 and resumed his life of crime. He was on a jail work gang in Montgomery County, Kansas, in 1931 when he escaped, robbed two pharmacies, and was shortly afterward found dead in a Garnett motel room from a drug overdose. Charles Earnest Underhill was finally paroled from his life sentence in 1936 after serving twenty-three years, but he died the next year from cirrhosis.[22]

Even after he'd killed Philip Burton back in 1913, some observers thought Earnest Underhill had just acted with the impetuosity of youth when he'd pulled the trigger on the tamale peddler—that he wasn't really a bad person. But nobody ever said that about his brother Wilbur. And despite the various criminal capers of Earl, Earnest, and George Underhill, the notorious outlaw career of their brother is why people still remember the Underhill name today. Wilbur Underhill was twenty-five years old and already a veteran criminal when he was released from his second term at Jeff City in November 1926. But he had yet to even hit his stride.

Less than a month after his release, he started pulling off a string of robberies, murders, and jailbreaks in Oklahoma and Kansas that would ultimately land him near the top of the list of

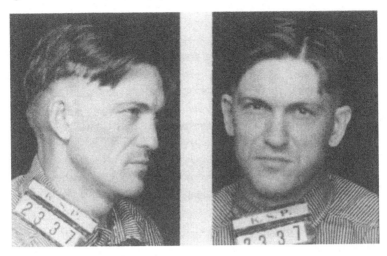

Kansas State Prison mug shots of Wilbur Underhill. *Author's collection.*

America's most wanted criminals. He was finally trapped in a house at Shawnee, Oklahoma, on December 30, 1933, and brought down by a barrage of lead from local and federal officers. He died a few days later in the Oklahoma State Penitentiary hospital. He was the first man killed by officers of the agency that would become the FBI. Underhill's body was brought back to Joplin for funeral services at Byers Avenue Methodist Church, where he had sometimes attended as a child. The service was reported at the time as the largest ever held in Joplin.[23]

Chapter 21

One of the Most Gruesome Mysteries Ever
William Webber's Murder of Louise Hagenbaugh

After the decomposing body of Louise Hagenbaugh was discovered on Friday evening, November 27, 1914, in her bed at the rooming house she kept on East Fifth Street in Joplin, it was thought at first that she might have died from asphyxiation, because the room was found to have a slow gas leak. However, other evidence pointed to robbery and murder. A dollar bill and an empty bag in which Mrs. Hagenbaugh, a wealthy fifty-nine-year-old divorcee, was known to have carried money were found on the floor near the bed, and a diamond ring with the stone missing was also discovered in the room. Upon closer inspection, investigators found fingerprints on the dead woman's neck. A *Joplin Globe* reporter considered the circumstances surrounding the woman's death "one of the most gruesome mysteries ever recorded in Joplin," and the coroner ordered an inquest for the next day to determine the exact cause of death.[1]

A post-mortem examination revealed the deceased had indeed met a violent death. In addition to the bruising around her neck, three of her ribs had been broken, and it was theorized that the murderer had crushed the ribs with his knee as he held her down and choked her. The coroner's jury concluded that Mrs. Hagenbaugh had met death at the hands of some unknown person, but suspicion was already settling on a man named William Webber.[2]

A two-time ex-convict from Illinois, the forty-year-old Webber, who also had a number of aliases, had come to Joplin a few weeks earlier and had taken a room at Mrs. Hagenbaugh's place. The woman had last been seen alive on the night of November 19, and Webber had flashed a large wad cash at a downtown saloon the next morning and then left Joplin.[3]

Webber had originally come to Joplin to meet an old Illinois acquaintance named Thomas Whitsell, and the two men had kept company during Webber's brief stay in town. Whitsell, who also roomed at Mrs. Hagenbaugh's, was arrested and held as a possible accomplice. Meanwhile, Webber, who'd already earned a reputation in Illinois four years earlier as "one of the most desperate criminals of the day," was nowhere to be found.[4]

Further investigation revealed that, after leaving Joplin on the 20th, Webber had traveled to Illinois to meet a woman named Helen Siders. He'd come back to Joplin with the woman and her little girl a couple of days after the murder but then had absconded again. It was learned that, in addition to having served one term in the Illinois State Penitentiary for burglary and another for armed robbery (the charge having been reduced from murder), Webber was also wanted for robbing a post office at Springfield, Illinois, just a month or so before he came to Joplin. Now, with the latest charge against him, Webber became the focus of a nationwide manhunt. The fugitive was described as about forty years old, 5'10" tall, weighing 215 pounds, with brown hair and hazel eyes. Rewards totaling $300 were offered locally for Webber's apprehension, and the Jasper County prosecuting attorney asked the Missouri governor to also offer a reward.[5]

A preliminary hearing for Whitsell was held in late December, and he was bound over for trial on a murder charge. Authorities admitted that they did not think he was the actual murderer and that they wanted to hold him primarily as a witness against Webber, and he was later allowed to give bond.[6]

Webber was finally tracked down and arrested in St. Paul, Minnesota, on February 20, 1915, when he was caught after passing a string of bogus money orders under the assumed name of Roy Miller. They were the same money orders he'd stolen from the bank in Springfield, Illinois, prior to coming to Joplin. Federal authorities turned him over to Missouri, and the Joplin police chief and other officers traveled to St. Paul to bring the accused killer back.[7]

The party reached Joplin on the evening of February 26, and Webber was lodged in the city jail. The next day, he spoke with reporters, declaring that the person who killed Mrs. Hagenbaugh should be hanged but that he didn't do it. He pointed to the fact that he had come back to Joplin with Mrs. Siders two days after Mrs. Hagenbaugh's death as evidence that he didn't kill her. "Would I have come back here knowing that I was facing a murder charge if I had actually committed the crime?" he asked rhetorically. "That is absurd."[8]

He expressed some doubt, however, that Mrs. Hagenbaugh had been killed and thought instead that she might have died from an accident or of natural causes. He admitted many of the circumstances that the police thought were incriminating, such as the fact that he had a large sum of money on him the morning he left Joplin, but he said it was money he had gotten from cashing bogus money orders. Indeed, the reason he hadn't come back to Joplin and turned himself in after he learned he was wanted for the murder of Mrs. Hagenbaugh, he said, was his fear of federal prosecution on the charge of robbing the post office and passing the phony money order. He said the reason he'd brought Mrs. Siders to Joplin was because he had made arrangements to rent Mrs. Hagenbaugh's rooming house under sublease and that Mrs. Siders was going to run the place for him while Mrs. Hagenbaugh was in Branson, Missouri, where she said she was going. When he and Mrs. Siders called at Mrs. Hagenbaugh's room and were unable to rouse her, he assumed she'd gone on to Branson without waiting to finalize the deal on the rooming house. Webber and Mrs. Siders then decided to leave Joplin rather than wait around.[9]

At his arraignment in early March, Webber waived a preliminary hearing, and his trial was set for the April term of the Jasper County Circuit Court. When the proceeding got underway in early May, the prosecution called the Joplin chief of police and the Joplin chief of detectives as its star witnesses. Both men testified that Webber had admitted to them shortly after he was brought back from St. Paul that he might have been partly responsible for Mrs. Hagenbaugh's death. According to their testimony, Webber told them that Mrs. Hagenbaugh was jealous because Webber was paying attention to another woman who lived in the Hagenbaugh rooming house, that they argued in a hallway when Webber started to go to the other woman's room, and that he struck her and knocked her against a bannister or stove. He carried Mrs. Hagenbaugh to her room and placed her in bed but did not think she was seriously hurt. The state said the reason Webber came back to Joplin with Mrs. Siders was that he planned to dispose of Mrs. Hagenbaugh's body, but when he learned that her building had been raided by police as a possible house of ill repute while he was gone and when he could not locate Thomas Whitsell, he again took flight.[10]

The defense pursued the theory that Mrs. Hagenbaugh had indeed died of asphyxiation as the man who discovered the body first thought. They called an expert witness who testified that a person who died of asphyxiation could well have spots on his or her neck similar to bruises made by choking. Seeking to undercut the motive of robbery advanced by the prosecution, Webber's lawyers also called witnesses who testified that Mrs. Hagenbaugh was not wealthy and often had trouble paying her bills. On rebuttal the prosecution pointed out that, when Mrs. Hagenbaugh's body was found, a bird was flying around in her room, and that, if she had died of asphyxiation, the bird would have died, too.[11]

The case was given to the jury on the evening of May 6, and they came back the next morning with a verdict finding Webber guilty of first degree murder and a sentence of life imprisonment. The vote stood nine for conviction and three for acquittal on the first ballot, and it took five more ballots to reach a unanimous vote for conviction. After Webber's conviction, the case against Whitsell was continued indefinitely, meaning it would only be revived if new evidence turned up. On June 1, Webber's motion for a new trial was overruled, and he was transported to the state prison in Jefferson City two days later.[12]

Webber's lawyers appealed to the Missouri Supreme Court, but in July 1916, the justices confirmed the verdict of the lower court. In late August of the same year, Webber and three other inmates escaped the state prison by sawing out of their cells, fleeing via a tunnel to the stockade, and then shinnying

WEBBER FOUND GUILTY OF MURDER IN FIRST DEGREE

JURY RETURNS VERDICT THIS MORNING AT NINE

GENTS LIFE SENTENCE IN THE PEN

Was Charged With Killing Mrs. Hagenbaugh In Joplin Only First Degree.

Webb City Register announces verdict in the Webber murder trial.

over the stockade wall. Webber was recaptured in January 1917 near his old stomping grounds of Springfield, Illinois.[13]

In October 1925, Missouri governor Sam Baker paroled Webber on the recommendation of the State Penal Board. The board had received numerous letters from character witnesses on Webber's behalf, and his conduct during his incarceration had been good, except for his escape back in 1916. Apparently nobody bothered to point out that the escape was a pretty big exception, because Webber was released after having served just over ten years of what was supposed to be a life sentence.

He was paroled to a supervisor in Kansas City, who was going to help him secure employment, and Webber vowed to make good.[14]

Apparently Webber did manage to stay out of serious trouble for the rest of his life, but his notoriety was not quite over. In 1937, his testimony as a government witness against the Progressive Miners of America, which had been accused of some coal train bombings, caused a stir when it was learned that John L. Lewis, president of the rival United Mine Workers, was one of the people who'd petitioned the Missouri governor for Webber's release twelve years earlier.[15]

Chapter 22

Arkansas Tom
Oklahoma Outlaw and Jasper County Bank Robber

Roy "Arkansas Tom" Daugherty already owned a reputation as a notorious outlaw when he made his criminal debut on the Jasper County stage in December 1916. Released in late 1910 after serving seventeen years behind bars for his part in a Wild West gunfight in Oklahoma, Daugherty made an attempt to go straight, but the lure of easy money soon drew him back into a life of crime. Graduating from horses to high-speed automobiles, he went from outlaw to gangster and carried out several bank heists in the Jasper County area over the next few years before being gunned down during a police shootout on Joplin's west side in 1924.[1]

A native of McDonald County, Daugherty left home in the mid 1880s, when he was just a teenager. He started going by an alias, Tom Jones, and probably spent time in Arkansas, because by the time he drifted into Oklahoma Territory in the early 1890s, he'd picked up the colorful nickname "Arkansas Tom." Hooking up with Bill Doolin's notorious Wild Bunch, Daugherty was captured and sentenced to fifty years in prison for his role in the gang's deadly shootout at Ingalls in September 1893.[2]

E. D. Nix, a US marshal who'd been instrumental in the capture of Daugherty, helped get him pardoned in 1910 and helped him find work. In 1915, Nix and his business partners made a movie called *The Passing of the Oklahoma Outlaws*, and they recruited Daugherty to play himself in the movie. They traveled throughout the Midwest presenting the film, with

Daugherty providing pre-movie commentary. Their itinerary included a stop at Joplin's Club Theater during July 1915.[3]

Roy "Arkansas Tom" Daugherty. *Photo courtesy of Jim Hounschell.*

But Daugherty apparently enjoyed being a robber more than playing the part of one. About 2:30 in the afternoon of December 13, 1916, two masked men; later identified as Daugherty and his cousin, Albert Johnson; walked into the Farmers and Miners Bank at Oronogo wielding revolvers and found assistant cashier A. W. Fuller talking on the phone. The taller of the two robbers, Johnson, walked up to Fuller and knocked the receiver from his hand. Pressing the barrel of his revolver against Fuller's ear, Johnson, a former Barry County deputy sheriff, demanded to know where the money was. Fuller said it was all in the counter, and the diminutive Daugherty scooped up about $1,700 in currency and coin from a counter drawer as Johnson stood guard over the cashier. Daugherty then went into the vault and grabbed another $750, but he overlooked about $12,000 more hidden elsewhere in the vault.[4]

The bandits forced Fuller into the vault, locked the door, and went outside to an awaiting getaway car driven by an accomplice, Harvey Painter. Fuller, using a screwdriver he'd previously placed inside the vault for just such an emergency, freed himself after about five minutes and gave an alarm. Nobody had seen the getaway vehicle leave Oronogo, but two witnesses said they saw a gray touring car sitting in front of the bank with its engine idling shortly before Fuller gave his alarm. Other witnesses reported that such a car had roared past them west of town at high speed. Officers went out in pursuit but lost the trail of the suspect vehicle near Carl Junction.[5]

Modern-day photo of the Oronogo bank building that Daugherty robbed. *By the author.*

The small bank robber (Daugherty) had momentarily removed his mask during the holdup, and Fuller described him as having a dark complexion, dark hair, and red, sore-looking eyes. He stood about five feet six inches tall, weighed about 150 pounds, and wore a cap and a brown overcoat. The taller man

(Johnson) was described as slender, and he wore light clothes and a felt hat. Rewards totaling $700 were offered for the capture and conviction of the bank robbers. About a month later, on January 15, 1917, Daugherty, Johnson, and two different sidekicks, Jesse Cutler and Willard Massee, teamed up to rob the First National Bank of Fairview about forty miles southeast of Joplin in eastern Newton County. On February 15, a man named Charlie Adams was taken into custody in Joplin on suspicion of committing a strong-arm robbery in the city the night before. As it turned out, he was part of the Daugherty gang but had not participated in the Fairview heist because he'd been arrested in Joplin the day before it took place. Upset that the rest of the gang had not shared the spoils with him, he implicated Daugherty, Johnson, and their partners in the Fairview bank job. Johnson, Cutler, and Massee were arrested on February 17, and Johnson gave a statement confessing to his part in both the Oronogo and Fairview heists and implicating Daugherty in both. Bank officials from Oronogo and Fairview came to Joplin and identified Johnson as a participant in both heists and Cutler as one of the Fairview holdup men. All three suspects were taken to Newton County.[6]

Two Joplin police officers, William Gibson and Charles McManamy, located Daugherty in a house at Ninth Street and Mineral Avenue in Galena, Kansas, on the evening of February 19. When Daugherty answered their knock at the door, Gibson saw a pistol lying on a nearby dresser and jumped between it and Daugherty before the wanted man could make a move for it. The officers then seized the intoxicated Daugherty, and he offered no resistance. At the time of his arrest, Daugherty was described as the leader and "the most desperate member of the gang," and his history as a Wild West outlaw was briefly chronicled in local newspapers.[7]

Brought back to Joplin, Daugherty talked freely of his own participation in the Fairview robbery, but despite the fact that Johnson and Cutler had implicated him, he refused to say what part, if any, the other suspects played in the heist. Remarking that "talking is one of the things Arkansas Tom does not believe in," the *Joplin Globe* described him as the "baddest bad man."[8]

Daugherty was also taken back to Newton County, and all four suspects were arraigned at Neosho on February 26 on charges of robbing the Fairview bank. All four pleaded guilty. Still clinging to a thieves' code of honor, Daugherty took most of the blame upon himself and asked the judge to go easy on his co-defendants. The judge did indeed give the others lighter sentences than he assessed Daugherty. However, Massee, the getaway driver at Fairview, got six years while Cutler, who went inside the bank, got only four, perhaps because Massee, like Daugherty, had refused to cooperate with authorities. Johnson also received a sentence of six years in the pen, while Daugherty took a fall for eight.[9]

Daugherty was transferred to the state penitentiary at Jefferson City in mid-March 1917. His sentence was commuted by the governor in November 1921, supposedly because of good behavior, and he was discharged after serving a little over half of his scheduled eight-year stint.[10]

He might have conducted himself well enough inside the walls to merit early release, but once on the outside, it took only a couple of years before he reverted to a life of crime. On Saturday, November 24, 1923, Daugherty and a sidekick hijacked a taxicab driver at Miami, Oklahoma, and made him drive out of town before stealing a watch from him and forcing him out of the vehicle near Commerce with a promise to return the watch when they were through with it.[11]

Pressing the taxi into criminal service, Daugherty and three partners; Jess Cockran, Len Brookshire, and Guy McKenzie; pulled up in the vehicle outside the Bank of Asbury about twenty miles northwest of Joplin on Monday, November 26, with robbery on their mind. Unknown to the outlaw foursome, though, a series of what the *Joplin News Herald* called "harrowing experiences" awaited them before they would finally make their escape late that night. "Gunplay and bold acts of banditry that would rival some of the daring works of outlaws in the days when the James boys terrorized Missouri" would figure in the flight of the desperadoes.[12]

Two of the bandits stayed in the getaway taxi, while two others entered the bank and flourished pistols. Daugherty was presumably one the gunmen, since the robbers' modus operandi was similar to the Oronogo and Fairview heists. The bandits herded three people who were in the bank into the vault, scooped up all the money they could lay their hands on, and put it in a satchel. The take totaled slightly over a $1,000 in currency and coin.[13]

Before the captives were driven into the vault, one of them was able to sound an automatic alarm system that alerted folks in nearby businesses and houses that a robbery was in progress. As the bandits emerged from the bank, they were met by shotgun fire from an Asbury citizen. The robber carrying the money satchel dropped it but picked it back up and jumped into the getaway car along with his cohort. The taxi sped away to the west amidst rifle fire from another citizen, R. C. Coleman.[14]

Coleman and two other men hopped into a vehicle of their own and gave chase. The pursuing vehicle got close enough to exchange fire, and the occupants of the two automobiles kept up a running fight for several miles. Five miles west of town, the bandit car turned south and soon came to a halt in the middle of the road. Two outlaws got out on the running boards of the vehicle to give battle. The pursuing vehicle stopped, too, and Coleman got out and fired several shots at the bandits. The robbers got back in their car, and the chase resumed briefly but was soon called off when the getaway car reached a wooded area. Armed only with Coleman's rifle, the pursuers were leery of going up against the heavily armed gang in an area that lent itself to ambush and offered many hiding spots.[15]

Authorities in surrounding towns were notified of the Asbury robbery almost immediately, and a number of officers from various agencies joined in the chase after the bandits. Just an hour or so after the holdup, Joplin motorcycle cop Clarence Allison intercepted the robbers on a road near Crestline, Kansas, and exchanged gunfire with them. The bandits abandoned their vehicle and took to a ravine that meandered across a field. Allison hopped in the outlaw car and drove it across the field to try to cut them off. After just a short distance, the car hit a ditch, and Allison alighted from the vehicle. Hurrying ahead, he intercepted three of the gang, and got the drop on them as they were walking down the ravine. He disarmed them and was marching them back up the ravine when the fourth gang member, Daugherty, sneaked up behind him. Allison felt the muzzle of a revolver pressed against his back. "Drop that gun!" Daugherty ordered, and Allison complied.[16]

The other gang members retrieved their weapons, and all four then marched their captive back toward the road. When they got there, they were met by local citizen J. A. Lucas and his son. The two had witnessed the initial gunfight between Allison and the bandits and had retrieved rifles in the meantime. However, they were afraid to use them for fear of endangering Allison's life, and the bandits quickly disarmed the father and son.[17]

Seeing the taxi they'd used for their getaway mired in the field, the robbers commandeered Lucas's car, took Allison as a hostage, and forced him to drive. After taking the officer through Galena and several other nearby small towns, they finally told him to stop the car not far from Devil's Promenade near the Missouri-Oklahoma border. As the bandits let Allison out of the vehicle, one of them asked him how much money he had on him. When the officer said he had four dollars, the outlaw told him he could keep it. Four dollars probably seemed like a puny sum, because the gang still had the currency they'd taken from the Asbury bank, although the coins had been left in the money satchel on the floor of the automobile abandoned in the Kansas field. The bandits also gave Allison the watch they'd taken from the taxi driver with instructions for him to return it in fulfilment of the promise they'd made when they stole it.[18]

The car the bandits took from Lucas turned up a few days later near Peoria, Oklahoma. A suspect in the holdup was arrested just before Christmas but later acquitted. In mid-January 1924, Jess Cockran was arrested in Tulsa for his role in the Asbury heist, and he admitted he was one of the four men who pulled off the job. Len Brookshire was also arrested near Tulsa a day or two later. Both men were brought back to Jasper County, convicted in the spring of 1924, and sentenced to fifty years apiece in the Missouri state prison. Cockran later died in prison, and Brookshire served about forty years, interrupted by an escape and a brief parole.[19]

About the first of August 1924, ex-con Guy McKenzie was arrested in Colorado as a third suspect in the Asbury bank robbery and brought back to Missouri a week or so later. Roy Daugherty had previously been identified from mug shots taken seven years earlier when he was sent to prison for the Fairview robbery as the fourth suspect, and on August 16, authorities received a tip that he was holed up at 1420 West Ninth Street in Joplin at the home of an acquaintance named "Red" Snow.[20]

About 6:30 that evening, Joplin detective Len VanDeventer and chief of detectives William Gibson, the same man who'd helped arrest Daugherty in Galena seven years earlier, drove to the address in one car while police chief V. P. Hine and two other officers approached in a separate vehicle. Knowing the desperate character of the man they were after, the officers arrived at the residence expecting that Daugherty would not be taken without a fight, and a fight is what they got.[21]

Alighting from their vehicle, VanDeventer started for the front door and Gibson headed toward the back door to cut off a possible escape route. Red Snow was not home, but Daugherty was there with Snow's wife and the couple's two kids, a twelve-year-old daughter and a baby. Seeing the police cars pull up outside, the fugitive made a move toward the back door with the baby tagging along at his feet.

Met at the rear entrance by Detective Gibson, Daugherty promptly opened fire, with one of his shots taking "a generous chip out of the officer's straw hat," but otherwise doing no damage. Gibson returned fire, and although two or three of the .32 caliber shots wounded Daugherty, they failed to bring him down. Daugherty darted back toward the front room, with the infant still trailing at his heels, while the mother and older sister stood off to the side screaming at the top of their lungs. In the front room, Daugherty encountered VanDeventer, who'd come in through the front door while his partner engaged the desperado at the rear exit. Daugherty leveled his pistol at VanDeventer, but the officer fired first, piercing the fugitive through the heart with a .44 slug on his first shot. The outlaw fell onto a nearby bed and died almost instantly. VanDeventer later said he beat Daugherty to the trigger, but Gibson qualified the claim, explaining that Daugherty had fired only two shots at him and that he thought the desperado's pistol had jammed after the second shot.[22]

Chief Hine and the two officers with him never approached the house during the shootout but instead took up strategic hiding spots in some woods surrounding the property. Hine was later fired by the mayor for his failure to go to the aid of Gibson and VanDeventer.[23]

Daugherty's body was taken to Hurlbut's Undertaking in Joplin, where it was viewed the next day, August 17, by an estimated 5,000 people, including women and children. "Most of the thousands who gazed upon the pallid face," said the *Joplin News Herald*, "were merely curious to view a man known to be of the type of fearless desperadoes who robbed, plundered and killed in the early days of outlawry when gunplay was not uncommon. They knew that few of his kind have survived." Arkansas Tom was later buried in an unmarked grave at Fairview Cemetery.[24]

Chapter 23

The Murder of a Carthage Taxi Driver
One of the Most Spectacular Cases in the Modern
History of Jasper County

Taxi driver William Spain left the Harrington Hotel in Carthage about one o'clock Monday morning, May 9, 1921, with two young male passengers dressed in military uniforms who said they wanted to be taken to the home of a Mrs. Tucker several miles northwest of Carthage on the Base Line Road (i.e. Highway M). When Spain did not return after a reasonable time, the owners of the cab company became concerned and instituted a search for the missing man. About nine o'clock the same morning, Spain's blood-smeared taxicab, a five-passenger Dodge, was found abandoned two miles northwest of Carthage on the Lower Bridge Road (i.e. Civil War Road). Foul play was immediately suspected, and a search that included the dragging of nearby Dry Fork of Spring River was undertaken.[1]

Suspicion quickly settled on twenty-one-year-old Earl Dewey Tucker. He was the son of the woman to whose house the taxi passengers had said they wanted to be taken, and he was home on leave from Camp Eustis, Virginia. He was roused from bed and arrested at his sister's home in Carthage later that morning. Tucker put on civilian clothes when he was arrested, and officers demanded to see his soldier's uniform. He could not produce his trousers, and the top part of the uniform showed signs of having been freshly laundered. Family members told conflicting stories about the young man's whereabouts the previous night. Tucker was taken back to the Harrington Hotel, but the witness who'd seen the two men get in Spain's cab said he could not positively identify the suspect now that he was wearing civilian clothes. Nonetheless, officers felt sure they had the right man, and Tucker was taken to the county jail in Carthage. Just an hour or two later, authorities, fearing mob violence, moved him to Joplin.[2]

Tucker stoutly maintained his innocence when he was grilled by law officers at Joplin Police headquarters that afternoon. He said he'd been with his girlfriend during the time the crime had allegedly been committed. Despite his denial and despite the fact that no body had been found and no clear motive established, Tucker was charged with first degree murder so that he could be held for further questioning. The next day, he clung to his story of innocence even after his mother came to Joplin and pleaded with him to tell the truth. Later that day, Tuesday, May 10, a partially burned military uniform was found during the search for Spain's body, but Tucker denied it belonged to him.[3]

On the evening of May 11, Tucker finally broke down and gave a confession, claiming he knew who had killed Spain but that he did not participate in the murder himself. He said he and a fellow soldier named William Mullen left Carthage shortly after midnight on Monday morning the 9th as passengers in Spain's cab and that north of town they picked up two other soldiers, whom they had met as they were leaving Camp Eustis. One of the other two he knew only as Harry, and he did not know the fourth man's name at all. When they got close to his mother's house, Tucker said, he left the rest of the group. He reunited with Private Mullen a couple of hours later, and Mullen told him that he had shot Spain and, with the help of the other two soldiers, dumped his body from a bridge over North Fork about a mile north of Purcell. The only motive for the crime was that the killers wanted Spain's vehicle, but they later abandoned it when it had a flat tire.[4]

After Tucker's confession, he was taken to Springfield for safekeeping. In Springfield, he repeated essentially the same confession he'd given in Joplin, and it was transcribed word for word by a stenographer. Authorities felt, however, that the suspect was still not telling the whole truth.[5]

William Spain, pictured with his three-year-old daughter shortly before his disappearance. *From the Joplin News Herald.*

Investigators went out on the evening of Wednesday, May 11, and found blood on the bridge Tucker had directed them to, but the search was hampered by darkness. The focus of the search had already turned to the North Fork of Spring

River even before Tucker's confession, and the next morning, workers began searching the river in earnest. About 8:20 a.m., Spain's body was found lodged in some willow trees a hundred yards below the bridge. An autopsy later in the day on the 12th found that Spain had been shot twice, once in the heart and once in the head, and that either wound would have been sufficient to cause death. From the angle of the wounds and the blood patterns, investigators concluded that Spain had been shot while behind the wheel by a passenger sitting beside him in the front seat. This strengthened their belief that Tucker was the person who killed Spain, since he was seen in the front seat of the cab as it left the Harrington Hotel, but they thought he might have had an accomplice.[6]

Tucker was brought back to Joplin during the weekend of May 14-15 for his arraignment in the Jasper County Circuit Court scheduled for Monday the 16th. On Sunday, with his mother and his girlfriend present, he broke down and gave an altered, more complete confession than his previous one. He admitted that he was present, along with Mullen and the two John Doe soldiers, when Spain was killed, but he still maintained that Mullen was the trigger man. The motive was that the foursome planned to steal Spain's car so they could use it to rob the Purcell Bank.[7]

On Monday morning, Tucker appeared before Judge Grant Emerson, waived a preliminary hearing, and pleaded guilty to complicity in the first-degree murder of William Spain. Emerson, declaring that he thought there were extenuating circumstances in Tucker's case and that he didn't think it was a good thing to condemn to death a man who pleaded guilty, sentenced the defendant to life imprisonment in the state penitentiary. Tucker was transported to Jefferson City later that same day.[8]

The decision to accept Tucker's guilty plea was not well received in Carthage. The *Carthage Press*, for example, said officials had made "a grave mistake" in allowing Tucker to plead guilty. He should have been forced to stand trial, said the newspaper, and, if found guilty, hanged.[9]

William John Mullen, the soldier whom Tucker had accused of shooting William Spain, did not return to his military post and was declared a deserter. He was apprehended in Canada on a burglary charge in mid-May, shortly after the Spain murder, but Jasper County officials did not learn of his arrest until mid-August. Sheriff Harry Mead traveled to Canada to interview Mullen but came back emptyhanded because Mullen was ill and Canadian officials balked at turning him over.[10]

Near the same time as his trip to Canada, Mead also traveled to Jeff City to take an amended statement from Tucker. The prisoner now admitted that he and Mullen were the only ones involved in Spain's killing, and he told the sheriff the murder weapon was hidden at his sister's house. He still maintained that Mullen was the one who'd shot Spain, but he admitted that he had helped throw the victim's body over the bridge and helped hide the weapon. On August 19, Jasper County officials received word from military authorities that the serial number of the pistol, which was found hidden where Tucker said it would be, matched the number of the weapon Mullen had been issued at Camp Eustis.[11]

In early November, Tucker announced he wanted to amend his confession yet again, and Sheriff Mead traveled to Jefferson City to listen to it. Tucker now said that Mullen was not involved in any way in the murder of Spain. The prisoner said he had purchased Mullen's revolver from a cook at Camp Eustis to whom Mullen had given it just before deserting. Tucker also said that Mullen's revolver, the one he'd pointed lawmen to back in August, was not the murder weapon. He still maintained that he was only an accomplice and that one of his sidekicks, whom he did not know by name, had done the actual shooting. Officials believed Tucker was now telling the truth about Mullen, because Mullen had previously been able to show that he was in Canada the day after the Spain murder, making it unlikely he'd been involved. Authorities also believed Tucker had accomplices, as he claimed, but they did not buy his story that he himself was only an aider and abettor. They felt he was the instigator of the crime and the person who'd actually pulled the trigger.[12]

Around the early part of September 1922, Tucker issued still another confession, claiming that thirty-two-year-old Neil

Implicated in the Spain murder, William John Mullen proved to be nothing but an Army
deserter and small-time crook. *From the Joplin News Herald.*

Mertins of Carthage was with him when Spain was killed and
was the man who actually did the shooting. Tucker further
implicated Mertins's father-in-law, Isaac Harmon, as an
accomplice in planning and carrying out the crime. The sixty-
seven-year old Harmon was married to Tucker's twenty-year-
old sister, Dolly, and the couple were going through a bitter
divorce. Many speculated that Tucker's latest confession was a
put-up job instigated at least partly by Dolly, and, indeed, the
charges against both Harmon and his son-in-law were later
dismissed.[13]

In May of 1929, Tucker escaped from a prison truck near
California, Missouri. He was recaptured in Ohio in March 1930
and returned to Jeff City, but he escaped again in October 1931.
A report from Traverse City, Michigan, reached Jasper County
in September 1932 that the fugitive had been recaptured there,
but, if so, he made his getaway before he could be brought back
to Missouri. He was finally recaptured for real at Kalamazoo,
Michigan in August 1933 and returned to the Missouri state
pen.[14]

Despite Tucker's multiple escapes, Missouri governor Forrest Donnell somehow deemed the prisoner worthy of a parole, and he was set free on November 4, 1941. In reporting the governor's action, the *Joplin Globe* recalled Tucker's crime as "one of the most spectacular murder cases in the modern history of Jasper County." Tucker had his civil rights restored in June 1952, but what happened to him after that has not been traced.[15]

Chapter 24

Jasper County's Only Double Hanging
Two Men Swing for the Murder of a Carthage Grocer

After Castille Stapleton (alias Ralph Long) and Sterling Jackson (aka Oscar Moore) were arrested on suspicion of killing Carthage storekeeper George Babcock in April of 1922, they revealed that they'd first gotten acquainted at the Missouri State Penitentiary just a couple of years earlier. Jackson got sent to Jefferson City in December of 1918 on a burglary conviction from Jackson County when he was twenty-one years old. Stapleton, twenty-two, joined Jackson at the big house six months later, also on a burglary charge from Jackson County. Stapleton was released in September of 1921 after serving three-fourths of his three-year term, and Jackson had his five-year term commuted by the governor in early March 1922.[1]

If part of the purpose of incarceration is meant to be rehabilitating the wrongdoers, the program failed miserably in Stapleton's and Jackson's cases. In fact, their time in lockup seems to have had the opposite effect. Almost as soon as Jackson was released, the two men got back together in Kansas City and decided to go into "the hold-up business." Shortly after forming their "partnership," they stuck up and robbed a taxicab driver in Kansas City and then absconded to Pittsburg, Kansas. From there, they came to Joplin on Saturday, April 8, and rented a room at 315 Kentucky Avenue. That night they traveled to Carthage looking for a hold-up target.[2]

About ten o'clock, the desperate pair walked into Babcock's store at 411 East Central Avenue with their faces uncovered. Jackson carried a knife, and Stapleton was packing a pistol. According to bystander Fred Beard, Jackson bought five cents worth of tobacco and then asked for some soda pop. When Babcock started toward the rear of the store to retrieve it, Jackson followed him, and Stapleton also shuffled in that direction. At the rear of the store, Jackson grabbed Babcock from behind and demanded money, but Babcock spun around and began scuffling with his assailant. Stapleton drew his revolver and ordered Beard to throw up his hands. After the customer complied, Stapleton also ordered Babcock to stick up his hands, and when he did not promptly do so, Stapleton fired a single shot that struck the storekeeper in the neck. He died soon afterward.[3]

The robbers fled through an alley and wandered around the streets of Carthage until they got their bearings and then headed toward Joplin. They walked all the way, following streetcar tracks and railroad tracks until they got to Lakeside Park. From there, they followed the paved road, dodging into roadside thickets to avoid being noticed each time a car passed. In that way, they reached Joplin undetected and went to the house on Kentucky Avenue.[4]

As soon as Joplin authorities learned of the hold-up attempt and the killing of Babcock, they suspected the perpetrators might turn up in Joplin, and they asked the black community to be on the lookout for them. Acting on a tip from a woman named Hazel Mitchell, officers arrested Stapleton and Jackson at the Kentucky Avenue address just minutes after the pair arrived on Sunday morning. The Ku Klux Klan, which was active in Joplin and elsewhere throughout the country at this time, later gave Ms. Mitchell a $40 reward.[5]

Stapleton, still going by the name Ralph Long, and Jackson were taken to the Joplin Police station, where they gave confessions and Stapleton revealed his real name. Fearing mob violence, officers then whisked them away in "a high powered motor car" to Miami, Oklahoma, and placed them in the Ottawa County Jail for safekeeping. The two were brought back to Joplin for arraignment the next day, Monday, April 10, on first-degree murder charges. After entering "not guilty" pleas, they were taken back to Miami. Later the same day, a coroner's jury in Carthage returned a verdict that George Babcock had come to his death by a gunshot wound inflicted by Ralph Long (i.e. Stapleton) and that Long was assisted by Sterling Jackson.[6]

Fearing mob violence, authorities moved the prisoners again on Tuesday the 11th, spiriting them away to Springfield, Missouri, where they were placed in the Greene County Jail. Later in the week, as lynch fever subsided, the accused murderers were brought back to Jasper County from Springfield and placed in jail at Carthage.[7]

Stapleton's trial was scheduled first, and it got underway on May 1 in Division 2 of Jasper County Circuit Court at Joplin. During jury selection, the defense attorneys challenged virtually every potential juror on whether or not he was a member of the Ku Klux Klan, and all answered in the negative. According to a local newspaper, it was the first time in Joplin for a man to be publicly challenged on the question of his membership in the secret society.[8]

Fred Beard, the customer who'd been in Babcock's store on the night of the crime, was the star witness for the prosecution. He positively identified Stapleton as the shooter, explaining that he was only about seven or eight feet away from him when he pulled out his revolver and ordered Beard to throw up his hands. Among the state's other witnesses was the detective who took Stapleton's and Jackson's statements confessing to their crime when they were first arrested.

Stapleton's lawyers offered no witnesses, and their only defense was a plea to spare their client the death penalty.[9]

After a trial that lasted less than two days and after only fifty-six minutes of deliberation, the jury came back on the afternoon of May 2 with a guilty verdict and a sentence of death by hanging. The only reason deliberations lasted as long as they did was that the jurors split 9-3 in favor of the death sentence at first, and it took three more votes to achieve unanimity. After the trial, Stapleton was taken back to jail at Carthage to await formal sentencing.[10]

Sterling Jackson's trial began in Division 1 of Jasper County Circuit Court at Joplin on May 3, the day after Stapleton's concluded. Jury selection consumed most of the first day, and by the end of the second day, all arguments and testimony on both sides had been presented. Prosecution testimony was virtually the same as it had been for Stapleton's trial, and the defense again offered no witnesses, although Jackson's attorneys made a strong plea to spare his life. The jury got the case in the late afternoon of the 4th and deliberated for five and a half hours without reaching a verdict before retiring for the night.[11]

On the morning of May 5, the jury reached a guilty verdict and sentenced Jackson to hang. As was the case with Stapleton's jury, several votes were required to achieve unanimity. The deadlock was over the sentence, not over the guilty verdict, with one or two jurors holding out for life imprisonment instead of death. The point that finally won over the holdouts was apparently the fact that, although Jackson had not fired the fatal shot, he was armed with a deadly weapon.[12]

Defense attorneys for both Stapleton and Jackson filed motions for new trials, but both motions were overruled on May 13. Immediately after the rulings, Judge Grant Emerson sentenced Stapleton to hang on June 23, 1922, and Judge J. D. Perkins pronounced the same sentence on Jackson. Both men's cases were then appealed to the Missouri Supreme Court, automatically staying their executions.[13]

The prisoners were returned to Carthage immediately after sentence was pronounced on them. They had to be brought back to Joplin in early June for safekeeping after a mob formed in Carthage and threatened vigilante violence, but they were again returned to Carthage after a couple of days.[14]

On June 21, 1923, the Missouri Supreme Court affirmed the lower court's verdicts in Stapleton's and Jackson's cases, rejecting the defense's claim that the condemned men had not received fair trials. At the same time, the high court also rejected a broader challenge to the constitutionality of capital punishment. The execution date for both men was set for dawn on August 3. Plans called for them to hang simultaneously on a double scaffold erected just west of the county jail surrounded by a fence or stockade to keep out uninvited spectators.[15]

On Tuesday night, July 31, Stapleton, through the medium of a *Joplin Globe* reporter, made an eleventh-hour appeal to Missouri governor Arthur M. Hyde to save his partner's life. He claimed that neither he nor Jackson got a fair trial, and he largely blamed the newspapers' biased reporting during the legal proceedings for the prejudice against him and his fellow defendant. He said that if he and Jackson had been white, they might have received life imprisonment but not death sentences, and he cited the recent case of Dewey Tucker, the young white man who'd killed William Spain in Carthage and received life imprisonment. He said he and Jackson were not given an opportunity to plead guilty in exchange for lesser sentences as Tucker had been.[16]

"If the governor don't give us a stay," Stapleton continued, "all I ask is that he give or commute the man who had nothing to do with the killing. I will go to the scaffold gladly and take the drop if they will only commute Jackson. They should not take two men's lives for one. The other man didn't do the shooting. He had nothing to do with it. I had the gun, and I did the shooting, and I should take the drop."[17]

The *Globe* and other news outlets had recently reported that the condemned men seemed unconcerned by the sights and sounds of the scaffold being built just outside their cells, but Stapleton dismissed "that stuff" as "newspaper talk." He said, of course, it bothered them and that he hadn't slept since Saturday night. During the reporter's visit, however, Stapleton, as if to belie his nervousness, sang and danced to the music of a phonograph that was brought into the corridor outside his cell, and as the reporter and other visitors got ready to leave, he told them to "be sure and come back for some more music before the big show Friday morning."[18]

On Wednesday, August 1, W. F. Maher, attorney for the condemned men, received word from Governor Hyde that he would not intervene on behalf of Stapleton and Jackson. Hyde said he had recently visited Carthage and talked to citizens there, and he admitted he was concerned that commuting the men's sentences might incite vigilante violence.[19]

On Thursday night, the eve of the double hanging, a curious crowd began to gather around the jail in Carthage. Stapleton and Jackson were reportedly holding up well under their ordeal and even appeared jovial at times. The prisoners asked for and received ice cream and watermelon for their final meal, a fact that the *Joplin Globe* deemed worthy of a headline.

Shortly after midnight, jailer Norman Bricker read the death warrants to the condemned men. Afterward, Jackson, who'd served briefly in the military during World War I, handed Brinker a letter in which he requested that any veteran's bonus due him be sent to his mother in Kansas City.[20]

NEGRO SLAYERS TO DIE ON SCAFFOLD AT 5 A. M.

Jailer Reads Death Warrant to Condemned Men at Midnight, Forestalling Any Chance for Reprieve—Blacks Eat Ice Cream and Watermelon on Eve of Hanging—Crowd Surrounds Jail Awaiting Hour of Execution.

Stapleton and Jackson's early-morning double hanging had already occurred by the time most readers saw these headlines in the August 3, 1923 *Joplin Globe*.

At about 4:45 Friday morning, August 3, 1923, Stapleton and Jackson, with their arms already bound, were led from their cells to the scaffold via a walkway through a west window of the jail. After the nooses and caps were adjusted around the men's necks and heads, Sheriff Harry Mead pulled a lever that sprung both traps simultaneously, and Stapleton and Jackson dropped to their deaths together at 4:56 a.m. They were pronounced dead about ten minutes later, and their bodies were taken down and turned over to local undertakers shortly afterward. Although a limited number of spectators had been allowed inside the enclosure to witness the double execution, crowds of curiosity-seekers viewed the bodies at the undertaking establishments. Stapleton's body was then taken to Fayette, Missouri, for burial, while Jackson was interred in Carthage's Cedar Hill Cemetery.[21]

Chapter 25

A Murder Mystery Solved
The Slaying of R. T. Thompson

On Wednesday evening, October 23, 1929, Robert T. Thompson. a thirty-one-year-old Joplin watchmaker, was out riding around with Miss Mary J. Quinn, a nurse at St. John's Hospital. The two had known each other for years, but they'd gotten better acquainted during Thompson's recent stay at the hospital for treatment of an eye illness. Divorced and the father of a young child, Thompson had continued to see the twenty-three-year-old Miss Quinn after his discharge, and the two had "been out driving on several occasions" in recent weeks.[1]

On this night, Thompson picked Mary up and drove east of town to Duquesne Road. He wanted to get away from Joplin, because the bright lights bothered his eye, which still required treatment. Turning north, the couple drove to the Wilhoit Refinery road (now Newman Road) and turned east. A half mile down the road, Thompson slowed and was preparing to stop so that Mary could put some medicine in his eye. Just as she turned on the dome light so she could see to administer the medicine, a car with several people in it pulled up alongside the Thompson car, and one of the passengers ordered Thompson to stop. Instead of complying, he started to pull away, and someone from the other car fired a shot that struck him in the left temple. Thompson slumped over the steering wheel, apparently lifeless, as the assassin car sped away. Mary, who'd never driven before, pulled Thompson over to the passenger's seat and took the steering wheel herself. Frantically, she drove her friend to the hospital, but it was too late. It was determined after they reached the hospital that Thompson had died almost instantly.[2]

In the aftermath of the murder, a large reward was offered for the apprehension of the gang responsible. One man was arrested on suspicion of having killed Thompson, but he was discharged after it was determined that he'd merely read about the crime and had given a false confession. With few clues to unlock the mystery of the crime, the real murderers of R. T. Thompson went unidentified.[3]

For two years.

Then in early October 1931, police got an anonymous tip that twenty-four-year-old Leslie Edgington of Joplin was somehow involved in Thompson's murder. Authorities were planning to take him into custody for questioning for the crime when he got into a fight at a Joplin pool hall on Sunday evening, October 11. Responding to a call to break up the fight, police arrested Edgington and held him for questioning in the two-year-old murder case.[4]

The tip had implicated four other people besides Edgington, and police began rounding them up as well. Thirty-seven-year-old Earl Osborn of Central City was lodged in jail at Joplin alongside Edgington, while forty-five-year-old George Herrelson and his forty-one-year-old wife, Bertha, who was Osborn's sister, were arrested at their Riverton, Kansas, home and taken to the Cherokee County Jail at Columbus. The fifth suspect, twenty-two-year-old Floyd Blinzler, fled when the police pulled up outside his Joplin home, and he was not immediately apprehended.[5]

On Monday evening, October 12, Edgington confessed to his part in the crime and confirmed the identity of the other four participants. He said Osborn and Herrelson had been operating as road bandits for some time prior to the killing of Thompson. On the night of the murder, Edgington said, he and Blinzler were at Fifteenth and Main in Joplin when Osborn and the Herrelson couple drove up and asked the two young men to accompany them on an expedition of robbery. Edgington said he did not want to go but that Osborn told him he had to because he knew too much. The two young men climbed into the back seat of Herrelson's Chrysler. In the front seat, the owner was driving, his wife was beside him, and Osborn was riding shotgun. As the gang drove east of town looking for someone in a parked car who might be an easy victim, Osborn, who had two pistols, handed one of them to Edgington.[6]

When the gang spotted the Thompson car coming to a halt with its dome light on, Herrelson pulled up beside it. Osborn and Edgington hopped out with their revolvers in hand. When Thompson refused the order to stop and began to drive away, Osborn opened fire. The two men hopped back in the Chrysler, and Herrelson sped away. Osborn later told Edgington that he shot Thompson because he thought Thompson was going for a gun. Osborn also threatened Edgington that if he "squawked," the rest of the gang would take him for "a long, long ride."[7]

Confronted with Edgington's confession, Osborn gave a statement of his own on Tuesday, October 13. He admitted being the gunman who'd actually shot Thompson, but he refused to implicate his sister or her husband. Later that day, Osborn and Edgington were arraigned before a Joplin justice of the peace, who charged them with first-degree murder and committed them to the Jasper County Jail at Carthage without bond.[8]

Osborn and Edgington shortly after their arrests. *From the Joplin Globe.*

Blinzler was captured at Crocker, Missouri, on October 15 and brought back to Carthage, where he gave a statement that night. He confirmed that Osborn was the slayer of Thompson, but he said Herrelson directed the operations of the gang. Blinzler also admitted that he and Edgington had accompanied Herrelson and Osborn on several robberies prior to the Thompson murder, a detail that Edgington had omitted in his confession. However, Edgington admitted that Blinzler's statement was true when confronted with it. Blinzler was arraigned the next day, October 16. Charged with murder, he joined Edgington and Osborn at the county jail.[9]

On October 17, George and Bertha Herrelson were extradited from Kansas, arraigned in Joplin on murder charges, and transported to Carthage, where they, like the other three gang members, took up lodging at the county jail.[10]

Mug shots of George and Bertha Herrelson. *Courtesy Missouri State Archives.*

At their preliminary hearings on November 4, Blinzler and the Herrelsons were bound over for trial in the Jasper County Circuit Court. Edgington and Osborn waived preliminary hearings and were also held for trial.[11]

When the circuit court opened in mid-November, Osborn initially pleaded not guilty to first-degree murder, but on November 24, he changed his plea to guilty rather than face a jury. The prosecution offered to reduce the charges against Edgington and Blinzler to second-degree murder in exchange for their testimony against the Herrelsons, and they took the deal, pleading guilty on November 30, 1931.[12]

Each in turn took the stand to testify against the Herrelsons when their joint trial got underway at Carthage later the same day. The testimony of the youthful accomplices was similar to the confessions they'd given when first arrested, with a couple of significant modifications. Edgington now said that he was carrying a flashlight when he and Osborn got out of the bandit car to accost Thompson and that Osborn did not hand him a revolver until after the two got back in the Chrysler. Blinzler said he'd never been formally introduced to the Herrelsons and, therefore, couldn't be positive they were the same couple he'd been with on the night of the murder. The defense attorney argued that his clients were not even at the murder scene on the night in question but were instead at home in Galena, Kansas, where they then resided. The lawyer trotted two or three witnesses to the stand to try to establish the alibi, and he suggested that Osborn, Edgington, and Blinzler had committed the crime by themselves.[13]

The case was given to the jury the next day, December 1, and they came back that evening after three hours of deliberation with a verdict convicting both Herrelson and his wife of first-degree murder. Two of the couple's grown daughters were in the courtroom, and they broke into tears as the verdict was read and sentences of life imprisonment were pronounced. A few days later, the sentences for Edgington and Blinzler were set at fifteen years apiece in the state prison.[14]

Edgington and Blinzler were paroled or had their sentences commuted after a few years, and they were both back in Joplin prior to 1940. Meanwhile, Osborn and the Herrelsons were still making their home at the big house in Jefferson City.[15]

Chapter 26

Irene McCann: Good Girl or Bad Woman?
The Murder of Jailer E. O. Bray

When Irene Scott was growing up in Alabama, she was a "good girl," according to her mother, and, as a teenager, she taught Sunday school in the local Baptist Church. Even after her life's path took a criminal turn, her charm and good looks earned her leniency, and when she subsequently broke out of the Missouri Penitentiary on two separate occasions, her pretty face was plastered on newspapers across the country like that of a celebrity. Only a handful of people saw beyond the pleasing facade to the devious scheming it disguised.[1]

Irene was born in DeKalb County, Alabama, where her father served as a deputy sheriff. He was killed in a gunfight with moonshiners when Irene was barely eight years old, and her mother, Velma, remarried shortly afterward. In the fall of 1929, at the age of eighteen, Irene, in the words of her mother, just "got a desire to pick up and run off." Irene wrote a letter from Dallas not long after she left home informing her mother she was working as a waitress there, but then the letters stopped.[2]

Irene, who started going by the name "Billie Lee," spent the next year crisscrossing the country working variously as a waitress, dancer, and "entertainer" in Texas, Florida, New Orleans, and Chicago. In May of 1930, she was arrested on suspicion in New Orleans when she and two men were spotted snooping around a Canal Street motion picture theater late at night. Quickly released, she struck out for parts unknown and landed in Springfield, Missouri, around August or September of 1930.[3]

She got a job working as a waitress and soon made the acquaintance of several desperate young men from Joplin, including Jess Biggs, Raymond Jackson, and Albert McCann. Biggs and Jackson were suspected of pulling off a string of holdups in the Joplin area, and Joplin authorities notified Springfield law officers to be on the lookout for the pair. In the early morning of October 9, 1930, Springfield Police raided a rooming house on West Walnut where the two suspects were thought to be holed up. Biggs and Jackson made a daring escape, but the officers found Irene and another young woman, Mildred Holman, in the men's apartment. Irene, who identified herself as Billie Lee from New Orleans, was questioned and released. Jackson was captured later that day and sent to the Jasper County Jail in Carthage, while Biggs was killed near Joplin a little over a month later by a fellow bandit in a quarrel over a woman.[4]

Meanwhile, Irene took up with McCann. An eighteen-year-old Joplin lad, McCann did not yet have the desperate reputation of Biggs and Jackson, but he was well known to local juvenile authorities and had a wild streak that matched Irene's own. The couple's whirlwind romance led quickly to a marriage proposal. When they went before a justice in Columbus, Kansas, on November 7 to apply for the license and have him perform the ceremony, McCann had to ask Irene what her last name was.[5]

The newlyweds promptly embarked on "a career of highway robbery," teaming up with Paul Hindman and his ex-wife, Peggy Moss. On or about November 20, the foursome stole a car in Tulsa and drove to Kansas City, where they attempted to hold up a drugstore that same night. The two women remained in the car, and McCann guarded the entrance as Hindman went inside. When the druggist pulled out a revolver, he was killed and Hindman gravely wounded in an exchange of gunfire.[6]

The four desperadoes fled to Joplin, where the three who'd escaped the Kansas City hijinks uninjured dumped Hindman on the steps of Freeman Hospital. Hindman died the next day, but, before expiring, he gave a deathbed statement implicating his ex-wife and the McCanns as his sidekicks. Peggy

Moss was quickly arrested for her part in the attempted holdup and murder of the druggist, while Albert and Irene McCann remained at large.[7]

On Sunday morning, December 14, Albert and Irene went to the Jasper County Jail at Carthage with the intention of trying to spring Raymond Jackson, who was awaiting transport to Jefferson City after being convicted of robbery in connection with the string of crimes he and Jess Biggs had carried out. Irene went into the jail alone to scout the place out, using the ruse that she wanted to see misdemeanor prisoner Bill Daggett. Informed that Daggett had already been released, she went back to the car, and then she and Albert returned to the jail together. McCann insisted that Sunday jailer E. O. Bray double check his record on Daggett's release. When Bray turned to oblige, McCann grabbed the jailer's revolver, and the two men began struggling over it.[8]

Irene pulled a .22 caliber pistol out of her purse and fired a shot at Bray, but the bullet struck McCann in the leg instead. McCann, however, managed to wrest Bray's revolver from him and shoot the jailer with his own weapon. When Bray continued to reach for the weapon, McCann shot him twice more, killing him almost instantly. Irene took Bray's jail keys from his belt and handed them to her husband, who raced upstairs. Realizing he was in the women's quarters of the jail and, therefore, not where Jackson was kept, McCann dropped the keys and hurried back downstairs, telling Irene they had to go. The couple made their escape, intimidating several bystanders with threats as they did so. In running through the jail gate, Irene lost a heel off one of her shoes.[9]

Albert and Irene McCann were suspected in the killing of Bray almost immediately after it happened, but the fugitives were nowhere to be found in Jasper County. Instead, they fled to Oklahoma, where they stopped in Chelsea so that Irene could purchase bandages and medicine to treat Albert's leg wound. Chelsea chief of police Tom Deem saw Irene come into a drugstore and make the purchase, and he noticed a heel missing from one of her shoes. He thought little of the incident, however, until a day or two later when he read a newspaper account of the attempted jail delivery at Carthage. When he again spotted the McCanns in Chelsea on December 30, he arrested them without incident. Deem took a .38 caliber revolver from McCann, later identified as having belonged to Bray. The police chief also confiscated two pistols from Irene, a .38 caliber she carried in her coat and a .22 caliber in her purse. Back in Joplin, Mildred Holman, the young woman who'd been in the rooming house at Springfield with Irene when officers raided it back in October, was arrested as a possible "source of information," but she was not held as a suspect in the crimes of the McCanns.[10]

Irene McCann and her husband at the time of their arrest. *From the Altoona (PA) Tribune.*

Neither McCann nor his wife would talk much when first arrested, except that Irene said she sure felt sorry "for that boy," meaning her husband. After the outlaw couple was returned to Jasper County the next day, however, they began to open up about their criminal escapades.[11]

On the afternoon of December 31 at the Joplin Police headquarters, Albert signed a written statement confessing both to the killing of Bray and to his participation in the holdup attempt in Kansas City during which Paul Hindman killed the druggist. McCann also admitted helping Hindman stage two drugstore holdups in Joplin in November previous to the Kansas City fiasco. Albert said he sustained the bullet wound in his leg when Irene fired a shot at Bray with a revolver Hindman had given her prior to his death. Irene also signed a confession admitting that she was with her husband when he shot Bray and when Albert and Hindman committed their crimes, although she did not go into detail.[12]

Later on the evening of the 31st, Albert and Irene pleaded not guilty to murder at their arraignment before a Joplin justice of the peace. They were then lodged in the city jail, because authorities felt emotion was too intense against them in Carthage to risk taking them to the county jail until after their preliminary hearings.[13]

On January 2, 1931, the pair waived preliminary hearings and were bound over to the circuit court for trial. County prosecutor Ray Watson announced he planned to seek the death penalty for both defendants, and they were transported to the county jail in Carthage.[14]

In mid-January, Albert McCann's lawyer filed a motion to have his client's case tried separately from Irene's, and the severance was granted. In early February, McCann's motion for a change of venue was denied.[15]

Also in early February, Irene's mother, Velma Richardson, arrived from Alabama to try to help in her daughter's defense. Irene had not wanted her lawyers to contact her mother, preferring that she face her troubles alone rather than disgrace her family, but they overruled her wishes and summoned Mrs. Richardson to Jasper County. Velma said that she'd lost track of her daughter shortly after she left home fourteen months ago and that she'd feared she was dead.[16]

Prosecutors elected to try Albert first, and his trial got underway on April 20. Sixteen-year-old John Dyer, son of the regular Jasper County jailer, was the prosecution's star witness. An eyewitness to the crime, young Dyer said he saw McCann wrest Bray's revolver away and fire three bullets into the relief jailer's body. McCann's lawyers pursued an insanity defense. The defendant's mother, Mrs. May McCann, took the stand to say that her son had been plagued by headaches ever since he was a baby, that he'd always been "queer and abnormal," and that mental disorders ran in his family. After a week-long trial, the jury came back on the evening of April 25 with a verdict finding McCann guilty of first-degree murder. Informed of the verdict that night in her cell at the Jasper County Jail, Irene seemed "broken up" by the news but made no statement.[17]

Irene's trial took place less than a month later, in mid-May 1931. The prosecution sought to show that Irene fired a shot during the struggle between her husband and Bray. A medical expert who examined Albert McCann's wound said it was caused by a small caliber weapon, but the judge disallowed testimony that Irene had a .22 pistol on her person when she was arrested in Oklahoma, because no evidence was offered to show that she carried such a weapon when Bray was shot. Indeed, John Dyer, who again served as a primary state witness, said on cross-examination that he did not see Irene fire a shot or display a weapon.[18]

The highlight of the trial came when Irene took the stand in her own defense. She said Albert was nice to her when they first met and she "learned to love him" but that he turned mean and abusive right after they married. She only stayed with her husband and participated in his crime spree, she said, out of fear. She wept as she told the jury of the many times McCann had beat her. Twice, she said, he had even tried to shoot her in a drunken rage, and she'd only saved herself by deflecting the barrel of the weapon at the last second so that the bullets missed their mark. Irene claimed she did not know her husband's real purpose in going to the county jail and thought he only wanted to visit Bill Daggett. She did not realize he actually meant to break Raymond Jackson out of jail. She denied even knowing Raymond Jackson, despite the fact that two Springfield policemen had testified for the prosecution that she was in the same room where Jackson and Biggs had been when the officers raided the place the previous October. She also denied firing a shot at Bray or having a small-caliber pistol in her possession at the time of the crime. In fact, she said, she'd never fired a gun in her life.[19]

Irene's case went to the jury on the evening of May 20, and the deliberative body came back on the morning of the 21st with a verdict finding her guilty of second-degree murder with a sentence of ten years in the state prison, the lightest punishment that could be assessed under the judge's instructions for first or second-degree murder. Receiving the verdict with a smile, Irene commented, "I was lucky. Although I told the truth on the witness stand, I think that under the circumstances the jury was kind to me and I thank them."[20]

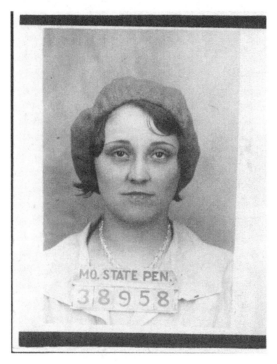

Mug shot of Irene McCann taken when she was admitted to the Missouri State Penitentiary. The photo later appeared in newspapers across the country when she escaped. *Author's collection.*

Albert McCann's lawyer appealed his case to the Missouri Supreme Court, and he was taken to the state prison in Jefferson City pending the outcome of the appeal. Meanwhile, Irene was also taken to the state penitentiary to begin serving her ten-year sentence.[21]

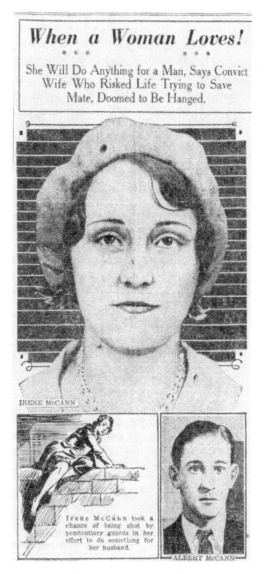

The story of Irene's escape was romanticized in the press. *From the El Paso (TX) Times.*

In the early morning of November 10, Irene escaped from the women's prison farm adjoining the main prison by scaling an eight-foot wire fence. She left two notes behind, one for Margaret Gorsuch, a prison matron, and the other for the warden. In her note to Mrs. Gorsuch, Irene apologized for causing the matron trouble and explained that she was escaping so she could get evidence to clear her husband, whom she said was innocent of killing Bray. "I should have told the truth at first," she said, "but I wasn't big enough."[22]

In her note to the warden, she thanked him and other prison officials for their kind treatment of her. Despite the affable tone of her notes, a report at the time of her escape said that most of the matrons at the prison considered her a "bad woman."[23]

The story of Irene's escape made headlines across the country, with photos of her and sketches depicting her escape accompanying the story. Irene's freedom, however, was short-lived. She was recaptured by a prison official on a road just east of Jefferson City the day after her escape. He stopped to offer her a ride, and she accepted. Recognizing her, he drove her back to town and delivered her to the prison. She offered no resistance.[24]

In February 1932, the state supreme court reversed the lower court's verdict in the Albert McCann case, mainly on the basis that he should have been granted his motion for a change of venue. A new trial began in Springfield in May 1932. Irene was brought to Springfield as a defense witness, and, contradicting her testimony at her own trial, she now said she did, indeed, fire the first shot during the jailbreak attempt and that the bullet struck Albert in the leg, just as he had said in his original confession. The jury again found McCann guilty of first-degree murder, but this time he was spared the death penalty and sentenced, instead, to fifty years in prison. Afterward, McCann said that he was happy with the sentence and that he hoped to get out someday.[25]

After her testimony, Irene was taken back to Jefferson City. Six and half months later, she teamed up with Edna Murray, known as the "Kissing Bandit" because of the "resoundent smacks" she bestowed on several of her victims, to make another sensational prison break. "Among the more notorious inmates of the women's prison," Irene and Edna, on the late night of December 12 or early morning of December 13, sawed their way out of a new cell building at the women's prison farm. Because of the difficult nature of their escapade, it was thought they probably had help from the outside.[26]

Irene again made news when she surrendered in 1934. *From the San Francisco Examiner.*

In contrast to her quick recapture after her previous escape, this time Irene made a clean getaway. She might have stayed on the lam indefinitely except that she simply walked into a Chicago police station on January 16, 1934, and gave herself up. "I'm tired of it all," she announced. "I want to go back to prison." The story of her surrender again made headlines, and the details of her criminal career, accompanied by photographs, were sensationalized in newspapers across the country.[27]

Irene was returned to the Missouri State Penitentiary two days after her surrender. Two years later, in January 1936, she became seriously ill, and the governor gave her a "sick parole" rather than risk her dying in prison. She was released into the custody of her mother, who was then living in Little Sioux, Iowa. Irene died at a hospital in nearby Sioux City on February 5, 1937, from complications of stomach cancer.[28]

Albert McCann escaped from the state prison in Jefferson City on December 22, 1954, by simply walking away from the prison farm. He was recaptured in Los Angeles in mid-November 1958 and brought back to Missouri. He was paroled two years later, went back to Los Angeles, and died there in 1964.[29]

Chapter 27

A Webb City Murder
The Killing of Coyne Hatten

When a stranger bumped into Coyne Hatten in Webb City near the rear of Morgan's drugstore late on the night of May 16, 1931, Hatten's natural inclination was to stand up for himself. A former star athlete from a well-to-do Webb City family, the twenty-seven-year-old Hatten wasn't used to being pushed around.[1]

If Hatten had known the desperate character of the man he was dealing with, he might have exercised a little discretion, but, instead, he demanded to know whether the stranger was looking for trouble. He'd scarcely gotten the words out of his mouth when the stranger pulled out a revolver and opened fire, shooting Hatten in the chest. After a pause, the man poured two more bullets into Hatten's body, killing him almost instantly.[2]

After the shooting, the assailant walked south on Webb Street to the front of the drugstore and went inside. He then exited through the rear door, walked past the body of his victim, and rendezvoused a block away with a male companion and two female companions who were waiting for him in an automobile. The four then sped away from the scene.[3]

The shooting was totally unexplained at first, and the shooter and his companions were unidentified. In the immediate wake of the crime, police arrested three young men who'd been seen arguing with Hatten shortly before the shooting, but all three denied any involvement in his death. Early the next morning, May 17, authorities got a break that put them on the right track when Mickey Carey, a forty-three-year-old ex-convict, appeared at the Joplin Police station. He said that he'd driven a man known to him as Jimmie Jones from Joplin to Webb City the previous night and that they'd been accompanied by Carey's wife and a Webb City waitress named Doris Adams. Carey said his wife had a wound on her arm and they'd gone to the drugstore to have the injury dressed. He and his wife had already gone inside, leaving the other couple at the car, when he heard three shots coming from behind the store. Rushing back outside, Carey and his wife saw Hatten lying dead, and Jones and Miss Adams were nowhere to be seen. Carey said he and his wife then returned to Joplin, but he denied driving Jones away from the scene.[4]

A young Coyne Hatten, right, with his older brother and sister. *Collection of Sara Easley McKibben, courtesy of Webb City Area Genealogical Society.*

Jones was arrested later that day at a Joplin rooming house. In his possession at the time was a pistol with three empty cylinders from which shots had recently been fired. Jones was identified at the time as an alleged Detroit hoodlum with several aliases, including Watkins and Geers (or Sheers).

The suspect admitted going to Webb City the previous night but denied killing Hatten.[5]

Police revealed that Jones, who'd come to Joplin about three weeks earlier, was associated with a gang of bootleggers at South Coffeyville, Oklahoma, where he was known as W. H. Geers, and a coroner's jury on the night of May 18 named Geers, alias Jones, as the slayer of Coyne Hatten. Doris Adams said she introduced Geers to Hatten, immediately heard a shot as she was walking away, and then looked back in time to see Geers shoot Hatten twice more.[6]

Geers was charged on May 19 with first degree murder, and Carey was charged as an accessory after the fact for allegedly driving the killer away from the scene. Questioned that same day, Geers not only denied killing Hatten but also repudiated his previous confession in which he'd admitted his movements on the night of the murder. He also denied even knowing Doris Adams, who'd given a written statement against him.[7]

Funeral services for Coyne Hatten were held the same day, May 19, at Sacred Heart Catholic Church in Webb City with a large crowd in attendance. Burial followed in Mount Hope Cemetery.[8]

On May 20, the suspect broke down and gave a full confession. He said his real name was James Edward "Jimmy" Creighton and he was twenty-six years old. Born in Hugo, Oklahoma, he'd served one term in a reformatory when he was a teenager, one term in the Oklahoma State Penitentiary for auto theft, and brief stints in a couple of city jails. He admitted he was wanted in connection with a daring bank robbery at Hastings, Nebraska, the previous February during which he and his partners bound and gagged several bank officials, took over $27,000, and shot it out with police to make their escape, kidnapping two officers in the process. He said he was also "wanted at several other places" for robberies and other crimes.[9]

Creighton said that, on the night of the Hatten shooting, he, Doris Adams, Mickey Carey, and Carey's wife had been drinking. The foursome drove to Webb City to have Mrs. Carey's wound dressed, and as Creighton alighted from the vehicle, he accidentally jostled into Hatten. Creighton claimed Hatten asked him whether he was looking for trouble and then gave him a shove. At that point, Creighton pulled out his revolver and started shooting.[10]

Newspaper photo of Jimmy Creighton. *From the Lincoln (NE) Journal Star.*

After his confession, Creighton requested that officials contact attorney Frederick Apt in Iola, Kansas, to represent him. Creighton's wife, Velma, came from a respectable Oklahoma family, and her parents were personally acquainted with Apt. The lawyer had already been retained to represent Velma on a charge of being an accessory in the Hastings bank job. When he was contacted, Apt immediately came to Joplin, where he spoke to newsmen after seeing his client. He said Creighton told him he had come to the Joplin area less than a month ago, that he'd had $10,000 when he arrived, but that he'd blown almost all of it on gambling and drunken orgies.[11]

At his arraignment before a Webb City justice of the peace the next day, May 21, Creighton waived a preliminary hearing and was held without bond on a first-degree murder charge. He was taken to the county jail at Carthage to await trial.[12]

Over the next few days, additional details about Creighton's spectacular crime career continued to emerge. It was learned, for instance, that one of the men he had roomed with while holed up in Joplin prior to the Hatten murder was the notorious Fred Barker, Ma's youngest son.[13]

Creighton's trial got underway at Carthage in late June 1931. Numerous witnesses who either saw or heard the shooting identified Creighton as the man who'd killed Hatten, and they suggested that he had little, if any, provocation. Creighton, on the other hand, took the stand to claim self-defense. He said that he and Hatten argued about his being with Doris Adams and that he shot Hatten after Hatten pushed him and made a move as though he were reaching for a weapon. The prosecution pointed out in closing arguments that Creighton had not claimed self-defense in his previous confessions, not until he got on the stand with his life hanging in the balance.[14]

The jury reached a verdict in the case on June 26, finding Creighton guilty of first-degree murder and sentencing him to hang. The vote for a guilty verdict was unanimous from the start, but the jury took four ballots to agree on the death penalty. Outwardly unmoved by the verdict, Creighton said he was glad he was sentenced to death because he thought such a verdict would make a successful appeal more likely.[15]

Appeal is exactly what his lawyers did, and the execution was stayed pending the outcome of their plea. In the meantime, Creighton was taken to the state prison in Jefferson City for safekeeping after a knife was found in his cell and he bragged that he would escape from the county jail.[16]

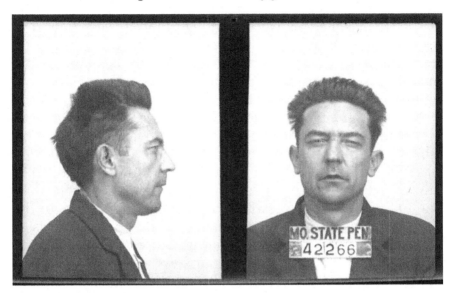

Mug shot of Jimmy Creighton. *Courtesy of Missouri State Archives.*

Taking up Creighton's case in August 1932, the Missouri Supreme Court reversed the verdict of the lower court on the grounds that the judge should have granted a change of venue and should have included an instruction that the jury might find the defendant guilty of manslaughter.[17]

Creighton was granted a change of venue to Barton County for his retrial, which occurred at Lamar in January 1933. On the early morning of the 17th, the jury came back after eleven hours of deliberation with a verdict finding the defendant guilty of first-degree murder and sentencing him to life imprisonment. The vote for the guilty verdict was unanimous from the beginning, with eleven jurors arguing for the death penalty. However, one held out for life imprisonment, and the others finally relented in order to reach an agreement.[18]

For the first few years after being transported to the state penitentiary at Jefferson City, Creighton had a reputation as a troublemaker. In February 1934, he tried to "gouge his eyes out" with a fingernail because he'd supposedly been driven insane by the monotony of the prison routine. Part of his sight was saved, and authorities thought his self-mutilation was a ploy to try to gain a parole. Creighton eventually calmed down and went to work as a prison barber.[19]

He became trustworthy enough that he was allowed to work on the prison farm, but he escaped from there in 1944. Recaptured the next year, he was returned to the main prison. In early 1954, he was moved to the State Asylum at Fulton but returned to the prison after a month and half.[20]

In September 1954, a riot at the state prison resulted in the death of one inmate and injuries to about twenty-five others, including Jimmy Creighton. Afterward, Creighton, who was in a cell next to the man who was killed, was moved from the prison to the nearby Cole County Jail for his own protection. The following year, he testified against the ringleaders of the riot, earning a reputation among fellow prisoners as a "squealer" but also scoring points with officers prosecuting the rioters. In January 1956, the Missouri governor agreed to parole Creighton on the recommendation of the prosecutors rather than return him to the penitentiary, where he would almost surely be killed by other prisoners. After Creighton's discharge, a group of citizens from southwest Missouri learned of his release and sent the governor a letter of protest, but by then it was too late. After twenty-four years in prison, Jimmy Creighton had skedaddled for parts unknown.[21]

Chapter 28

Typical Ozarks Hillbillies
The Worden Brothers Hang for Rape

During a single night in the fall of 1931, Elmer "Pete" Stevenson and brothers Lew and Harry Worden waylaid at least three carloads of people at gunpoint in Jasper County, Missouri, and raped three high school girls in the process.

But they paid a dear price for their criminal spree.

About eight o'clock on Sunday evening, November 15, 1931, twenty-year-old Norman Parks, eighteen-year-old George Mimms, and their fifteen-year-old girlfriends, Bettie Hefley and Catherine Morris, were parked near the abandoned Coahuila mine about three and a half miles northwest of Carthage when a strange car pulled up beside them and stopped. Three men got out carrying revolvers and ordered the young people out of their automobile. Parks, who was behind the wheel, was struck on the head and shoulder when he didn't obey the order fast enough to suit the assailants.[1]

One of the holdup men, later identified as thirty-one-year-old Pete Stevenson, escorted the two young men at gunpoint to the other side of a nearby chat pile, while his two accomplices, later identified as thirty-four-year-old Lew Worden and twenty-six-year-old Harry Worden, held the girls prisoner a short distance from the automobiles. The Worden brothers threatened to kill both girls if Bettie didn't do as she was told. Lew then held the Morris girl at gunpoint while Harry escorted the Hefley girl into the nearby woods and sexually assaulted her.[2]

After the attack, the three assailants took off in both vehicles. Seeing no sign of Parks and Mimms, Bettie and

Catherine ran to a nearby farmhouse and frantically asked for help; the farmer took the girls back to Carthage. Bettie was crying when she got home, her hair was disheveled, and her clothes were soiled. She immediately told her mother the awful news. The police were notified of the crime, and a physician was summoned to examine the girl.[3]

Meanwhile, the highwaymen abandoned the Parks vehicle just south of Webb City. An hour and a half after the first attack, they held up a taxi cab near Carl Junction, about fifteen miles west of Carthage. They took the cab driver and his four passengers, two male and two female, to a wooded spot, where they beat the driver about the head with a pistol and stole ten dollars each from him and his two male passengers. They also took some personal items from the three male victims. The two young women were not molested.[4]

Then, at ten p.m., the three desperadoes accosted another carload of young people near Peace Church Cemetery northwest of Joplin. The young victims were seventeen-year-old Arthur Poundstone, twenty-year-old Tom Wills, and their sixteen and seventeen-year-old female companions. All four were taken to an isolated spot west of the Jasper County Tuberculosis Hospital (near the present-day Joplin Regional Airport). This time Harry Worden guarded the young men while Lew Worden and Pete Stevenson raped the two girls. The villains then stole Poundstone's car and again drove away in two vehicles.[5]

The holdups and assaults on November 15 were just the latest in a recent outbreak of attacks and highway robberies in the Jasper County area. Public outrage prompted an intense investigation, and suspicion quickly settled on the Worden brothers, who'd previously lived in Joplin, where Harry had worked as a barber. During a police standoff with four road bandits a few years earlier, only one of the highwaymen was captured, and Harry Worden was suspected of being among the three who got away. He and his brother had been under police scrutiny ever since, but they had disappeared from Jasper County several months prior to the recent crimes.[6]

A picture of Lew Worden was located, and the victims of the November 15 assault near Carthage tentatively identified him as one of the men who'd perpetrated the outrage. The license number of the bandit car, as taken down by one of the victims, was matched to a tag stolen from an automobile near Birch Tree, Missouri, 170 miles east of Carthage, the previous July, and the Wordens were soon traced to nearby Mountain View. Lew Worden was taken into custody there on November 24, but local officers, under the impression that only Lew was wanted, allowed Harry Worden to escape.[7]

Lew Worden was brought back to Carthage on November 25 and lodged in the Jasper County Jail. That evening he admitted his participation in the two holdups ten days earlier during which the three girls were sexually assaulted. He implicated his brother in the crimes but didn't know whether Harry or his other companion (whom he did not identify) had criminally assaulted any of the girls. He denied that he himself had raped any of them, admitting only that he had attempted to assault one of girls from the Poundstone vehicle but was unsuccessful. He explained that he and his companions had driven from Mountain View on the evening of the attacks, arriving shortly before the first assault, and that they'd returned to Mountain View in the wee hours of the following morning, abandoning Poundstone's automobile near Mountain View.[8]

Brought to Joplin on the night of the 26th, Worden also confessed to the holdup of the taxi driver and his passengers. Poundstone, Wills, and their two young women companions viewed the suspect in the Joplin City Jail and identified him as one of the men who had waylaid them. Charged with criminal assault on one of the girls, Worden was taken back to Carthage the next day and arraigned the day after that.[9]

Harry Worden and Pete Stevenson were arrested in Illinois in early December after Stevenson got drunk and started bragging to two young women that he was a "bank bandit." Both men were returned to Missouri, but Stevenson, who'd still not been named as a suspect in the Jasper County assaults, was taken to Van Buren and held in the Carter County Jail on a robbery charge.[10]

Worden, meanwhile, was brought to Carthage on December 7, 1931. When he was interrogated concerning the November 15 attacks on the young women, he admitted that he'd had sexual intercourse with one of the girls, but he denied that he'd used force.[11]

Although both Wordens pleaded not guilty at their initial appearances, Lew changed his tune when his trial came up in Division One of the Jasper County Circuit Court at Joplin on January 27, 1932. Throwing himself on the mercy of the court, he changed his plea to guilty, and his lawyers argued that his admission of guilt and the consequent sparing of the victim the ordeal of having to testify should warrant consideration for leniency. However, Judge Harvey Davis was in no mood to show mercy. "Any man who will go out on the highway and ravish a young girl deserves the death penalty," Davis declared in sentencing Worden to hang on March 3 at Carthage.[12]

The next day, January 28, Harry Worden's trial began in Division Two before Judge Grant Emerson. The defense filed motions for a continuance, for a change of venue, and to have the jury panel quashed. In arguing the case for a change of venue, Worden's lawyers said the guilty plea in Lew Worden's case had prejudiced Jasper County citizens against their client, but Emerson denied all the defense motions. The rest of the day and most of the next were spent in picking a jury.[13]

Late on the afternoon of the 29th, Bettie Hefley took the stand as the first state witness. She said she pleaded with Harry Worden to leave her alone but that he threatened to kill Catherine Morris, the best friend she had in the world, if she didn't do exactly what he told her to do. It was only then, fearing for her friend's life, that she quit trying to resist. Bettie said that one of the Worden brothers also threatened, as they were leaving, to look her up if she said anything about what had happened. Catherine Morris and George Mimms followed Bettie to the stand and confirmed her story in virtually every detail. (Norman Parks had taken a job in Detroit and moved away.)[14]

Prosecution testimony continued the next morning, January 30, with Deputy Glenn Stemmons testifying that Harry Worden had confessed to criminal assault shortly after being brought back to Carthage. Harry Worden's lawyers then presented their case the same day. The main defense witness was Worden's wife, Blanche, who testified to her husband's lack of education and dull-wittedness.[15]

The case went to the jury in the late afternoon, and they came back that evening with a guilty verdict after deliberating about three hours. A unanimous jury vote fixed the penalty at death, and the judge formally pronounced the sentence on February 1. When a motion for a new trial was denied, the verdict was appealed to the Missouri Supreme Court, and the execution date indefinitely postponed.[16]

After several weeks of negotiations between Jasper County and Carter County officials, Pete Stevenson was finally brought to Carthage on February 18, lodged in the Jasper County Jail, and charged as the third assailant in the November 15 assaults.[17]

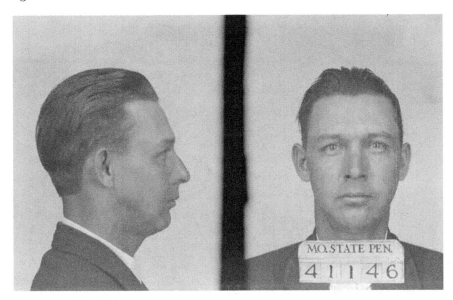

Mug shot of Pete Stevenson. *Courtesy Missouri State Archives.*

Meanwhile, Lew Worden's lawyers appealed to the Missouri governor to commute their client's sentence to life imprisonment or at least grant a stay of execution until after Harry Worden's case was settled. They argued that it was grossly unfair to execute a man who had pled guilty to an offense before executing a partner in crime who had pled not guilty to the same offense. Stanley Clay, Lew's lead lawyer, described his client as a "typical Ozarks hillbilly" and "a moron" who was incapable of understanding why he should be hanged for what he had done. The governor, however, declined to intervene in the case, declaring that it should not be a foregone conclusion that a person could escape the death penalty just by pleading guilty.[18]

As Lew Worden's execution day approached, family members, including his mother, visited him in his cell at the Carthage jail, and Lew helped make his own funeral arrangements. As an honorably discharged veteran of World War I, he was accorded military rites, although the local American Legion declined to participate in the planned service. Worden, who'd recently professed religion, blamed his troubles on "sin and whiskey."[19]

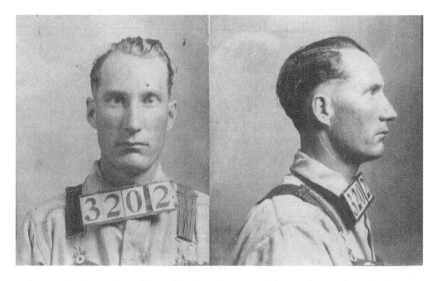

Front and side profiles of Lew Worden. *Courtesy of Jasper County Records Center.*

On the early morning of March 3, 1932, Lew Worden walked calmly to the gallows erected just outside the county jail at Carthage. About 100 observers, including the father of the girl Worden attacked, were allowed inside the stockade surrounding the gallows, while a crowd of about 500 thronged around the enclosure. After the preparations were made, Worden dropped through the trap at 6:02 a.m. and was pronounced dead twelve minutes later. A Carthage funeral home took charge of the body, services were held in Joplin a couple of days later, and Worden was buried in Joplin's Forest Park Cemetery.[20]

Coverage of the Worden case had been the lead headline in recent editions of the local newspapers, but Lew's execution was relegated to a subhead by the kidnapping of the Lindbergh baby.[21]

At the April 1932 term of Jasper County Circuit Court, Pete Stevenson was granted a change of venue to neighboring Lawrence County. He pled guilty there on May 23, was sentenced to 99 years in the state penitentiary, and was taken to Jefferson City a few days later.[22]

On December 14, 1932, the Missouri Supreme Court affirmed the lower court's decision in Harry Worden's case and reset his execution for January 20, 1933. Worden's lawyers then appealed to newly elected governor Guy B. Park for clemency, and a number of people from Jasper County wrote letters supporting the appeal. Worden's wife, Blanche, and his spiritual advisor, the Rev. Dow Booe, traveled to Jefferson City to deliver several of the letters to the governor and make a personal plea for leniency. On January 18, less than forty-eight hours before Worden was scheduled to die, Park issued a stay of execution until February 10, announcing that he needed more time to study the case.[23]

As the February 10 deadline approached, Worden's lawyers renewed their appeal to the governor asking that he commute their client's sentence to life imprisonment, but this time Park declined to interfere. Worden was put on a death watch, and he was visited regularly by his wife and the Rev. Booe, a Pentecostal preacher who had also been Lew Worden's minister during his final days. On the evening of February 9, Harry issued a public statement, confessing to the crime he'd been convicted of and asking for God's mercy.[24]

On the early morning of February 10, Harry Worden, like his brother before him, marched to the gallows with outward calm. After he stepped on the trap and the noose was adjusted around his neck, he bid the sheriff goodbye but made no further statement. The trap was sprung at 5:59 a.m., and Worden was

Harry Worden Is Hanged For Attack on a School Girl

Former Joplin Barber Goes to Gallows Calmly at Carthage Jail.

Headline announcing Harry Worden's execution. *From the Maryville Daily Forum.*

pronounced dead after twelve minutes. The execution took place inside the jail building in a room on the second floor with about 50 witnesses in attendance. It was the same room from which Lew Worden had begun his death march to an outside scaffold 49 weeks earlier.[25]

Harry Worden's body was taken to a funeral home in Galena, Kansas, Rev. Booe's hometown. He was interred in Galena's Hill Crest Cemetery.[26]

At the time of Worden's execution, a Carter County newspaper lamented the fact that Pete Stevenson, despite being "generally regarded as the leader of the gang," had escaped the death sentence. But his reprieve didn't last long. He died in prison at Jefferson City in May of 1934.[27]

Chapter 29

Bonnie and Clyde Invade Jasper County
A Bank Robbery, a Kidnapping, and A Shootout

Gangsters Bonnie Parker and Clyde Barrow were little known outside their home state of Texas when they made their first appearance in Jasper County in late 1932. Leaving Dallas on Halloween night, the pair drove to Carthage, Missouri, where they met up with two of Clyde's Texas pals, Frank Hardy and Hollis Hale. The gang rented tourists cabins to use as a base of operations while the three men committed a series of minor burglaries and robberies throughout the month of November.[1]

On Tuesday, November 29, Clyde set his sights on the Farmers and Miners Bank at nearby Oronogo and sent Bonnie into town to scout out the place. About nine o'clock the next morning, the gang stole a Chevy sedan from a Carthage residence and drove it and a Ford V-8 to Oronogo. Bonnie waited in the high-powered Ford a mile and quarter west of town, while the three men went into Oronogo in the Chevy and parked in front of the bank. Hale stayed in the car, as Barrow and Hardy strode into the bank with Barrow toting a submachine gun.[2]

Clyde leveled the submachine gun at cashier R. A. Norton and ordered him to throw up his hands. Norton had been robbed three times previously and was used to dealing with gunmen. Disregarding the command, he ducked behind the teller's cage and came up firing with a .38 caliber automatic pistol. Clyde returned fire, said the *Joplin Globe*, "directing a barrage of lead at the wooden panel behind which the cashier was crouched." As Norton moved along the inside of the cage,

Clyde trailed him with a stream of submachine gunfire, but the bullets failed to penetrate the steel casing that lined the cage.[3]

Clyde Barrow showing off part of his arsenal. *Author's collection.*

Norton's gun jammed after he'd fired three shots, and when Clyde realized the teller was no longer shooting, he, too, ceased fire. Poking out the glass of a door that led into the cage, Clyde leveled his weapon at the cashier and demanded his surrender. Norton rose to his feet with his hands raised and explained that his gun had jammed.[4]

The bandits then smashed a large, glazed window in a different partition door and entered the cage. Clyde stepped up to Norton and placed the barrel of his gun against the cashier's ribs. "I ought to pump you full of lead," he threatened.[5]

Hardy said they should leave the cashier alone and just "get the money and let's get out of here."

Clyde guarded Norton while Hardy scooped up a pile of money on the teller's cage. Out on the street, Hale had started honking the horn of the getaway car as soon as the shooting started, and the two bandits inside, anxious to make their escape, ignored the bank's vault, where a much larger sum of money was located. Hurrying outside, they saw two townsmen approaching the bank carrying weapons, but the bandits ordered the men back and sprayed lead toward them to reinforce their command.[6]

Barrow and Hardy piled into the Chevy, and the three robbers drove away to the west. Alerted by the sounds of gunfire, a number of other townspeople had also armed themselves and taken up strategic positions near the bank. As the robbers drove away to the west, the impromptu posse, several of whom had taken cover behind an oil truck, opened fire on the bandit car. Clyde, still wielding the submachine gun, returned fire, shooting the truck's tank and windows full of holes.[7]

A mile and a quarter west of Oronogo, the three bank robbers reunited with Bonnie Parker. Abandoning the Chevy, they got into the Ford V-8 and sped away.[8]

Later that morning, a local citizen who'd passed the Ford while Bonnie sat behind the wheel by herself, described her as wearing a blue dress, a red hat, and a black jacket. Although the identity of the gang was unknown, the bank robbers were described as well dressed young men between twenty and twenty-five years of age. One local citizen speculated that the bandits might have been from the general Oronogo vicinity, because he'd seen an automobile matching the description of the Ford V-8 in the area the day before, but police officers thought the robbers were from elsewhere, perhaps Kansas City. A few days later, Cashier Norton mistakenly identified Herman Barker's brother Fred as one of the robbers, but their true identity remained a mystery until Bonnie and Clyde's next escapade in Jasper County early the following year. In reporting the Oronogo robbery, the *Joplin Globe* said it was the first time a submachine gun had been used during a Jasper County crime.[9]

Each time the Farmers and Miners Bank had been held up in the past, the bandits had made off with only a few hundred dollars at most, and this time was no exception. The *Globe* reported that the current robbers stole something less than $500, but it was actually a good deal less than that—only about $115. From the backseat of the bandit car, Hardy counted the money as the gang drove back toward Carthage, and he reported to Clyde that the heist had yielded only eighty dollars. Clyde said to go ahead and divide it three ways, and Hardy made the split, cheating Clyde out of his fair share. After the gang got back to the cabins, Hardy and Hale insisted on going out to buy more ammunition. They left on foot and stole a car, and Clyde never saw them again.[10]

About six o'clock on the evening of January 26, 1933, Bonnie, Clyde, and new sidekick W. D. Jones were driving a Ford V-8 with an Oklahoma license plate slowly back and forth in the vicinity of the Shrine Mosque in Springfield, Missouri, when motorcycle cop Tom Persell pulled them over on suspicion. Clyde hopped out of the car armed with a sawed-off shotgun and ordered Persell into the front seat between Jones and the driver's seat. Then Clyde hopped back in behind the steering wheel and took off. Bonnie sat in the backseat with a .45 revolver in her hand. In addition to Clyde's shotgun and Bonnie's revolver, the car was stocked with other "pistols too numerous to count," a submachine gun, a couple of rifles, and another sawed-off shotgun. Persell also noticed several sacks of money in the car.[11]

Barrow and Jones told Persell to climb over the seat and get in the back. Taking his seat beside Bonnie, the officer got a good look at the woman whose name would soon become notorious throughout the land. He later described her as "red-haired and freckled" with a very white face. She had on a coat and a turban-like hat cocked to one side. She was slender but wore no makeup, and Persell found her "not the least bit beautiful."[12]

Persell recalled that all three of the gang members were profane and "hardly said anything without cussing." Clyde called Bonnie "Babe" or "Hon," while W. D. called her "Sis." She called Jones "Bud."[13]

W. D. Jones was one of several sidekicks Bonnie and Clyde had during their criminal career. *Author's collection.*

The gang forced Persell to pilot them out of Springfield. After wandering around north and east of town for a while, Clyde, who did most of the talking, demanded that Persell show them a back route to Joplin. The motorcycle cop guided the gang north to the Pleasant Hope turnoff near Crystal Cave. From there, Clyde worked his way north and west, clipping along at fifty miles an hour, even though the roads were narrow and muddy.[14]

The gang stopped for gas at Golden City. Continuing west, they came out on Highway 71 between Lamar and Jasper, and suddenly Clyde seemed to know exactly where he was. Dodging from one country road to another, he worked his way south and drove into a residential area of Carthage, where the gang started looking for a car to steal, because the battery was running low on the Ford they were driving. Calling over his shoulder to Bonnie, Clyde asked, "Hon, do you think there are any cars we can get at Webb City?"

When Bonnie said yes, Clyde struck out again on the back roads to Webb City. Clyde stopped twice in Webb City to let W. D. get out and scout around, but both times he came back emptyhanded. The gang then drove to Oronogo, where Clyde told W. D. about the gun battle he'd gotten into a couple of months earlier. When Persell asked what Clyde was talking about, the gang leader said, "Some monkey in the bank took a shot at us."[15]

Leaving Oronogo, the gang drove to the Roanoke neighborhood of Joplin, where W. D. tried to steal five different cars but couldn't get any of them started. Finally, Bonnie spotted someone standing in a nearby home watching them through a window, and she told Clyde they needed to "scram" before the police came.[16]

Clyde didn't smoke, but Bonnie, "who was just as profane as her companions," according to Persell, "simply ate fags." After she and W. D. ran out of cigarettes, they started bumming them from Persell.[17]

Clyde went back to Oronogo and drove past the bank, and one of the men remarked, "There's the bank all lit up."

The gang stopped beside a Chevrolet they'd spotted during their previous pass through Oronogo. Clyde got out to

Bonnie Parker didn't actually smoke cigars, but she did like cigarettes. *Author's collection.*

try to steal it himself but found it was locked. He then briefly disappeared in the darkness, and when he came back, he said he'd spotted a Model-T Ford. Taking the submachine gun and a pair of pliers, he went away again and returned about fifteen minutes later with an old battery, which he set on the running board. Clyde got back behind the wheel and took off. After driving a few miles in the direction of Joplin, he stopped, and Persell helped him replace the bad battery with the stolen one. The officer walked behind the vehicle to try to get the license plate number, but it was covered with mud.[18]

After replacing the battery, the gang drove through the intersection at Stone's Corner and headed west. A few miles past the intersection, Clyde stopped to let his hostage out. It was thirty minutes after midnight on Friday morning, January 27. Clyde told Persell that, if he would walk back to the intersection and go south toward Joplin for a mile or so, he would find a filling station where he could phone for help. Displaying an almost-reckless gumption, the motorcycle cop asked whether he could have his gun back. Clyde refused and told him to consider himself lucky. As the bandit car sped away, Persell set out on foot and reached the service station about two o'clock in the morning.[19]

Describing his captives the next day, Persell said the driver (Clyde) "seemed to be a foreigner of some sort." He had a swarthy complexion and appeared about twenty-six years old. He wore a tan hat and a dark suit and weighed about 140 pounds. The other man (W. D.) was several years younger and was stocky, weighing about 160 pounds. He wore a dark suit, overcoat, and hat, and he talked very little.[20]

A couple of days after Persell's kidnapping, the car that the outlaw gang had used during the caper was found abandoned at Cherryvale, Kansas, and Persell trekked from Springfield to positively identify the vehicle. He was sure it was the same automobile by a broken fan shaft, which had caused the generator to disconnect and the battery to run down, and by other distinctive characteristics.[21]

Barely over two months after the kidnapping, Bonnie, Clyde, and W. D. Jones once again invaded the Jasper County area. It would prove to be the gang's most infamous incursion of all. About the first of April 1933, the threesome, along with Clyde's brother Buck and Buck's wife, rented an apartment on South Oak Ridge Drive in Joplin just across the county line in Newton County. Reports of suspicious activity at the apartment led law officers to raid the place on April 13, resulting in a bloody shootout that left two lawmen dead. Found in the apartment after the gang escaped were several rolls of film containing photos that would lead to positive identification of the gang members and make Bonnie and Clyde household names across the country.[22]

Chapter 30

A Robbery Gone Bad
Carthage Capitalist Slain in His Home

Around the first of March 1934, W. R. Murray borrowed a trailer from wealthy Carthage businessman Brooks Van Hoose, and about noon on Sunday the 4th he brought the trailer back to Van Hoose's estate four miles southwest of town in the Morgan Heights neighborhood. Murray, who did odd jobs for Van Hoose, tried to rouse his employer but got no answer when he knocked on the door or rang the doorbell. Murray noticed what looked like a bullet hole in the door of Van Hoose's automobile, but he didn't become unduly alarmed at the time. Thinking the situation over, though, he became apprehensive for Van Hoose's safety, and the next morning he went to the real estate agency Van Hoose and George Biemdick operated together in Carthage to see whether Van Hoose was there. Informed that he hadn't showed up for work yet, Murray told Van Hoose's partner what had transpired the day before. Biemdick and some of his employees tried to telephone Van Hoose but got no answer. Biemdick, his nephew Gerald, and a couple of other employees drove out to the Van Hoose place to investigate. After they found all the doors locked and failed to rouse anybody, Gerald Biemdick knocked out a window to gain entrance to the home. Inside, he discovered Van Hoose lying dead on the floor just inside the front doorway of his massive stone house. He'd been shot multiple times. [1]

The Biemdick party immediately called authorities, and Sheriff Oll Rogers arrived to investigate. A revolver Van Hoose owned was found on the floor beside his body. Rogers said Van Hoose had bought the weapon about eight months earlier after receiving threats from extortionists. Van Hoose and his wife had been robbed at their home once before a couple of years earlier, but he was determined not to let the threat of another robbery scare him away. Even after his wife had left a few months earlier for an extended stay in Washington, D. C., Van Hoose insisted, against the advice of friends, on staying alone in his house in Morgan Heights.[2]

And now he was dead.

Van Hoose home as it looks today. *Photo by the author.*

Van Hoose's revolver had been fired one time, and Rogers concluded the victim had been killed when he showed fight. The sheriff believed there was more than one assailant. He thought Van Hoose had probably fired the errant shot that struck his automobile when he'd opened the door to find the gunmen facing him and that the assailants had immediately returned fire. Rogers placed the time of death as approximately 9:30 Saturday night, March 3, because Van Hoose was still fully clothed, having not yet dressed for bed, and a neighbor woman reported hearing what sounded like gunshots coming from the direction of the Van Hoose home about that time. Because Van Hoose was still wearing a $4,000 diamond ring and had over a hundred dollars in his pocket and because of the prior threats he'd received, authorities concluded at first that the assailants had planned to kidnap him. Officials later decided, however, that the motive was probably robbery but that the assailants panicked and fled after killing Van Hoose in the act of resisting.[3]

Sheriff Rogers revealed that he'd received a tip early Saturday evening that a gang was going to meet near the Broadview Country Club not far from Van Hoose's home and "pull something" later that night. Rogers, a deputy, and members of the state highway patrol had gone out to the country club to investigate shortly before the likely time of Van Hoose's murder, but they found no suspicious activity.[4]

On Monday evening, March 5, eight or ten hours after Van Hoose's body was discovered, Charles Napper, a forty-one-year-old ex-convict, turned himself in at the county jail after learning he was wanted as a suspect in the murder. He confessed he was with a gang of five men who were in the vicinity of the Van Hoose home on Saturday night, but he denied participating in the actual crime. He named the other four men as former Carthage restaurant operator L. B. Harmon, L. B.'s brother Glenn Harmon, and two acquaintances of Glenn Harmon whom he did not know. Napper said he and L. B. Harmon were in one car, while Glenn Harmon, an ex-convict and current fugitive from the law, was in a second car with his two sidekicks. They met and parked near Van Hoose's house, and L. B. Harmon walked off with the other three men leaving Napper alone in L. B.'s car. Napper said he knew the gang was up to something but he was not in on the scheme. After a few minutes, the four men "came back in a hurry." The five men took off in the same cars they'd arrived in, and Napper said he never saw Glenn Harmon or his two pals after that.[5]

Glenn Harmon had "a long crime record" dating back to 1922 and was currently wanted for robberies in Joplin, St. Louis, and Kansas. He was also suspected of being one of the men who'd held up Van Hoose and his wife two years ago.[6]

Arrested about the same time as Napper, L. B. Harmon gave a story similar to Napper's except he said that he and Napper, after stopping at the rendezvous spot near Van Hoose's home, left for Joplin without waiting for Glenn Harmon and his sidekicks to show up. He claimed to know nothing about the murder of Van Hoose. After talking to both Napper and L. B. Harmon, officers concluded that a sixth man might have been in on planning the robbery of Van Hoose.[7]

On the evening of March 7, a coroner's inquest concluded that Van Hoose had died from two pistol shots, either one of which could have been fatal. The next day, first-degree murder charges were filed against Napper, L. B. Harmon, Glenn Harmon, and three unidentified associates of Glenn Harmon.[8]

In mid-March, thirty-one-year-old Victor Powell, identified as one of Glenn Harmon's accomplices in the murder of Van Hoose, was apprehended in Denver. The identity of another accomplice, nineteen-year-old Byron Wolff, was announced at the same time. Sheriff Rogers traveled to Denver to bring Powell back to Jasper County, and during the return trip the prisoner admitted that he'd been in the Carthage area with Glenn Harmon at the time of Van Hoose's murder but, like Napper, denied involvement in the actual crime. After reaching Carthage on March 26, Powell further admitted that he was in the immediate area of the Van Hoose home, but he named Harmon and Wolff as the men who'd actually gone to the door and shot Van Hoose when he resisted being robbed. He said Harmon and Wolff came running back to the car and Harmon said, "We had to kill him."[9]

Wolff was captured in Los Angeles on the evening of March 26 when he was overpowered by a tailor whom he attempted to hold up. The next night, Glenn Harmon was killed in a gunfight with a Los Angeles detective after Wolff led officers to the hideout where the fugitive was holed up. Jasper County officials announced that all the suspects in the Van Hoose slaying had now been captured or killed except for the still unidentified sixth man. Then, just a couple of days later, William Moors was arrested as the mysterious sixth accomplice. He was a taxicab driver who had brought Powell, Wolff, and Glenn Harmon from Kansas City to Carthage on the day of Van Hoose's murder.[10]

In mid-April, Wolff was brought back to Jasper County from Los Angeles. Shortly after his arrival, he and the other four suspects were jointly arraigned at Carthage on charges of first-degree murder. The preliminary hearing for Powell, Wolff, and Moors took place on April 19, while Napper waived preliminary examination, and all four were held for trial. Meanwhile, L. B. Harmon's preliminary hearing was continued. A couple of weeks later, he, too, was bound over for trial.[11]

In early June, the cases of Napper, Powell, Wolff, and Moors were severed, while L. B. Harmon was granted a change of venue to Barton County. Powell's trial was held first, in mid-June. One of the main state witnesses, in addition to the officers who investigated Van Hoose's murder, was R. E. Dugan, the informant who'd originally tipped Sheriff Rogers that a crime was afoot on the night of March 3. Operator of the Sleepy Hollow tourist camp east of Carthage on Route 66, Dugan said he overheard the six men at his place of business planning to pull some sort of robbery in the Morgan Heights area. The defense tried unsuccessfully to get the confession Powell had given when he was brought back from Denver thrown out. He was convicted of first-degree murder and sentenced to life imprisonment.[12]

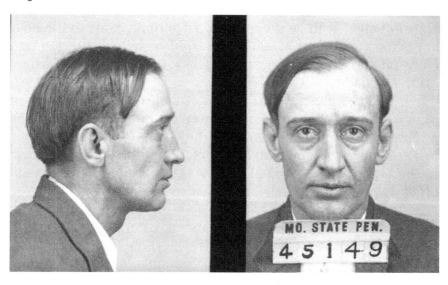

Victor Powell was the first to go on trial for the murder of Van Hoose. *Mug shot courtesy of the Missouri State Archives.*

At Wolff's trial in late June, Napper testified for the prosecution under an agreement to dismiss the murder charge against him. Napper repeated the story he'd told after he was first arrested, saying he'd been left alone near the Van Hoose place in L. B. Harmon's car while the other men, including Wolff, marched off together and came back "in a hurry." Like Powell, Wolff was convicted and sentenced to life imprisonment. Napper was released on parole a couple of weeks later.[13]

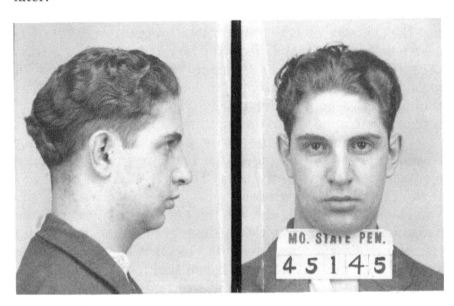

Like Powell, Byron Wolff received life imprisonment for the murder of Van Hoose, but he had his sentence reduced on retrial. *Courtesy Missouri State Archives.*

Both Powell and Wolff appealed their verdicts to the Missouri Supreme Court after their motions for new trials were denied in early August. L. B. Harmon's trial at Lamar in September ended in a mistrial when one of the jurymen was dismissed because his wife became gravely ill.[14]

In late March 1935, Moors, who'd been adjudged insane in Kansas a few years earlier, was again declared insane and committed to the state hospital at Nevada. The murder charge against him was nol prossed.[15]

At L. B. Harmon's retrial at Lamar in September 1935, Harmon testified in his own defense. He admitted he was in the general area of the Van Hoose residence on the Saturday night of the crime, but he said he was only there to try to talk his brother into leaving the territory without causing trouble. The defendant said he did not get nearer to the house than three-quarters of a mile. Napper also took the stand as a defense witness. He testified that, earlier in the day on Saturday, Harmon protected him from the other four men when they wanted to rob him and that Harmon told him afterward, "We'd better get away from this bunch." Harmon was acquitted.[16]

In November 1935, the Missouri Supreme Court ruled that the evidence on which Byron Wolff was convicted of first-degree murder was insufficient, and he was granted a new trial. On retrial at Carthage in March 1936, he was convicted of second-degree murder and given a sentence of ten years in the penitentiary. A motion for a new trial was denied, and the defense again appealed to the supreme court.[17]

In late June 1936, the state supreme court denied Victor Powell's appeal and sustained his sentence of life imprisonment. Jasper County prosecutor Charles R. Warden remarked at the time that the high court's decision probably ended the Van Hoose case but that he was not entirely satisfied with the outcome. Warden said officials thought all along that Glenn Harmon was the ringleader of the gang that killed Van Hoose and that his youthful sidekick, Byron Wolff, was probably the trigger man. At the time of Wolff's second trial, Warden had traveled to Jefferson City to try to get Powell to turn state's evidence and testify against Wolff in exchange for a recommendation of clemency in his own case, but Powell had refused, gambling that the supreme court would also grant him a new trial. He'd lost the bet, and now he had to pay the price.[18]

Warden was right that the upholding of Powell's life sentence closed the Van Hoose case for all practical purposes, but in a footnote to the story, the supreme court also upheld Wolff's ten-year sentence in February 1937.[19]

Chapter 31

Jealousy and a Quarrel
The Murder of Daisy Esmond and Execution of
Chester Jackson

Journalists have always loved a sensation, and murder is one of the biggest sensations of all. But not all murders are equally newsworthy. Varying circumstances obviously make some of them more interesting than others, but throughout much of America's history, one of the criteria editors often used to decide the newsworthiness of a homicide had little to do with the circumstances of the case and a lot to do with the color of the victim's skin. If a white person killed another white person, it generally caused a stir and was widely reported in the newspapers. And if a black person killed a white person, it was almost certain to make front page headlines. But if a black person killed another black person, the attitude seemed to be "So what?" and the incident often was not widely reported.

A case in point was Chester Jackson's killing of his former paramour, Daisy Esmond, in Joplin on Wednesday night, August 3, 1938. The murder warranted just a brief item on page five of the next day's *Joplin News Herald* and was not even mentioned in the *Joplin Globe* until Saturday, August 6, when that paper reported on Jackson's arraignment for killing "a Negress" named Daisy Esmond three days earlier.[1]

Daisy wasn't the first woman the thirty-year-old Jackson had tangled with. Just a couple of months earlier, Theola Isaac, his previous romantic interest, had received a five-year suspended sentence for wounding him during a quarrel, but recently Jackson had been living with Ms. Esmonds. Two years divorced and the mother of two kids, Daisy had left Jackson just a few days before the fateful night and gone to stay with her brother-in-law and her sister, Mamie. On the evening of August 2, 1938, Jackson called at Mamie's house in the 1200 block of West Tenth and asked Daisy to come back, but she refused.[2]

About 11:30 the next night, Jackson returned packing a .38 caliber pistol and called Daisy outside. Speaking to her in front of Mamie's home, he again implored Daisy to come back to him, but she still refused. They quarreled, and when she turned to go inside, he pulled out his pistol and shot her in the back. An ambulance was summoned, but Daisy died on the way to St. John's Hospital.[3]

Meanwhile, Jackson turned himself in at the police station shortly after the shooting and was held on suspicion of murder, although no formal charge was immediately filed, because the prosecuting attorney was out of town. After questioning the suspect, Joplin detective chief Ed Portley said that the shooting apparently resulted from "jealousy and a quarrel." When Jackson appeared for arraignment on August 5, he again admitted the shooting but claimed he didn't intend to kill Daisy and was only trying to scare her. Dismissing the suspect's dubious claim, Justice Vernon Sigars ordered him held without bond on a first-degree murder charge for trial at the September term of the Jasper County Circuit Court in Joplin.[4]

Appearing for trial in Division Two of the circuit court on September 26, Jackson announced through his court-appointed attorney that he wished to plead guilty, but as soon as he learned that Prosecutor Roy Coyne intended to seek the death penalty, he requested and was granted permission to withdraw the guilty plea. Jury selection then began and consumed the rest of the day.[5]

Testimony began on September 27 before "a packed courtroom, consisting principally of Negroes," according to the *Joplin Globe*. Daisy's sister, Mamie Ransom, was the state's key witness. She said that Jackson had previously threatened Daisy, that he appeared at the Ransom home on the night of August 3 to renew the threat, and that he shot her as she attempted to flee from him. Taking the stand in his own defense, Jackson admitted he was jealous and angry when he went to the

Ransoms' house on the night in question, but he said he had a "lapse of memory" and had no recollection of shooting Daisy. He claimed the last thing he recalled was her threatening to kill him.[6]

The trial featured what the *Joplin Globe* called "the unusual spectacle of a Negro attorney...making a closing argument in which he asked the jury of white men to assess the death penalty" on another black person. William M. Bradshaw of Topeka, who'd "been engaged by a group of Joplin Negroes to assist the prosecution," said he was requesting the death sentence in order to establish that "one Negro has no more right to kill another Negro than has one white man to kill another."[7]

After just one day of testimony and arguments, the case was given to the jury late on the afternoon of the 27th. The jury deliberated three hours and came back about 9:00 p.m. that evening with a guilty verdict and a sentence of death. It was the first death sentence imposed in Jasper County since the state legislature had outlawed hangings in the individual counties and declared that all executions should be carried out in the gas chamber at Jefferson City.[8]

Jackson displayed no emotion when the verdict was read but later remarked that it was a "gross miscarriage of justice." He was taken to the county jail at Carthage to await formal sentencing. A week or so later, Judge Wilbur Owen pronounced sentence and set Jackson's execution date for November 28. Owen denied a motion for a new trial, but an appeal to the Missouri Supreme Court automatically stayed the execution. In the meantime, Jackson was transported to Jefferson City to await the high court's decision.[9]

In early July 1939, the supreme court reversed the verdict of the lower court on the grounds that the trial judge should have granted the defense's request for a continuance and should have included in his instructions to the jury an option of finding the defendant guilty of second-degree murder. The case was remanded to Jasper County for a new trial, and Jackson was brought back to Carthage.[10]

Jackson's second trial took place in Joplin in late September in Division One of the Jasper County Circuit Court. On the 29th, the jury again convicted him of first degree murder and sentenced him to die. Judge Ray Watson pronounced sentence two weeks later, setting the execution date for December 8, and he denied the defense motion for a new trial. Jackson's lawyer, Ralph Baird, again appealed the case to the supreme court, and the prisoner was taken back to the state prison to await the outcome of the appeal.[11]

Mug shots of Chester Jackson. *Courtesy Missouri State Archives.*

Through a clerical error, word of the appeal was not forwarded to the warden of the Missouri State Penitentiary, and on Wednesday, December 6, he telephoned Baird from Jefferson City that if he didn't receive official notice of Jackson's appeal, the lawyer would have "a dead client here Friday morning." Judge Watson promptly contacted the state attorney general, who instructed the supreme court clerk to officially notify the warden of the appeal, and Jackson thus dodged a premature execution at the last minute.[12]

On July 3, 1940, the supreme court upheld the verdict in Jackson's second trial and reset his execution date for August 16. The appeal of Robert West, a convicted killer from St. Louis, was overruled at the same time, and he was scheduled to die at the same time as Jackson. Less than a week before Jackson was supposed to meet death, the Missouri governor granted the

Joplin man a five-week stay at the behest of his attorney, setting a new execution date of September 20. A few days later, West, a white man, was given a similar reprieve.[13]

But both men had run out of postponements. Visited at the state prison on the eve of their executions, each said he was "trying to take it like a man," and the two appeared calm throughout most of the day and evening. Shortly after 12:00 a.m. on the morning of September 20, they were led into the gas chamber and strapped into the death chairs. West bid goodbye to the warden, but Jackson didn't say a word. The gas was released at 12:24 a.m., and Jackson died at 12:28. West took two minutes longer to die.[14]

Chapter 32

Eula Gipson Slain at a West Seventh Nightclub
One of the Most Gruesome Murders
in Joplin Police History

On Wednesday evening, February 21, 1940, Harold Saunders, a twenty-eight-year-old Joplin truck driver, had a date to go bar hopping with Dorothy Hill. They met at Draeger's Beauty Shop, where Eula Gipson, a "comely" twenty-six-year-old divorcee, had just finished giving Dorothy a perm. Eula was acquainted with both Dorothy and her date, and they invited her to come along. The threesome went first to Wimpy's tavern in East Joplin and then to Metzger's bar in the 600 block of Main Street. There they ran onto Delmar Petty, who, like Saunders, drove a truck for United Transport Company. A thirty-two-year-old married man and the father of three children, Petty was also acquainted with Saunders's female companions, and he joined the three in a booth. Petty had been drinking and already appeared to be intoxicated.[1]

About 10:30, the four took a taxi to the Rodenia Night Club on West Seventh, which had a reputation as a "disorderly place." The four resumed drinking at a booth, and after a while, Petty and Ms. Gipson got up and started dancing. When the couple didn't return straightway, Saunders and Miss Hill went looking for them and, stepping outside, finally saw Petty staggering back toward the club by himself about one o'clock in the morning. When they asked where Eula was, Petty said she was inside dancing.[2]

The three went back into the Rodenia, but Eula was nowhere to be seen. "I'll bet you a quarter she'll be back in five minutes," Petty remarked as the three sat back down. When she didn't show up as Petty predicted, they went back outside and looked for her some more but still couldn't find her. Saunders and Miss Hill finally decided Eula might have caught a ride back into town with somebody else; so, they picked up her coat and purse to take to her and started for home.[3]

As the couple left, they told the nightclub owner, S. D. "Kate" Melton, that Eula was missing, and Melton immediately undertook a search of his own. But he, too, had no luck finding the missing woman. Meanwhile, Petty fell into a drunken stupor in a booth, and Melton decided to let him sleep it off. Melton finally aroused him at 5:00 a.m., and Petty called a cab and went home.[4]

When Eula didn't come home and didn't show up on Thursday morning at the beauty shop where she worked, her parents became concerned. They talked to Saunders and Miss Hill and, after learning what had transpired the previous night, contacted the police.[5]

Two detectives were dispatched to Petty's home in the 800 block of Pennsylvania to interrogate him. They found Petty still wearing the trousers he'd worn the night before, and they noticed blood on them. Asked about the shirt he had worn the previous night, Petty admitted that he'd asked his wife to wash it because it, too, had blood on it.[6]

Petty was arrested and brought to the Joplin Police station for further questioning. Detective Chief Gerald Stults then directed the two detectives who'd arrested Petty to take him to the nightclub to help look for the missing woman.[7]

Meanwhile, Saunders had already returned to the nightclub to resume looking for Eula, and Melton joined in the search. About 2:30 in the afternoon, Melton found the young woman's crumpled, nude body in some tall grass about 150 yards north of the nightclub. The grass had been beaten down all around the body, suggesting that the diminutive Miss Gipson had struggled mightily with her assailant. The *Joplin Globe* described the scene:

> There was blood everywhere and bits of torn clothing were found strewn over an area twenty feet square.... The torso of the body had been ripped wide open, as though with a sharp knife. There were

numerous other deep knife wounds about the body, and her nose was fractured where a knife blade apparently had been thrust into her face and ripped under one eye. There was also evidence…that she had been horribly beaten about the mouth, eyes, and face before death occurred, because the face was badly swollen.[8]

The detectives arrived with Petty shortly after the grisly discovery, and the suspect covered his eyes and turned away in horror when he was shown the victim's body. The detectives and policemen who went to the scene described it as "one of the most horrifying sights they had ever witnessed," and the *Globe* called the crime "one of the most gruesome murders in Joplin police history."[9]

Melton told the officers he'd seen Petty arguing with Miss Gipson at the front door of the nightclub about midnight the previous evening and that he saw Petty "pull her outside." Although investigators found only a single small knife on Petty when they searched him, Saunders said he knew the suspect had also been carrying a larger knife the night before, because he'd seen Petty take both knives out as he was retrieving change from his pocket.[10]

Taken back to the police station for further inter-rogation, Petty admitted that he'd had a second knife but he didn't know what had happened to it. He said he'd been so drunk that he could remember hardly anything after he left Metzger's bar. Asked how he thought he got blood on his clothes and scratches on his hands, he said he figured he must have gotten into a barroom brawl, as he'd done on a couple of previous occasions.[11]

Faced with all the evidence against him, Petty finally broke down. Did he kill Eula Gipson, the police interrogators demanded. "I guess I must have," he said, "but I can't remember what happened."[12]

Arraigned on Friday, February 23, on a charge of first-degree murder, Petty did not deny that he might have killed Miss Gipson, but he repeated that he didn't remember anything and asked for a lawyer. Denied bail, he was committed to the Jasper County Jail at Carthage to await a preliminary hearing the next week, and an attorney was appointed to represent him.[13]

An inquest into Eula Gipson's death took place on Monday the 26th. The county coroner testified that an autopsy revealed the victim had been "criminally assaulted." Although both Saunders and Melton testified that Petty was the last person seen with Eula, the jury returned a verdict that she came to her death by the hands of an unknown party or unknown parties.[14]

Testimony at Petty's preliminary examination on February 28 was little different from that at the inquest except that both Melton and his wife, Mae, who was a waitress at the nightclub, testified that Petty did not appear to be "real drunk" on the night in question. At the hearing's conclusion, Justice Vernon Sigars ruled that the accused should be held for trial without bond.[15]

Shortly after Eula Gipson's murder, samples of her blood and the blood found on Petty's clothes were sent to the Missouri State Highway Patrol for analysis, and the patrol reported to Jasper County authorities in mid-March that the two samples matched in type.[16]

In early April, Petty appeared before Jasper County circuit judge Wilbur Owen and entered a "not guilty" plea. Owen set Petty's trial for May 9, but when the case came up, it was transferred from Judge Owen's Division Two to Judge Ray Watson's Division One. The trial was reset for May 13. Over a hundred and sixty spectators packed the courtroom when the proceeding got underway in Joplin on that day, and hundreds more were turned away. Prosecutor Roy Coyne announced that he was seeking the death penalty, and he marched a whole procession of witnesses to the stand to build a case against the defendant. One witness, Charles Busby, who testified that he had served drinks to Petty and Saunders and their female companions at the Metzger bar on the night in question, might not have helped the state's case when he added that he himself had been taking Miss Gipson to the Rodenia nightclub almost every night for the previous week.[17]

When it came time for the defense to present its case, Petty's attorneys put Miss Evelyn Garrett, a waitress at the Rodenia, on the stand as their star witness. She said she'd seen

Eula Gipson and Delmar Petty, the man accused of killing her. *Author's collection.*

three or four "rough-looking" men at the nightclub during the time Petty and his companions were there, including during and after the time Eula Gipson disappeared. One of them, she continued, had what appeared to be blood on his hand, and he stuck the bloody hand in his coat pocket when he saw her looking at him. Miss Garrett also testified that she talked to Delmar Petty about an hour and a half after Eula disappeared and that, although she could tell he'd been drinking, he "acted normal" and did not have any blood on his clothes or scratches on his hands. On cross-examination, Coyne aggressively challenged Miss Garrett's testimony, getting almost in her face at one point. When Petty's attorneys objected, the courtroom audience burst into hoots and applause, and Judge Watson cleared the courtroom. Several customers of the Rodenia who saw Petty after Eula's disappearance also testified that they did not see blood on his clothes.[18]

Another key defense witness was a Kansas City coroner who had examined the clothes purportedly worn by the defendant on the night of the crime. He said he found no substance on them that could be positively identified as blood. The defense also introduced a number of witnesses who testified that Petty had a good reputation in the community. On cross-examination, Coyne demanded of several of them whether they had not heard of Petty having molested or assaulted two or three other young women prior to Eula Gipson's murder, but they all denied having heard such rumors.[19]

The highlight of the trial came when Petty took the stand in his own defense. He maintained he did not kill Eula Gipson because he "wouldn't do such a thing," although he admitted he did not remember anything about the night in question after he left Metzger's bar. He claimed that he'd been dosed with whiskey from a "mystery glass" while he was at Metzger's. "Every time I turned around," he said, "the glass was filled with whiskey." He denied that he'd admitted shortly after he was first arrested that he must have killed Eula. He also said a handkerchief with blood on it that the state had introduced as having been taken from Petty was not his because it had a laundry mark on it unlike anything he had on any of his handkerchiefs.[20]

During rebuttal, the state recalled Mae Melton, who said that the men whom Evelyn Garrett had described as "rough-looking" were actually well dressed and that Evelyn had admitted to her that the stain she saw on one of the men's hands could have been nicotine instead of blood. Kate Melton and one or two other rebuttal witnesses also said Evelyn had told them she wasn't sure the stain was blood. In addition, the prosecution recalled one or two witnesses to testify that the bloody handkerchief did not have the laundry mark on it when it was taken from Petty but that it was the same handkerchief, suggesting that defense attorneys had tampered with the evidence while it was in their hands.[21]

In his instructions to the jury, Judge Watson reduced the charge against Petty to second-degree murder, explaining that a first-degree charge was not warranted by the facts presented during trial. He told the twelve jurymen that they could find Petty guilty of second-degree murder or a lesser charge or they could acquit him.[22]

During closing arguments, the defense argued that Eula Gipson had been killed by an "unidentified maniac" and that the blood found on Petty's trousers was probably planted there by the real killer while Petty was zonked out in the booth at the Rodenia in the wee hours of the morning. Describing the slaying of Eula Gipson as the "most dastardly murder ever committed in Jasper County," Prosecutor Coyne countered that all the facts in the case pointed to Petty's guilt and that his only defense was "I don't remember."[23]

The case was given to the jury at ten o'clock Friday morning, May 17, and the foreman reported back at 5:00 p.m. that the body was hopelessly deadlocked at eight to four. Whether the majority favored conviction or acquittal was not officially reported, but rumor had it that the eight favored a guilty verdict. Judge Watson declared a mistrial and set a new trial for the September term. A couple of days later, since the charge against him had been reduced to second-degree murder, Petty was released on $10,000 bond. At the fall term, the defense was granted a continuance until the January 1941 term.[24]

The handling of the Petty case became an issue in the fall 1940 contest for county prosecutor between Coyne, the Democratic incumbent, and Ralph Baird, his Republican challenger. Baird, who had been co-counsel for Petty, won the election. When the case came up again in January, Baird disqualified himself as prosecutor but announced that he also would not defend Petty a second time. However, assistant prosecutor C. S. Walden, who had been Petty's other lawyer the first time around, disqualified himself as prosecutor so that he could again represent Petty. Ben Kesterson was appointed special prosecutor, and the case was again postponed to give him time to prepare for trial. He resigned two months later, however, citing lack of cooperation and financial support from the county court and the prosecutor's office. Kesterson said he believed Petty was guilty of the crime with which he was charged but that Baird and other county officials were hindering his effort to prosecute the case and that he would "not be a party to making a farce of the most gruesome crime ever committed in this county."[25]

At the request of Judge Watson, who was now serving in the military, the Missouri attorney general took charge of the case, sending an attorney from Springfield to Jasper County as a special prosecutor, and the trial was again delayed to give him time to prepare.[26]

Petty's second trial finally got underway in Joplin in late September 1941. Both sides presented evidence and arguments similar to what they'd introduced at the first trial. The trial concluded late on the evening of September 27, and the jury came back with an acquittal after only twenty-five minutes of deliberation. When the verdict was read, much of the courtroom audience burst into applause. An outraged J. V. Gipson, Eula's father, stood up and waved his hands in protest, but Mrs. Gipson restrained him and he slumped back into his seat.[27]

Delmar Petty lived the rest of his life in Joplin and mostly stayed out of trouble, although he was suspected of receiving stolen property in a 1944 case. He ran a filling station and was accused of buying some tires from a man who'd stolen the vehicle that the tires came from. Petty later worked as an office manager of a truck lines. He died in 1949 and was buried in Osborne Cemetery.[28]

Chapter 33

Badman Bill Cook and the Murder of the Mosser Family

Between 1:30 and 2:30 in the morning, January 2, 1951, Joplin police officers Nathan Keaton and Floyd Cline were patrolling the southwest part of town when they turned north off County Line Road (i.e. 32nd Street) onto Maiden Lane and headed downhill into a sparsely populated area of abandoned mines. At the bottom of the hill near an old railroad track that had previously served the mines, the officers spotted a blue, two-door Chevrolet sedan parked on the other side of the road heading south. They looked the vehicle over as they passed and noticed it had an Illinois license plate. At 26th Street, the patrolmen turned around and made another pass, this time throwing their spotlight on the car, but when they saw children in the car and no one standing outside the vehicle as if the occupants needed roadside assistance, the officers drove on.[1]

What Keaton and Cline had no way of knowing was that, if they'd been a little more curious, they might have prevented what became at the time one of the worst mass murders in US history. On the other hand, if the officers had pressed their investigation a little further, they might have wound up dead themselves. Because inside the car was droopy-eyed desperado Bill Cook holding hostage the Carl Mosser family he'd kidnapped at gunpoint in Oklahoma two and a half days earlier.[2]

And the anger and resentment pent up inside the twenty-one-year-old Cook from a lifetime of neglect and abuse was about to explode.

Cook, the third-youngest child in a family of ten children, was born in Joplin on December 29, 1929, to William E. Cook and his wife, Laura. The family lived in the mining district of Chitwood at the west edge of Joplin, where the elder Cook tried to scratch out a living doing odd jobs. Billy Cook was born with a growth on one eye that caused him to have to lift his eyelid with his hand in order to see. Although the growth was finally removed for free by a kindly doctor, the eye still drooped, and the boy was stuck with the ignominious nickname Cockeye Cook.[3]

Young Cook's mother died in 1933, when the boy was only three or four, and after her death, the father left the kids to fend for themselves. Not long after Laura's death, a probation officer found Billy and some of his siblings living in a cave in the Chitwood area, where the old man would drop by on occasion to bring food.[4]

Billy and his siblings were removed from the old man's custody, and over the next several years, Billy boarded with various families. When he was about ten, he was taken in by a foster mother. She adopted him in 1939, but a rift developed between the two shortly afterward. In 1940, when Bill was about eleven, he walked into the juvenile office and announced that he wouldn't live with his foster mother any longer. He accused her of taking clothes from him and said that on two different occasions bicycles she had purchased for him had been repossessed by the credit man.[5]

Placed in another foster home, Billy refused to stay there and went instead to live with an older, married sister. A short time later, the sister brought him back to the juvenile authorities, saying she couldn't control him. Billy was then taken before a judge and given an option of going to another foster home with a promise to stay there or else going to a reformatory. He chose the reformatory.[6]

After spending eleven months in the state reformatory at Boonville, Bill returned to Joplin in late 1941 and again lived with his sister for a while. But most of the time he was cast adrift, living on the streets. In 1943, the thirteen-year-old Cook slugged a Joplin taxicab driver and robbed him of $11. The next day, the cab driver spotted the boy in downtown Joplin, overpowered him, and turned him over to police. He was sent back to the reformatory for five years, and his behavior while there was bad. He fought with the other boys and once struck another boy with a baseball bat. He ran away from the reform school in early 1946 but was recaptured in Joplin and taken back. He ran away again and attempted to steal a car while he was on the loose. Given a new five-year sentence, he was sent on September 17 to the Algoa Work Farm, a medium security facility near Jefferson City. He still behaved in an unruly manner, and, after an escape attempt, he was transferred on October 16, 1946, to the state penitentiary as incorrigible.[7]

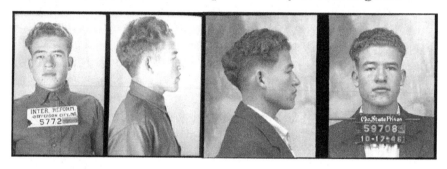

Mug shots of Bill Cook when he was admitted to the Algoa Work Farm in September 1946, left, and to the state prison a month later, right. *Missouri State Archives.*

Released in June of 1950 under the state's three-quarters law, he came back to Joplin sporting an array of tattoos, including the words "Hard Luck" on the fingers of his left hand. Already embittered at the age of twenty, he proposed to his father a partnership of crime. He said he planned to "live by the gun," and he wanted his dad to provide him with alibis. The elder Cook declined to cover for his son; so, Bill looked up Harold Martin, a young Joplin man he'd been in prison with, and suggested they go into a criminal partnership. When Martin balked at the opportunity, Bill took him to an abandoned mine shaft in west Joplin and threatened to kill him and throw his body in the shaft if he didn't agree to the plan. Martin, though, was able to get away and to avoid Cook after that.[8]

Bill, or "Cookie" as he was sometimes called, left Joplin soon afterward, crisscrossing the country. He came back to

Joplin briefly in November but then took off for California, where he got a job washing dishes at a cafe in the desert town of Blythe. On Christmas Day 1950, he got drunk and hitchhiked to Mexico with plans to "buy" a Mexican girl and bring her back to the United States. He found a girl, but she said she couldn't go with him because she had no passport.[9]

Cook hitchhiked back to the US and abducted a motorist named Lee Archer near Lubbock, Texas, on December 30. He made Archer drive him to Oklahoma, where, later the same day, he forced Archer out of his car near Luther, just east of Oklahoma City, and commandeered the vehicle. Cook drove east along Route 66 but had gone but a short distance when he realized the stolen vehicle could be easily traced. Abandoning Archer's car, he flagged down a westbound 1949 Chevy driven by thirty-three-year-old Carl Mosser of Atwood, Illinois. Mosser, his wife (Thelma), and their three children, ranging in age from seven to three, were headed to Albuquerque, New Mexico, to visit Mosser's brother. Cook forced his way into the car at gunpoint and ordered Mosser to drive.[10]

Thus began a frenetic journey back and forth across the Southwest, with Mosser first driving through Oklahoma into Texas. When Cook and Mosser went into a grocery store at Wichita Falls, Mosser started scuffling with Cook and screaming for help, but the storekeeper thought the two men were just playacting or else getting ready to hold him up. Brandishing his pistol, Cook forced Mosser back into his car, and the pell-mell trip continued. Mosser made another attempt to escape at Carlsbad, New Mexico, but Cook again got the situation under control and told Mosser he'd kill him and his family if he tried anything else. At El Paso, Texas, Cook ordered Mosser to turn around and head back east. The ill-fated journey took the Mossers back through Texas and across Oklahoma into Arkansas, where the kidnapper and his hostages stopped at a cafe in DeQueen to eat on the afternoon of January 1, 1951.[11]

Heading north along Highway 71, Cook reached Joplin with his captives late on the night of January 1 or shortly after midnight on the 2nd. According to Cook's later confession, he and the Mossers stopped on Maiden Lane so that he could bind

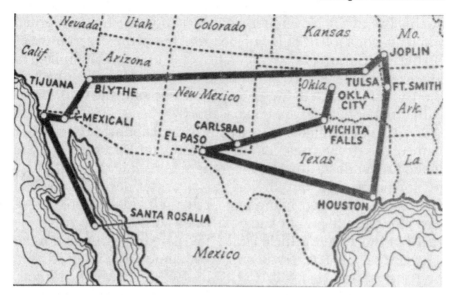

Map showing route Cook took after kidnapping and then killing the Mosser family. *From the Carbondale Southern Illinosian.*

and gag his hostages, preparatory to releasing them unharmed. When the Joplin police car made its second pass and its tail lights receded in the distance, though, the mother and children grew hysterical and started screaming. A porch light at a nearby house came on, and Cook panicked, or so he said, and started shooting. He put a bullet through Carl Mosser's brain and then shot Thelma Mosser through the chest. Seven-year-old Ronald Dean, who, like his parents, was already bound and gagged, was shot four times. Cook then shot the two youngest kids, five-year-old Gary Carl and three-year-old Pamela Sue, as they struggled in his arms.[12]

Cook took the wheel of the Mosser car and, for the next hour or so, drove aimlessly around Joplin with his gruesome cargo. About 3:00 a.m., he drove to an old mine shaft less than two blocks from the home of the foster mother he'd stayed with when he was ten to twelve years old. Located about a hundred yards north of West Fourth Street on the west side of Oliver Street, it was the same shaft he'd threatened to throw Harold Martin into the previous summer. Lugging the bodies of the Mossers to the shaft, Cook dropped them in, and they fell thirty-four feet to a watery grave.[13]

Carl and Thelma Mosser and children Ronald, 7, Gary, 5, and Pamela, 3. *Photo from Jim Hounschell's Lawmen and Outlaws: 116 Years in Joplin's History.*

Back in the Mosser car, Cook fled to Tulsa, where he abandoned the vehicle north of town. He then headed back to Blythe, hitchhiking part way and taking a bus the rest of the way. At Blythe, Cook kidnapped a deputy sheriff, Homer Waldrip, and stole his vehicle, leaving the deputy stranded along the highway almost seventy miles south of town. Using the cop car as a decoy, he waylaid a motorist named Robert

Dewey and later killed him. He then fled in Dewey's car to Mexico.[14]

Meanwhile, the Mossers' Chevrolet, abandoned near Tulsa, was found on January 3 with bloody clothes and several bullet holes in the seats. Drivers licenses belonging to Carl and Thelma Mosser and other identifying information were also found in the car. The odometer showed the vehicle had been driven 3,100 miles since it had been serviced in Illinois just a few days earlier. Authorities made a connection between the apparent kidnapping of the Mossers and the hijacking of Lee Archer when a farmer living near Luther, Oklahoma, came forward to say he'd seen a young man abandon the Archer vehicle and almost immediately flag down a car matching the description of the Mosser automobile. A receipt for a pistol purchased in St. Louis and bearing the name of Bill Cook was found in the Archer vehicle, and Archer's description of his hijacker matched the description a witness gave Oklahoma authorities of the man who'd abandoned the Mosser car near Tulsa. Tracing Bill Cook's background, officers learned their suspect had a record of delinquency and crime in Joplin going back to his pre-teen years.[15]

On January 6, Deputy Waldrip made his way back to Blythe and told the story of his narrow escape from Bill Cook, the thick-lipped killer from Joplin. He thought Cook had spared his life only because he and his wife, who worked at the same cafe where Cook had been employed, had befriended the young man. He said Cook had admitted killing the Mosser family and said he dumped their bodies in the snow somewhere in Oklahoma. Combined with the fact that the abduction of the Mossers and the abandonment of their car had both occurred in the Sooner State, Waldrip's story caused authorities to focus their hunt for the Mosser bodies in Oklahoma.[16]

On January 15, Cook was captured in Mexico and brought back to California. Pleading mental blackouts, he claimed to have no knowledge of killing anybody. On the same day, law officers expanded their search for the Mossers to include the Joplin area, and they were about to uncover evidence that belied Cook's claims of amnesia. Acting on a tip from Harold Martin, whom Cook had threatened the previous

Bill Cook, immediately after his capture in Mexico. *Author's collection.*

summer, officers went to the abandoned mine shaft just off West Fourth Street, lifted the boards covering the shaft, and saw two or three bodies floating on the surface of the water thirty feet below. Ultimately, all five bodies of the Mosser family were retrieved from the shaft, laid out in a ghastly array, and photographed for newspapers.[17]

A few days later, Cook retracted his claim of mental blackouts and gave a full confession. He told in some detail not only the story of the Mosser murders but also the story of his kidnapping of Waldrip and killing of Dewey in California.[18]

Bill Cook photographed at the US marshal's office in L.A,. a few days after his capture in
Mexico, enroute to Oklahoma. *Author's collection.*

Cook was first prosecuted in Oklahoma on federal
kidnapping charges. He was convicted in the late spring of 1951
and given a sentence of 300 years in prison at Alcatraz. At the
same time, the US attorney general authorized that Cook also
be tried in California for murdering Dewey. At the second trial
in November 1951, Cook was convicted of first-degree murder
and sentenced to death.[19]

"Badman Billy" was put to death in the gas chamber in
the California State Prison at San Quentin on December 12,
1952. "Sullen to the end," the "squatty killer" refused to see a
chaplain and died "with a false show of boredom." Original
plans called for a funeral to be held in Oklahoma, but Cook's

family called off the event because of the "Roman holiday" atmosphere surrounding it. Cook's body was then brought back to Joplin and buried in an eerie, after-dark ceremony in Peace Church Cemetery on the northwest outskirts of town with just a handful of family and friends in attendance. The Rev. Dow Booe, the same man who had been a spiritual advisor to the Worden brothers twenty years earlier, conducted the brief ceremony.[20]

Chapter 34

The Brutal Assault on Lisa Schuh
One of the Most Heinous Rapes
in Jasper County History

Lisa Schuh, a pretty thirteen-year-old schoolgirl from Wichita, was visiting her grandmother, Eula Childs, in Joplin on Sunday afternoon, July 23, 1961, when she decided to take her little dog for a walk. Leaving her grandmother's house at 730 Porter about 4:15 p.m., she started down an alley behind the house and had gone but a short distance when a man in a green and white 1956 Chevrolet pulled up beside her and asked her a question.[1]

Vernon Stephens, who was painting inside a garage that fronted on the alley, looked out a window and saw the man pull out a road map as if asking the girl for directions. Stephens heard the girl reply that she couldn't help. Suddenly the girl clasped her hand over her mouth in horror, and the man jumped out of the car, grabbed her by the arm, and hustled her and her dog into the automobile. When the man got back in the car, Stephens saw what had caused the girl's alarm. The man held a pistol in his right hand and was waving it threateningly at the girl, as she cowered in terror on the other side of the front seat. Stephens got a look at the man's face and also hurried into the street as the kidnapper drove away in time to see that the car bore a Kansas license with the tag number SU-1-0204.[2]

Stephens quickly notified the girl's grandmother, who told Lisa's older brother to call the police. A manhunt involving hundreds of officers from all over the Tri-State area was launched almost immediately. Detective Charles Hickman of the Joplin Police came on duty about 5:00 p.m. and promptly joined the search. After driving around for several minutes in the area of the chat piles at the northwest edge of Joplin, Hickman spotted a car near the intersection of Belle Center Road and Schifferdecker that seemed to fit the description Stephens had given. Hickman, driving an unmarked car, followed the vehicle south on Schifferdecker and confirmed that the license plate number also matched. The officer radioed for backup, and he and Sergeant Jack Fay stopped the vehicle near the intersection of Seventh and Schifferdecker.[3]

The officers found a girl's bloody blouse, a pair of shorts with a flowered design, a pair of panties, and a pair of blue, ballet-type slippers piled in a heap on the floorboard of the backseat. Beneath the front seat the officers found a .22 caliber automatic pistol. Also found in the car were some men's clothes with bloodstains on them and a large rock that had bloodstains on it as well. The policemen placed the driver under arrest and took him to the station for interrogation.[4]

The suspect, identified as twenty-nine-year-old Charles Harvey Odom, said he'd been to Springfield to visit his mother and was on his way back to his home in Wellington, Kansas. He had stopped on Seventh Street at a filling station just west of Maiden Lane to get gas, but he denied abducting the girl or knowing anything about it. Investigation into Odom's background revealed that he was a three-time loser, having served two brief terms in the Missouri State Penitentiary for Greene County burglaries and a term in the Kansas State Penitentiary

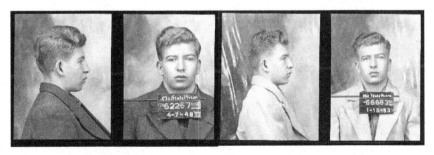

Mug shots of Charles Harvey Odom from two previous stays in the Missouri State Penitentiary, left 1949 and right 1953. *Courtesy of the Missouri State Archives.*

for a Wichita burglary. In addition, he'd served a stint at the Boonville Reformatory for a burglary committed when he was just fourteen. According to a Springfield newspaper, he'd spent only one Christmas outside jail since he turned fourteen, and even then he was out on bond.[5]

When asked directly whether he might have committed the crime in question, Odom said, "It's possible, but I don't think so."

Hoping the suspect might lead them to the girl, officers loaded him into a police cruiser and took him to the area northwest of Joplin where he'd first been spotted, but he said he had no recollection of the area and no knowledge of where the girl might be. He was taken back to police headquarters after the girl's older brother appeared on the scene and wanted to "get at" the suspect.[6]

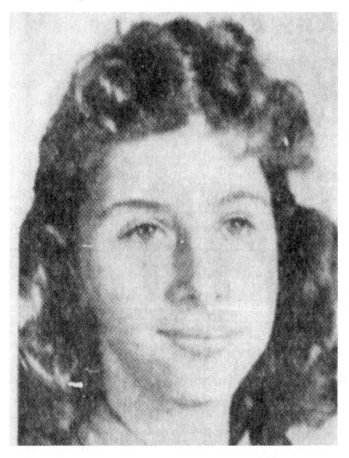

Lisa Schuh at the time of her abduction. *From the St. Louis Post-Dispatch.*

Meanwhile, those looking for the missing girl continued to concentrate their search northwest of Joplin, and shortly after 7:00 p.m., three Kansas lawmen and an area resident spotted her little dog on the east side of JJ Highway about a mile north of Belle Center. Looking around, they found Lisa in some dense underbrush, near death and clad only in a brassiere. She had been bludgeoned repeatedly, and one large wound on top of her head had laid open her skull and exposed her brain. She was rushed to Freeman Hospital in Joplin and soon forwarded to St. John's Hospital in Springfield, where she underwent brain surgery.[7]

Although Odom still maintained his innocence, he was charged with rape on Monday the 24th. Then, on Wednesday, July 26, he admitted the crime to the Rev. Dr. Jack Wilson, minister of the First Community Church in Joplin, with whom he had spoken the day before. Later on Wednesday, he also admitted the crime to police officers and signed a written confession. In part of his statement, Odom claimed the gun he pointed at Lisa was not loaded. He also said that she asked him for a cigarette and that, after she smoked it, she took off her own clothes when he asked her to and did not resist his advances. However, he became frightened after having intercourse, beat the girl over the head with the big rock found in his car, and "left the scene in a panic." According to Dr. Wilson, Odom broke into tears and kept saying he was sorry during his initial confession. On Thursday the 27th, the prisoner was escorted to Carthage and lodged in the Jasper County Jail.[8]

Lisa stayed in a coma for several weeks and underwent more surgery. She finally began to show signs of recovery about the first of September, although she remained partially paralyzed on the right side of her body. Told that Lisa was showing signs of improvement, Odom said he was glad to hear it. "I guess I hate myself worse than anyone else because of this."[9]

In mid-September, Odom waived a preliminary hearing and was bound over for trial on a charge of forcible rape. About the same time, Lisa was released from the Springfield hospital and taken home to Wichita. At arraignment a week or so later, Odom pled innocent, and trial was set for November in Jasper

County Circuit Court before Judge Ray Watson, the same man who'd conducted Delmar Petty's first trial. In mid-October, Watson denied a defense motion for a change of venue to Lawrence County.[10]

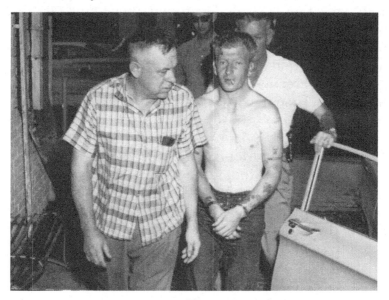

A bare-chested Charles Odom escorted by police after his arrest. *Author's collection.*

At the beginning of Odom's trial in November, Jasper County prosecuting attorney Stewart Tatum announced that he would seek the death penalty, while Odom's attorneys said they would plead insanity. The defense tried to get testimony about Odom's confession excluded on the grounds that he had initially given his statement in confidence to a minister, but Dr. Wilson, who held a degree in psychology and had previously worked as a consultant for the Kansas City Police, said he was not acting as a minister or spiritual counselor when he talked to Odom. The judge ruled that Odom's statement could be entered into evidence, and the testimony of Wilson and others as to its content was allowed. Odom's mother took the stand as the only defense witness. She testified that her son had to be "taken with instruments" when he was born, which left him with permanent marks on his head and neck. The boy's birth name was Charles Harvey Swan, but he'd taken his stepfather's name after she remarried. She said Odom had been shunted back and forth between relatives when he was growing up and that he had attempted suicide when he was just a lad. In closing arguments on November 9, assistant prosecutor Ben Pyle called the rape of Lisa Schuh "one of the most heinous, despicable crimes I have ever heard of." Later the same day, the jury came back with a guilty verdict and a sentence of death after deliberating only forty minutes.[11]

Mug shot of Charles Harvey Odom when he was admitted to the Missouri State Prison on January 4, 1962. *Courtesy of the Missouri State Archives.*

On December 28, Judge Watson overruled a defense motion for a new trial and set the execution date for February 8, 1962. Odom's attorneys, however, appealed to the Missouri Supreme Court, thereby staying the execution. In the meantime, Odom was delivered to the state penitentiary at Jefferson City to await the high court's ruling. On July 8, 1963, the supreme court upheld the verdict and reset the execution date for August 23. Addressing the defense's main contention that Odom should have been granted a change of venue because of prejudice against him in Jasper County, the state justices observed that in this era of widespread media coverage, citizens in an adjoining county are just as aware of high-profile crimes as those in the county where they happen.[12]

On August 19, four days before Odom was slated to die in the gas chamber, US Supreme Court justice Hugo Black stayed the execution to give the full court time to consider the case. The *Joplin Globe* reported that Odom's Jasper County lawyers did not initiate the appeal to the US Supreme Court and knew nothing about it. The supreme court clerk's office revealed the next day that Black acted in response to a letter Odom himself had written, and later in the week, the *Globe* editorialized against the high court's interference.[13]

Despite Justice Black's intervention, the US Supreme Court declined to review Odom's case, and the state supreme court reset the convict's execution date for March 6, 1964. Odom then petitioned for a stay of execution in federal court, but that motion, too, was denied.[14]

On March 5, the eve of his date with death, Odom declined to speak with the prison chaplain, saying, "I don't think we have anything to talk about." Later that night, after walking with "steady strides" into the gas chamber and being strapped into the death chair, he again declined spiritual solace, shaking his head when the chaplain approached. Shortly after midnight, the poisonous gas was released. The convicted rapist breathed deeply and died almost instantly.[15]

In early 1965, Lisa Schuh spoke to a Wichita civic group. She had come a long way in three and a half years but was still partially paralyzed on her right side and was still in physical therapy. Joking that her recovery was easy, she said, "I just see something I can't do and set out to do it. And pretty soon I can." A couple of months later, Lisa, now seventeen, also spoke briefly in Joplin at a meeting of the local Sertoma Club, which had raised funds for her medical treatment. "I give my thanks, many of them," she said, "to you persons who were so good to me."[16]

By the age of twenty, Lisa had regained enough of her verbal and quantitative skills to graduate from high school. Afterward she worked briefly in a hospital cafeteria, but her lingering health issues cut short her working years. In 1994, when she was forty-six, a *Joplin Globe* reporter interviewed her for a story about capital punishment. She was living in Barton County and had a twenty-two-year-old son. Her right arm was still unstable, she still spoke in broken patterns, and her ordeal had left her jaded on the question of the death penalty. She wondered only why Odom had not been executed promptly after raping her and leaving her for dead. Speaking of the crime, she said, "It just doesn't go away. I think of it every day, every night."[17]

Chapter 35

Murder at the Cold Spot
The Case of Fourteen-Year-Old Bobby Sinderson

"Gunman Pumps Nine Slugs into Store Manager," read the Friday afternoon headline of the March 3, 1967, *Joplin News Herald*. Earlier that day, about 1:45 in the morning, five men had walked into the Cold Spot, an all-night grocery store at 527 West Tenth in Joplin, and discovered the body of the night manager, sixty-four-year-old Merrill Nichols, riddled with bullets. A police officer who had stopped at the store at 1:15 to buy cigarettes and a candy bar said that about twenty-five minutes later, while he was parked three blocks away, he'd heard the sound of what he thought at the time was a car backfiring coming from the direction of the store. So, it was theorized the murder took place about 1:40, although the five men said they'd seen no one leaving the area as they arrived. About $30 had been taken from a cash register, and Nichols's billfold was also missing.[1]

Several men were questioned in the case before suspicion began to settle on a fourteen-year-old lad from Saginaw, whose identity was not made public at first. The youth had run away from home on Thursday, taking his stepfather's .22 caliber revolver, and he had turned up at the home of a paternal uncle in St. Louis about noon on Friday, ten hours after the crime. The pistol taken from the stepfather was found on Saturday in a restroom of the Greyhound Bus Station in Joplin and identified as the likely murder weapon. After talking to the boy's mother, the uncle brought him back to Joplin on Monday, March 6. The young suspect was questioned at the police station for about six hours that evening in the presence of his mother and uncle, but the boy staunchly denied any knowledge of the crime. He was nonetheless retained in the custody of Jasper County juvenile authorities.[2]

The former Cold Spot Grocery on West 10th Street was a barbershop for many years and is now an air conditioning contractor. *Photo by the author.*

His parents consented to let the boy be taken to Springfield for a polygraph test, and the results further implicated the lad. At a hearing on April 14, juvenile judge Woodson Oldham ruled that the youngster's case should be transferred from juvenile to adult court, and the boy, now named as Robert Eugene "Bobby" Sinderson, was immediately charged with first-degree murder and ordered held without bond in the juvenile section of the county jail until trial.[3]

At Sinderson's preliminary hearing in early May, a signed statement he'd made during questioning at the Joplin Police station upon his return from St. Louis was entered into evidence. He blamed the actual murder on an older boy named Jack Marcus, whom he'd met at a bowling alley a couple of weeks earlier, but he admitted that he supplied the murder weapon. He said he rode to the store with Marcus in the latter's car but remained in the vehicle when Marcus went inside and committed the murder. Efforts to locate the mysterious "Jack

Marcus" proved unsuccessful, however, and a prosecution witness said he'd seen Sinderson inside the store about 1:15 or 1:20 a.m. on the morning of the crime. After a week-long continuance, the hearing concluded in mid-May with the judge declaring that Sinderson should be held without bond. Trial was set for June but later continued.[4]

The trial finally got underway at Carthage in February 1968 before circuit court judge H. A. Kelso, who was appointed by the Missouri Supreme Court to hear the case after three previous judges had either disqualified themselves voluntarily or been disqualified on motion. The confession Sinderson had signed shortly after the murder was admitted as evidence, but the boy took the stand in his own defense to repudiate it. He said he left his mother and stepfather's house late on the night of March 2, 1967, and walked straight to the Greyhound Station, a distance of six or seven miles. He denied taking the .22 revolver with him and denied meeting anybody named Jack Marcus. He said he'd given the previous statement only because he grew tired after several hours of interrogation and he was afraid the weapon found at the bus station might implicate some other member of his family. The case was given to the jury on Friday night, February 16, 1968, and after deliberating three and a half hours, they reported they were hopelessly deadlocked. The split was seven to five, but no word was given on which number favored conviction and which favored acquittal. Judge Kelso declared a mistrial.[5]

Judge Kelso recused himself before Sinderson's next trial, because his schedule would not allow him to hear the case in a timely manner, and Judge Henry Riderer was appointed as his replacement. At a pre-trial hearing in April 1968, Riderer sustained a defense motion to suppress the confession Sinderson had given at the Joplin Police station three days after the crime on the grounds that it was coerced and violated the juvenile code. In the face of the court ruling, an angry Robert Warden, Jasper County prosecutor, dismissed the first-degree murder charge against Sinderson, saying he could not get a conviction without the confession, which he felt had not been coerced. Sinderson was released, but Warden filed a new charge of first-degree murder against him in early June in the magistrate court of Jasper County's Eastern District.[6]

Young Sinderson surrendered a few days later and was released on bond. At the conclusion of his preliminary hearing in August and September, magistrate judge Herbert Casteel bound him over to the circuit court. At the November term of circuit court, a grand jury indicted him for robbery with a firearm. Trial was set for January 1969, and Sinderson was returned to jail in lieu of $5,000 additional bond. He was later indicted for murder as well, but both cases were continued.[7]

Sinderson went on trial in Joplin in March 1969 on the robbery charge before Judge Paul Carver of Neosho, who'd been appointed to hear the case. The statement the boy had given in the wake of the crime was admitted into evidence over the objections of the defense. On March 14, the jury returned a verdict of guilty and sentenced Sinderson to five years in the penitentiary. Commenting on the lenient sentence, Prosecutor Warden said he thought the jury probably believed the boy's original confession that he was only an accomplice in the crime and not the actual murderer. Based on this conclusion, Warden dropped the murder charge against Sinderson a few days later.[8]

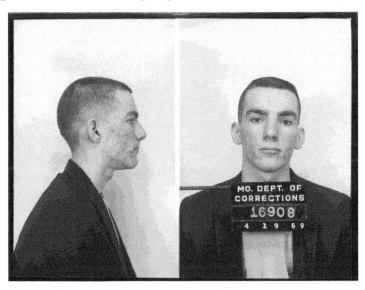

Mug shots of Bobby Sinderson when he was received at the state prison. *Courtesy Missouri State Archives.*

Despite the lenient verdict, Sinderson's lawyers filed a motion for a new trial, and when the motion was denied in April, they appealed to the Missouri Supreme Court. Their main argument was that admitting Bobby's confession into evidence violated the juvenile code. In the meantime, Sinderson was taken to Jefferson City to serve his time in prison, pending the outcome of the appeal. Taking up the case in June 1970, the high court ruled that the confession was admissible, and the justices affirmed the verdict.[9]

Despite the supreme court's ruling against him, Sinderson was destined to gain his freedom long before his full term expired. The question of commuting his sentence came up for review in October 1971. Missouri governor Warren E. Hearnes received a report from the Department of Corrections' Classification Committee showing the lad had accumulated 433 days of earned time through work, going to school, and good behavior during his incarceration and had only five days deducted for the minor offense of having another inmate bring cake to him from the food service section of the prison. Based on the report, Hearnes commuted Sinderson's sentence to two years and six and a half months, and he was released in mid-November.[10]

Chapter 36

Satanism, Heavy Metal Music, and
Ritualistic Killing
The Beating Death of Steven Newberry

The front-page headlines of the *Joplin Globe* on Wednesday, December 9, 1987, were horrific enough: "Authorities seek answers in brutal beating of 19-year-old" and "3 teens accused of killing classmate." Horrific enough, even without the disturbing rumor mentioned below one of the headlines that the murder was tied to satanic cult activity.[1]

The beating death of Carl Junction High School senior Steven Newberry happened recently enough that many readers probably remember it. A modern-day horror, it stands as one of the most gruesome crimes in Jasper County history, a dreadful bookend to the ghastly slaughter of the Fisk family and subsequent burning of two slaves in Carthage over 130 years earlier.

Steven Newberry had started school late because of hyperactivity and had been held back another year. Now nineteen, overweight, and immature for his age, he struggled to fit in among his younger classmates at Carl Junction High. Too eager to be liked, he was what the kids called a wannabe.[2]

By the fall of 1987, though, he thought he'd finally found his place, having been accepted into the periphery of a group of stoners led by fellow senior Jim Hardy. President of the student body, Hardy had been elected to the position not for his qualities of leadership and citizenship but because he stood out as a rebel and was voted in by the other students on a lark to confound the teachers and principals. The second-oldest of five children in an upper-middle class family, Hardy had been an altar boy and honor student in elementary school, but he began misbehaving about the time he was eleven, and he lost interest in academics. He was given to angry outbursts in his relations with family and friends, especially his father, and he started using drugs regularly. Increasingly drawn to heavy metal music, he found sadistic pleasure in torturing animals, and he started dabbling in devil worship. Other classmates in Hardy's inner circle included Ron Clements and Pete Roland, both of whom shared Hardy's fascination with heavy metal music, animal sacrifice, and the satanic. The three had killed several small animals, and they had begun to openly wonder what it would be like to kill a human being.[3]

Steven's mother, Marlys Newberry, worried about her son hanging around with Hardy and his friends. She worried about the drug use and the heavy metal music with its disturbing lyrics. She'd tried to get her son to stay away from the other boys, but he was nineteen. There wasn't much she could do.

And late on Sunday night, December 6, 1987, she grew especially worried. Steven had left with Jim Hardy, Ron Clements, and Pete Roland late that afternoon with a promise to be home early, but he still wasn't back, even though tomorrow was a school day.[4]

When Steven still hadn't come home the next morning, his mother called Carl Junction High School and learned that Steven was absent but that Jim Hardy and the other boys with whom Steven had left home were present. She called the sheriff's office, and law officers went to the school to question the three young men and any other students who might shed light on Steven's disappearance.[5]

At first, Hardy, Roland, and Clements insisted they'd dropped Steven off at a convenience store Sunday night, but when Clements was called back to the Carl Junction police headquarters for further questioning on Monday night, he broke down and admitted his part in killing Steven. He led investigators to an old abandoned cistern west of Joplin near the state line on the property of Farmer's Chemical Company (now Nutrien Joplin Phosphate). In the wee hours of Tuesday morning, Steven's body, weighted down by a rock, was pulled from the cistern. Further investigation showed that Steven had been bludgeoned to death by approximately seventy blows to the head and body, and four bloody baseball bats found discarded in some nearby weeds were thought to be the murder weapons.[6]

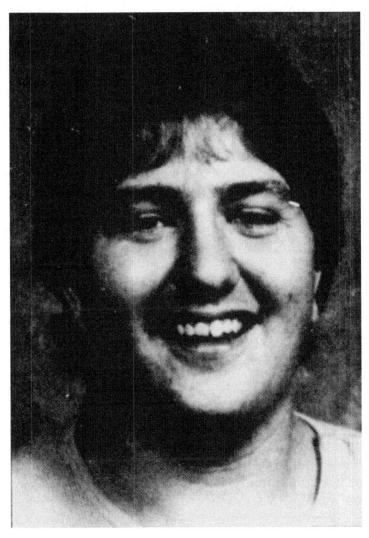

Newspaper photo of Steven Newberry near the time he was killed. *From the Joplin Globe.*

Warrants were issued for the arrest of James Hardy and Pete Roland later Tuesday morning. Roland was arrested at school the same morning, and Hardy turned himself in later that day.[7]

When news of the murder and the arrests was first released to the media, police were reluctant to talk about the ongoing investigation. They confirmed they had received several reports of cult-like activity in the Carl Junction area during the past couple of years, such as satanic graffiti and animal sacrifice, but they refused to confirm whether they thought the Newberry murder was tied to the earlier incidents. The only definite clue indicating that the Newberry killing was tied to cult-like activity was a dead cat found in the cistern alongside the young man's body. It, too, had been beaten to death.[8]

A horrifying story emerged over the next few weeks, however, as bits and pieces of new evidence were uncovered and statements from the three seventeen-year-old youths charged with Steven's death were made public. The three accused killers had arrived at Steven's house in Roland's car, and the four had driven from the Newberry home on Black Cat Road to the Farmer's Chemical property with Roland behind the wheel. In the floorboard lay four baseball bats, one of which had the word "Ultraviolence" written on it. Hardy had brought along a cat he had captured in a net bag. The four got out of the car and walked down some railroad tracks toward the old cistern, each carrying one of the bats. At the "well of hell," as Hardy and his pals called the cistern, they suspended the trapped cat from a tree limb, and each took turns beating the animal to death, with Steven joining in on the "fun."[9]

The other three had lured Steven out to the remote cistern intending all along to kill him. In fact, they'd planned to do it on a couple of previous occasions but had either backed out or had their plans otherwise thwarted. Now, they stood around waiting to see which one was going to strike the first blow. "What're we going to do now, Jim?" Ron Clements asked.[10]

After a moment's hesitation, Hardy swung his bat and hit Steven in the face. Steven started to run, turning to cry out, "Why me?" as the other three chased after him. "Because it's fun," Ron said with a laugh. Steven stumbled and fell, and the other three set upon him with a flurry of blows from the baseball bats. He was still moaning faintly when they dragged him back to the cistern, where they tied a stone to his body and dropped him in the murky water.[11]

Hardy originally pleaded not guilty by reason of mental defect, but when his case came up in Camden County on a change of venue in late April 1988, he changed his plea to guilty in an agreement with the prosecution to take the death penalty off the table. He later was sentenced to life imprisonment.[12]

At Clements's trial in Carthage in early May, the confession he gave to officers in the immediate wake of the killings was read to the jury. Among the statements he made in recounting the murder was a chilling acknowledgement that Newberry had been killed because "he just seemed inferior."[13]

Clements had pleaded not guilty by reason of mental defect, and his lawyer introduced some writing from the young man into evidence in an effort to establish the insanity defense. "What if I were to kill someone?" the writing said. "Would I feel remorse? What if violence were a way of life?" The papers were signed by "Alex Frost," a principal character in *A Clockwork Orange*, a book and movie about violent British youth gangs of the twenty-first century.[14]

Clements's mother took the stand to tell the court that she and Ron's father had an off-and-on relationship since the boy was less than a year old, and they often fought. The father never held a steady job because of his drug and alcohol abuse, and she herself was often away from home working the evening shift as a waitress. She knew Ron had been drinking alcohol for several years, and she suspected his use of other drugs. She and her son often clashed over his addiction to heavy metal music by groups like Megadeth and over the way he decorated his room in black and had webbing hanging from the ceiling with a wolf's head attached. Mrs. Clements said she sought help for her son but the counselor assured her after just a few sessions that there was nothing to worry about. Also testifying for the defense, two psychiatrists said that because of Clements's chaotic home life, his addiction to drugs and heavy metal music, and his involvement in Satanism, he was unable to appreciate the difference between right and wrong. The expert witnesses said they believed Clements was under the spell of Hardy, who, as the group's leader, had a magnetic hold on his followers.[15]

On May 4, the jury came back with a verdict finding Clements guilty of first-degree murder. During the subsequent sentencing phase of the trial, Clements took the stand to say he was sorry for what he had done, and the jury recommended a sentence of life imprisonment without the possibility of parole.[16]

Pete Roland's trial was held in June 1988 at Sedalia on a change of venue. He, too, had pleaded not guilty by reason of mental defect, and his attorney pursued a similar line of argument as Clements's lawyer had. The defense claimed that because of Roland's unstable home life, his obsession with heavy metal music, and his belief in satanism, he was predisposed to participate in the beating death of Steven Newberry. Taking the stand in his own defense, Roland agreed that listening to heavy metal music put him in a frame of mind to commit the murder, and, contradicting what he'd said in a taped confession shortly after the murder, he also said the murder was a ritualistic, cult-like killing.[17]

On June 18, the jury came back with a verdict of guilty of first degree murder after deliberating five hours. As was the case at Clements's trial, the state sought the death penalty for Roland, but the jury recommended life imprisonment without parole instead. In July, the judge in the case followed the jury's recommendation and sentenced Roland to life imprisonment. Hardy and Clements had already begun serving their sentences, and Roland shortly afterwards joined them at the state prison.[18]

Both Roland and Clements appealed their verdicts. Roland's conviction was affirmed, but Clements was granted a new trial by the Missouri Court of Appeals, which ruled that the jury in his case should not have been allowed to consider a psychiatrist's testimony that the murder was premeditated. At his retrial in Carthage in March 1991, Clements was once again found guilty and sentenced to life imprisonment.[19]

As of this writing, Hardy, Roland, and Clements are all still in prison serving life sentences, but a federal judge, in response to a class-action lawsuit, ruled in October 2018 that Missouri's system of life imprisonment without the possibility of parole was unfair to inmates whose crimes were committed when they were minors and that those individuals should be given a "meaningful and realistic opportunity" for eventual release.[20]

End Notes

List of abbreviations for frequently cited sources:

CB	*Carthage Banner*
CEP	*Carthage Evening Press*
FSDM	*Fort Scott Daily Monitor*
GET	*Galena (KS) Evening Times*
GWR	*Galena (KS) Weekly Republican*
JDH	*Joplin Daily Herald*
JDN	*Joplin Daily News*
JG	*Joplin Globe*
JNH	*Joplin News Herald*
MSPRD	Missouri State Penitentiary Records Database
SLPD	*St. Louis Post-Dispatch*
WCR	*Webb City Register*

Chapter 1
An Awful Spectacle

[1] *Liberty Tribune*, Aug 5, 1853 quoting the *Boonville Observer; An Illustrated Historical Atlas Map of Jasper County, Mo.*, 18.

[2] *Liberty Tribune*, Aug. 5, 1853, quoting the *Boonville Observer*.

[3] *Historical Atlas Map*, 18; *Liberty Tribune*, Aug 5, 1853, quoting the *Boonville Observer*

[4] *Liberty Tribune*, Aug. 5, 1853, quoting the *Boonville Observer*.

[5] *Liberty Tribune*, Aug. 5, 1853, quoting the *Boonville Observer; New Albany (IN) Daily Ledger*, Aug. 4, 1853, quoting *St. Louis Republican; Historical Atlas Map*, 18.

6 *Historical Atlas Map*, 18.

7 *Liberty Tribune*, Aug. 5. 1853, quoting *Boonville Observer*; *Historical Atlas Map*, 18.

8 *Liberty Tribune*, Aug. 5. 1853, quoting *Boonville Observer*; *Historical Atlas Map*, 18.

9 *Liberty Tribune*, Aug. 5. 1853, quoting *Boonville Observer*; *Historical Atlas Map*, 18

10 *Historical Atlas Map*, 18.

11 *Ibid.*

12 *Ibid.*

13 *Liberty Tribune*, Aug. 19, 1853, quoting the *Springfield Advertiser*; *Historical Atlas Map,* 18; *Carthage Mornin' Mail*, Sep. 26, 1997, reprint of an 1897 article.

14 *Historical Atlas Map*, 18; *Carthage Mornin' Mail*, Sep. 26, 1997.

15 *Carthage Mornin' Mail*, Sep. 26, 1997.

16 *Historical Atlas Map*, 18.

17 *Ibid.*

18 *Historical Atlas Map*, 18, *Carthage Mornin' Mail*, Sep. 26, 1997.

Chapter 2
The Disappearance of Mary Margaret Fullerton

1 *Sydney (Australia) Morning Herald*, Aug 24, 1868, quoting the May 12, 1868 *St. Louis Times*; Ohio Marriage Records, 1774-1993, Ancestry.com.

2 *Sydney Morning Herald*, Aug 24, 1868, quoting *St. Louis Times*; Missouri Marriage Records, FamilySearch.org.

3 *Sydney Morning Herald*, Aug 24, 1868, quoting the *St. Louis Times*.

4 *Ibid.*

5 *CB*, June 11, 1868.

6 *Sydney Morning Herald*, Aug. 24, 1868, quoting the *St. Louis Times*.

7 *Cincinnati Enquirer*, May 16, 1868, quoting the *St. Louis Democrat*; *Mt. Vernon Spring River Fountain*, Apr. 23, 1868.

8 *Cincinnati Enquirer*, May 16, 1868, quoting the *St. Louis*

Democrat; *Mt. Vernon Spring River Fountain*, Apr. 23, 1868.

9 *Cincinnati Enquirer*, May 16, 1868, quoting *St. Louis Democrat*; *CB*, Apr. 30, 1868; *History of Newton, Lawrence, Barry and McDonald Counties*, 454.

10 *CB*, Apr. 30, 1868.

11 *Sydney Morning Herald*, Aug. 24, 1868, quoting the *St. Louis Times*; *CB*, June 11, 1868, quoting the *Mt. Vernon Spring River Fountain*.

12 *Sydney Morning Herald*, Aug. 24, 1868, quoting the St. Louis Times.

13 *Sydney Morning Herald*, Aug. 24, 1868, quoting the *St. Louis Times*; *Cincinnati Enquirer*, May 16, 1868, quoting the *St. Louis Democrat*.

14 *Sydney Morning Herald*, Aug. 24, 1868, quoting the *St. Louis Times*; *CB*, June 11, 1868, quoting the *Mt. Vernon Spring River Fountain*.

15 *Cincinnati Enquirer*, May 16, 1868, quoting *St. Louis Democrat*; *CB, June 4, 1868*, June 11, 1868, quoting the *Mt. Vernon Spring River Fountain*.

16 *Sydney Morning Herald*, Aug. 24, 1868, quoting the *St. Louis Times*; *Cincinnati Enquirer*, May 16, 1868, quoting the *St. Louis Democrat*.

17 CB, June 11, 1868, quoting the *Mt. Vernon Spring River Fountain*.

18 *Ibid*.

19 *CB*, June 4, 1868.

Chapter 3
Dr. Taylor Gets His Neck Lengthened

1 *Richmond (VA) Dispatch*, June 8, 1870, quoting the *Kansas City Journal*.

2 *Ibid*.

3 *Ibid*.

4 *Ibid*.

5 *Ibid*.

6 *Ibid*.

7 *Ibid*.

[8] *Huntsville (AL) Advocate*, June 24, 1870.

Chapter 4
Murder at a Joplin Bawdy House

[1] *CB*, Nov. 20, 1873.
[2] *Neosho Times*, Feb. 27, 1873, quoting the *Joplin Mining News*; *CB*, Nov. 20, 1873; US Census, 1870 and 1880.
[3] *CB*, Nov. 20, 1873.
[4] *Ibid.*
[5] *Neosho Times*, Feb. 27, 1873, quoting *Joplin Mining News*.
[6] *CB*, Nov. 20, 1873; *Neosho Times*, Feb. 27, 1873, quoting *Joplin Mining News*.
[7] **Missouri's Judicial Records**, Elizabeth Greenma file.
[8] *CB*, Nov. 20, 1873.
[9] *Ibid.*
[10] *Ibid.*
[11] MSPRD; Missouri's Judicial Records, Edward Daugherty file.

Chapter 5
A Robber Hung at Minersville

[1] *CB*, Nov. 13, 1873; US Census, 1870.
[2] *CB,* Nov. 13, 1873.
[3] *Ibid.*
[4] *Ibid.*
[5] *CB*, Nov. 13, 1873; *Sedalia Democrat*, Nov. 29, 1873; US Census, 1850, 1860. Although Bryson was linked to guerrilla chief Bill Anderson by some Union reports just prior to Anderson's massacre at Centralia in the fall of 1864, Bryson was, in fact, a commissioned Confederate officer on recruiting duty at the time and in command of a separate body of men.
[6] *CB*, Nov. 13, 1873.
[7] *Ibid.*

Chapter 6
The Lynching of Daniel Reed

[1] *FSDM*, October 1, 1874.

[2] *FSDM*, Oct. 3, 1874; *Mt. Vernon Fountain and Journal*, Oct. 15, 1874, quoting the *Joplin Bulletin*.

[3] *Mt. Vernon Fountain and Journal*, Oct. 15, 1874, quoting the *Joplin Bulletin*.

[4] *FSDM*, Oct. 3, 1873.

[5] *FSDM*, Oct. 17, 1874.

[6] *Lexington (MO) Weekly Caucasian*, Oct., 17, 1874.

[7] *Mt. Vernon Fountain and Journal*, Oct. 15, 1874, citing the *Granby Miner*; *FSDM*, Oct. 17, 1874.

[8] *FSDM*, Oct. 17, 1874.

[9] *CB*, Sep. 16, Oct. 14, 1875.

Chapter 7
The Webb City Riot

[1] Wood, *Desperadoes of the Ozarks*, 27-43.

[2] *Fort Scott Weekly Monitor*, Jan. 25, 1877; *Columbus (KS) Courier*, Jan. 25, 1877, quoting the *Webb City New Century*.

[3] *Galena (KS) Messenger*, July 25, 1879; *Cincinnati Daily Star*, Jan. 29, 1877, quoting the *Joplin News*.

[4] *Columbus Courier*, Jan. 25, 1877, quoting *Webb City New Century*; *Cincinnati Daily Star*, Jan. 29, 77, quoting *Joplin News*; *FSDM*, Jan. 21, 1877.

[5] *Cincinnati Daily Star*, Jan. 29, 1877, quoting *Joplin News; Columbus Courier*, Jan. 25, 1877, quoting *Webb City New Century; FSDM,* Jan. 21, 1877.

[6] *Columbus Courier*, Jan. 25, 1877, quoting *Webb City New Century*.

[7] *FSDM*, Jan. 21, 1877; *Cincinnati Daily Star*, Jan. 29, 1877, quoting *Joplin News; Columbus Courier*, Jan. 25, 1877, quoting *Webb City New Century*; *CB*, Feb. 1 1877.

[8] *CB*, Feb. 1, 1877; *Columbus Courier*, Jan. 25, 1877, quoting *Webb City New Century*; *FSCM*, Jan. 21, 1877.

9 *Galena Messenger*, July 25, 1879.
10 *Mt. Vernon Lawrence Chieftain*, Apr. 11, 1877, quoting the
    Neosho Journal; Wood, *Desperadoes*, 37-43.
11 Wood, *Desperadoes*, 27-36.

Chapter 8
The First Legal Hanging in Jasper County

1 US Census, 1870; Indiana Marriage Index, Ancestry.com; *Mt.
    Vernon Lawrence Chieftain*, Feb. 27, 1878.
2 *Mt. Vernon Lawrence Chieftain*, Feb. 27, 1878; *Sedalia
    Weekly Bazoo*, Jan. 22, 1878; Sturges, *Illustrated
    History*, 120-122.
3 *Sedalia Weekly Bazoo*, January, 22, 1878.
4 *CB*, Jan. 17, 1878.
5 *Ibid.*
6 *CB*, Feb. 21, 1878
7 *Ibid.*
8 *Ibid.*
9 *CB*, Jan. 17, Feb. 21, 1878.
10 *CB*, Feb. 21, 1878.
11 *Ibid.*
12 *Ibid.*
13 *Ibid.*
14 *Ibid.*

Chapter 9
Britton the Bold

1 *JDH*, Feb. 10, 1880; Wood, *Desperadoes*, 62-64.
2 *JDH*, June 30, 1883.
3 Wood, *Desperadoes*, 64-65; *JDH*, June 29, 1883.
4 *JDH*, June 29, 1883.
5 *Ibid.*
6 *Ibid.*
7 *Ibid.*
8 *Ibid.*
9 *JDH*, June 30, July 3, 1883; *Neosho Miner and Mechanic*,

July 7, 1883.
10 *JDH*, July 3, 1883.
11 *Ibid.*
12 *JDH*, July 10, 1883.
13 *JDH*, July 11, 13, 1883.
14 Wood, *Desperadoes*, 67-71.

Chapter 10
Lynching of Joe Thornton

1 *GWR*, July 25, 1885, quoting *Joplin News*.
2 US Census, 1880; *GWR*, July 25, 1885.
3 *GWR*, Apr. 4, May 24, 1884.
4 *GWR*, Oct. 4, Dec. 13, 1884.
5 *GWR*, May 23, June 27, 1885.
6 Jasper County Circuit Court Records, Joseph Thornton
indictment, Mar. 1885; *GWR*, July 25, 1885, citing
Joplin News.
7 *GWR*, July 25, 1885, citing *Joplin News*.
8 *Ibid.*
9 *Ibid.*
10 *Ibid.*
11 *Ibid.*
12 *Ibid.*
13 *JDH*, July 19, 1885.
14 *GWR*, July 25, 1885, citing *Joplin News*.
15 *Ibid.*
16 *Neosho Miner and Mechanic*, July 25, 1885, quoting the
Joplin News; *GWR*, July 25, 1885, quoting the *Joplin
News*; Find a Grave, Memorial #21748538.

Chapter 11
Midnight Assassination

1 *Joplin Sunday Herald*, Aug. 1, 1897.
2 *Joplin Sunday Herald*, Aug. 1, 1897; *Springfield Leader-
Democrat*, Apr. 27, 1898.
3 *Springfield Leader-Democrat*, Apr. 27, 1898; *Joplin City*

Directory, 1896-1897.

4 *Springfield Leader-Democrat*, Apr. 27, 1898.

5 *Springfield Leader-Democrat*; Apr. 27, 1898; *Joplin Sunday Herald*, Aug. 1, 1897.

6 *Joplin Sunday Herald*, Aug. 1, 1897.

7 *Ibid.*

8 *Joplin Sunday Herald*, Aug. 1, 1897; *JG*, Aug. 3, 1897.

9 *JG*, Aug. 3, 1897; *Cape Girardeau Democrat*, Aug. 12, 1897; *Springfield Leader-Democrat*, Apr.. 27, 1898.

10 *Galena (KS) Daily Republican*, May 5, 1898, quoting *Carthage Democrat*; *Springfield Leader-Democrat*, June 6, 1898.

11 *Springfield Leader-Democrat*, Mar. 8, 1899, quoting the *Carthage Press*; *JDN*, July 6, 1899.

12 *JDN*, July 6, 1899.

13 *Ibid.*

14 *Ibid.*

Chapter 12
Fate of a Defamer

1 *GET*, Dec. 21 1899, quoting *JG*; *JDN,* Dec. 21, 1899.

2 *GET*, Dec. 21, 1899, quoting *JG*; *JDN,* Dec. 21, 1899.

3 *GET*, Dec. 21, 1899, quoting *JG*; *JDN*, Feb. 8, July 18, 1900.

4 *GET*, Dec. 21, 1899, quoting *JG*.

5 *GET*, Dec. 21, 1899, quoting *JG*; *JDN*, Feb. 8, 1900.

6 *GET*, Dec. 21, 1899, quoting *JG*; *JDN*, Dec. 21, 1899.

7 *GET*, Dec. 21, 1899, quoting *JG*.

8 *Ibid.*

9 *Ibid.*

10 *Ibid.*

11 *Ibid.*

12 *GET*, Dec. 21, quoting *JG*; *JDN*, Feb. 7 1900.

13 *JDN*, Feb. 8, 1900.

14 *JDN*, Feb. 9, 1900.

15 *Ibid.*

16 *JDN*, Feb. 9, 1900; *GET*, July 19, 1900, citing *JG*.

17 *GET*, Feb. 13, 1900, citing the *Joplin Herald*.

18 *JNH*, July 17, 1900.

[19] *JNH*, July 18, 1900.
[20] *Ibid.*
[21] *GET*, July 19, 1900, citing *JG.*
[22] *JNH*, July 19, 1900; *GET*, July 20, 1900, citing *JG.*
[23] *GET*, July 20, 1900, citing *JG.*
[24] *GET*, Aug. 14, 1900; MSPRD; US Census, 1920.

Chapter 13
Came Out Here to Die Like a Man

[1] *Reports of Cases Determined in the Supreme Court of the State of Missouri,* 162:313-314.
[2] *JG*, July 6, 1901; *Cases Determined,* 313.
[3] *Cases Determined,* 313.
[4] *JG*, July 6, 1901; *CEP*, June 20, 1900.
[5] *CEP*, June 20, 1900.
[6] *Ibid.*
[7] *CEP*, June 20, Nov. 16, 1900.
[8] *CEP*, June 20, 21, 1900.
[9] *CEP*, June 20, 1900.
[10] *CEP*, June 20, Nov. 16 1900; *Cases Determined,* 314.
[11] *CEP*, June 21, 1900.
[12] *Ibid.*
[13] *CEP*, Nov. 16, 1900.
[14] *Ibid.*
[15] *Ibid.*
[16] *Ibid.*
[17] *JG*, July 6, 1901.
[18] *Ibid.*
[19] *CEP*, July 5, 1901.
[20] *Ibid.*
[21] *Ibid.*
[22] *CEP*, July 5, 1901; *JG*, July 6, 1901.
[23] *CEP*, July 5, 1901.
[24] *CEP*, Nov. 16, 1900; July 5, 1901.

Chapter 14
Killing of Leslie and Lynching of Gilyard

[1] *JG*, Apr. 15, 1903.
[2] *Ibid.*
[3] *Ibid.*
[4] *Ibid.*
[5] *Ibid.*
[6] *Ibid.*
[7] *JG*, Apr. 16, 1903.
[8] *Ibid.*
[9] *Ibid.*
[10] *Ibid.*
[11] *Ibid.*
[12] *Ibid.*
[13] *Ibid.*
[14] *Ibid.*
[15] *Ibid.*
[16] *Ibid.*
[17] *Ibid.*
[18] *Ibid.*
[19] *JG*, Apr. 17, 1903; Harper, *White Man's Heaven,* 87-88; Abe Sauer, *The Awl,* "100 Years Later: A Black Man Finally Loves Joplin," https://www.theawl.com/2011/05/100-years-later-a-black-man-finally-loves-joplin/; *WCR,* Nov. 20, 21, 1903.

Chapter 15
Foot and a Half Butler and the Killing of Claude Brice

[1] *WCR*, Dec. 31, 1904.
[2] "Patrolman Claude Brice"; *WCR*, Jan. 5, 18, 1905.
[3] *WCR*, Jan. 21, 1905; US Census, 1900.
[4] *JG*, Mar. 23, May 23, 1905.
[5] *Chanute (KS) Sun*, Feb. 28, 1905; *Sedalia Democrat*, June 8, 1902; *JNH*, Jan. 16, 1906; MSPRD; Kansas State Penitentiary at Lansing Records.
[6] *JG*, Mar. 23, 1905.

[7] *JG,* May 19, 1905.

[8] *Ibid.*

[9] *JG,* May 20, 1905.

[10] *Ibid.*

[11] *JG,* May 23, 1905.

[12] *Ibid.*

[13] *Ibid.*

[14] *Ibid.*

[15] *Ibid.*

[16] MSPRD; *JG,* October 21, 1905.

[17] *JG,* May 23, 1905.

[18] *JG,* May 24, 1905.

[19] *JG,* October 21, 1905.

[20] *Ibid.*

[21] *JG,* Oct. 21, 22, 1905.

[22] *JG,* Oct. 21, 1905.

[23] *JG,* Oct. 22, 1905.

[24] *Ibid.*

[25] *JG,* Oct. 22, 1905; *GWR,* Nov. 17, 1905.

[26] *JNH,* Jan. 15, 16, 1906.

[27] *SLPD,* Jan. 17, 1906.

[28] *Sedalia Evening Democrat,* Jan. 17, 1906; *Lincoln (NE) Journal Star,* Sep. 17, 1920; *Kansas City (KS) Kansan,* Apr. 11, 1921.

[29] *Lincoln Journal Star,* Feb 11, May 8, 1922, Jan. 18, July 16, 1924, Apr. 28, 1928.

Chapter 16
The Green-Eyed Monster

[1] US Census, 1900; *JG,* Sep. 8, 1906; Missouri Marriage Records, Ancestry.com.

[2] *JNH,* Sep. 9, 1906; *JG,* Sep. 8, 1906.

[3] *JNH,* Sep. 9, 1906; *JG,* Sep. 8, 1906.

[4] *JNH,* Sep. 9, 1906.

[5] *JG,* Sep. 9, 1906; *JNH,* Sep. 9, 1906. During the late 1800s and early 1900s, saloons were generally off limits to women, but some of them had special rooms attached called wine rooms, where women were allowed.

6 *JG*, Sep. 9, 1906; *JNH*, Sep. 9, 1906.
7 *JG*, Sep. 8, 1906.
8 *JNH*, Sep. 9, 1906; *JG*, Sep. 9, 1906.
9 *JNH*, Sep. 9, 1906.
10 *JG*, Sep. 8, 1906.
11 *JG*, Sep. 8, 1906; *JNH*, Sep. 9, 1906.
12 *JG*, Sep. 8, 1906; *JNH*, Sep. 9, 1906.
13 *JNH*, Sep. 9, 1906.
14 *Ibid.*
15 *JG*, Sep. 8, 1906; *JNH*, Sep. 9, 1906.
16 *JNH*, Sep. 9, 1906.
17 *JG*, Sep. 9, 1906.
18 US Census, 1910, 1920.

Chapter 17
God Don't Love a Liar

1 *Cherokee (KS) Sentinel*, July 17, 1908.
2 *Reports of Cases Determined in the Supreme Court of the State of Missouri*, 223:173-194.
3 *Ibid.*
4 *Ibid.*
5 *Ibid.*
6 *Ibid*; *Cherokee Sentinel*, July 17, 1908.
7 *WCR*, Sep. 1, Dec. 17, 1908.
8 *Fort Scott Daily Tribune and Monitor*, Dec. 19, 1908; *Cases Determined*, 173-194; *WCR*, Nov. 24, 1909; *JG*, Nov. 25, 1909.
9 *JNH*, Feb. 18, 1910; *JG*, Feb. 19, 1910.
10 *JG*, Feb. 19, 1910; *JNH*, Mar. 3, 4 1910.
11 *JNH*, Mar. 4, 1910.

Chapter 18
Will Costley and the Unwritten Law

1 *WCR*, Dec. 9, 1909.
2 *WCR*, Oct. 25, 1909; *JG*, Jan. 13, 1910.
3 *WCR*, Oct. 25, Nov. 20, 1909.

4 *WCR*, Oct. 30, 1909.
5 *Ibid.*
6 *WCR*, Oct. 26, Oct. 29, Nov. 16, 1909; *JNH*, Feb. 18, 1910.
7 *WCR*, Nov. 20 1909, Jan. 6, 1910.
8 *WCR*, Jan. 6, 26, 1910.
9 *JNH*, Feb. 17, 1910.
10 *JG*, Feb. 18, 1910.
11 *Ibid.*
12 *Ibid.*
13 *JNH*, Feb. 20, 1910; *WCR*, Feb. 21, 1910.
14 *JG*, May 19, 20, 1910.
15 *JNH*, May 20, 1910.
16 *JG*, May 22 1910.

Chapter 19
Herman Barker's Jasper County Antics

1 Wood, *Ozark Gunfights*, 194; *WCR*, Oct. 31, 1906.
2 *WCR*, Oct. 31, 1906, Sep. 19, 1908.
3 *WCR*, Sep. 19, 1908.
4 *Ibid.*
5 *WCR*, June 25, 1909.
6 *JG*, Oct. 29, Nov. 17, 1912.
7 *JG*, Oct. 29, Nov. 5, 1913.
8 *WCR*, Mar. 9, 10, 16, 1915.
9 *WCR*, Mar. 9, 1915; *JG*, Mar. 10, 1915.
10 *WCR*, Mar. 10, 16, 1915.
11 *JNH*, Nov. 8, 16, 1915; *JG*, Nov. 16, 1915.
12 *JNH*, Nov. 16, 1915; *JG*, Dec. 17, 1915.
13 Wood, *Gunfights*, 194-195; *Springfield Republican*, Jan. 15, Aug. 13, 22, 1916; Montana State Prison Records.
14 *JG*, Jan. 18, 19, 1927; Oklahoma State Prison Records; "Kimes-Terrill Gang."
15 *JG*, Jan. 18, 1927.
16 *Ibid.*
17 *Ibid.*
18 *Ibid.*
19 *JG*, Jan. 20, 23, 1927.
20 *JG*, Apr. 1, Aug. 30, 1927.

21 Wood, *Gunfights*, 197-200.

Chapter 20
Training Ground for the Underhill Brothers

1 US Census, 1870, 1880, 1900; *JNH*, May 22, 1912.
2 MSPRD.
3 *JG*, Jan. 12, 1912; *JNH*, May 22, 1912.
4 *JNH*, May 22, July 4, 1912.
5 *JNH*, Jan. 19, 1913.
6 *JNH*, Feb. 11, 1912.
7 *JNH*, Oct. 29, 1913; MSPRD.
8 JG, Feb. 11, 1919.
9 *JG*, Mar. 18, 1919; MSPRD.
10 *JNH*, Apr. 15, May 23, 1919; Underhill, *Criminals,* 6.
11 *JNH*, Oct. 19, 1919; *JG,* Oct. 21, 1919.
12 *JNH*, June 8, 1920; *JG,* June 8, 1920.
13 *JNH*, June 8, 1920; *JG,* June 8, 1920.
14 *JG*, June 17, 1920; *JNH,* Oct. 15, 1920.
15 *JG*, Oct. 17, 1920.
16 *JG*, Apr. 21, June 21, 1922.
17 *JG*, Dec. 27, 28, 1922.
18 *JG*, Dec. 31, 1922.
19 *JG*, Jan. 11, 12, 1923.
20 *JG*, Feb. 11, 1923.
21 MSPRD.
22 "Wilbur Underhill: He Was Known as the 'Tri-StateTerror,'"
    JG, Nov. 7, 1931.
23 Wood, *Desperadoes*, 185-190.

Chapter 21
One of the Most Gruesome Mysteries Ever

1 *JG*, Nov. 28, 29, 1914.
2 *JG*, Nov. 29, 1914.
3 *JG*, Nov. 29, 1914; *Decatur (IL) Herald*, Jan. 27, 1906; July 1,
    1908, Feb. 13, 1915.
4 *JG*, Nov. 29, 1914; *Bloomington (IL) Pantagraph*, Oct. 13,

1911.

[5] *JG*, Dec. 1, 1914; *Decatur Herald*, Feb. 15, 1915.

[6] *JG*, Dec. 31, 1914, Feb. 10, 1915.

[7] *JNH*, Feb. 22, 1915; *JG*, Feb. 24, 1915.

[8] *JG*, Feb. 28, 1915.

[9] *JNH*, Feb. 28, 1915.

[10] *JNH*, Mar. 2, May 7, 1915; *JG*, May 5, 1915.

[11] *JG*, May 6, 1915; *JNH*, May 7, 1915.

[12] *JG*, May 11, June 4, 1915; *JNH*, May 7, June 1, 1915.

[13] *JG*, July 8, 1916; *JNH*, Aug. 27, 1916, Jan. 21, 1917; MSPRD.

[14] MSPRD; *Jefferson City Daily Capital News*, Oct. 3, 1925.

[15] *SLPD*, Nov. 27, 1937.

Chapter 22
Arkansas Tom

[1] Wood, *Gunfights*, 185-192.

[2] *Ibid.*, 181-184.

[3] *Ibid.*, 186; *JNH*, July 12, 1915.

[4] *JG*, Dec. 14, 1916.

[5] *JG*, Dec. 14, 1916.

[6] *JG*, Feb. 20, 21, 1917; *JNH*, Feb. 19, 1917.

[7] *JG*, Feb. 20, 1917; *JNH*, Feb. 20, 1917.

[8] *JG*, Feb. 21, 1917.

[9] *Neosho Daily Democrat*, 27 Feb., 1917.

[10] MSPRD.

[11] *JG*, Nov. 27, 29, 1923; Wood, *Gunfights*, 189.

[12] *JNH*, Nov. 27, 1923; Wood, *Gunfights*, 189.

[13] *JG*, Nov. 27, 1923; *JNH*, Nov. 27, 1923.

[14] *JG*, Nov. 27, 1923.

[15] *Ibid.*

[16] *Ibid*; Wood, *Gunfights*, 191.

[17] *JG*, Nov. 27, 1923.

[18] *Ibid.*

[19] *JG*, Dec. 1, 25, 1923, Jan. 16, 17, Feb. 6, May 4, 1924.

[20] *JG*, Aug 2, 9, 17, 1924.

[21] *JG*, Aug 17, 1924.

[22] *Ibid.*

[23] *JNH*, Aug 18, 1924.

24 *Ibid.*

Chapter 23
One of the Most Spectacular Cases

1 *JNH*, May 9, 1921; *JG*, May 10, 1921.
2 *JNH*, May 9, 1921; *JG*, May 10 1921.
3 *JG*, May 11, 1921.
4 *JG*, May 12, 1921; *JNH*, May 13, 1921.
5 *JNH*, May 12, 1921; *JG*, May 12, 1921.
6 *JNH*, May 9, 12, 13; *JG* May 13, 1921.
7 *JNH*, May 16, 1921.
8 *Ibid.*
9 *JNH*, May 17, 1921, quoting *Carthage Press.*
10 *JG*, Aug 19, 20, Oct. 22, Nov. 11, 1921.
11 *JG*, Aug. 19, 20, Oct. 22, Nov. 11, 1921, May 26, 1929.
12 *JG*, Nov. 11, 1921.
13 *JG*, Sep. 21, Oct. 1 1922; Apr. 6, 1923.
14 *JG*, May 26, 1929; Oct. 27, 1931, Aug. 27, 1933.
15 *JNH*, Nov. 1, 1941, *JG*, Nov. 2, 1941; MSPRD.

Chapter 24
Jasper County's Only Double Hanging

1 *JG*, Apr. 11, 1922; MSPRD; Soldiers Records; US Census, 1900.
2 *JG*, Apr. 1, 1922.
3 *GWR*, Apr. 14, 1922.
4 *JG*, Apr. 11, 1922.
5 *JG*, Apr. 11, Apr. 14, 1922.
6 *JG*, Apr. 11, 1922.
7 *JG*, Apr. 11. 1922; *Springfield Missouri Republican,* Apr. 15, 1922.
8 *JG*, Apr. 30, May 2, 1922.
9 *JG*, May 2, 3, 1922.
10 *JG*, May 3, 1922.
11 *JG*, May 3, 4, 5, 1922.
12 *JG*, May 6, 1922.

[13] *JG*, May 14, 1922.
[14] *JG*, May 14, June 10, 1922.
[15] *Springfield Leader*, June 21, 1923; *JG*, June 22, 1923.
[16] *JG*, Aug. 1, 1923.
[17] *Ibid.*
[18] *Ibid.*
[19] *JG*, Aug. 2, 1923
[20] *JG*, Aug. 3, 4, 1923.
[21] *JG*, Aug. 4, 5, 1923.

Chapter 25
A Murder Mystery Solved

[1] *JNH*, Oct. 24, 1929.
[2] *JNH*, Oct. 24, 1929.
[3] *JG*, Dec. 25, 1929, Oct. 14, 1931.
[4] *JG*, Oct. 14, 1931.
[5] *JG*, Oct. 14, 1931; US Census, 1900, 1910, 1930.
[6] *JG*, Oct. 14, 1931.
[7] *Ibid.*
[8] *Ibid.*
[9] *JG,* Oct. 16, 17, 1931.
[10] *JG,* Oct. 18 1931.
[11] *JG,* Nov. 5, 1931.
[12] *JG,* Nov. 25, Dec. 1 1931.
[13] *JG,* Dec. 1, 2, 1931.
[14] *JG,* Dec. 2, 1931.
[15] US Census, 1940; *JNH*, Apr. 13, 1940.

Chapter 26
Irene McCann

[1] *JNH*, Feb. 3, 1931.
[2] *JNH*, Feb. 3, 1931; *Gadsden (AL) Daily Times-News*, Feb. 27, 1919.
[3] *JG*, Jan. 8, Apr. 26, 1931; *JNH*, Feb. 3, 1931.
[4] *Springfield Leader*, October 9, 10, Nov. 20, 1930.
[5] *JG*, Dec. 31, 1930, Jan. 28, May 21, 1931; US Census, 1910,

1930.

6 *JNH*, Feb. 3, 1931; *Kansas City (KS) Masonic News*, Nov. 21, 1930; *Jefferson City Post-Tribune*, Nov. 22, 1930.

7 *Council Grove (KS) Republican*, Nov. 22, 1930; *Galena (KS) Journal*, Dec. 5, 1930; *JG*, Dec. 31, 1930, Jan. 1, 1931.

8 *JG*, Jan. 1, 1931; *Neosho Daily News*, Dec. 15, 1930.

9 *JG*, Dec. 31, 1930, Jan. 1, May 20, 1931; "State v. McCann."

10 *Sedalia Democrat*, Dec. 15, 1930; *JG*, Dec. 31, 1930.

11 *JG*, Dec. 31, 1930, Jan. 1, 1931.

12 *JG*, Jan. 1, 1931.

13 *Ibid.*

14 *JG*, Jan. 3, 1931.

15 *JNH*, Jan. 19, Feb. 3, 1931.

16 *JNH*, Feb. 3, 1931.

17 *JG*, Apr. 21, 23, 26, 1931.

18 *JG*, May 20, 1931.

19 *JG*, May 21, 1931.

20 *JG*, May 22, 1931.

21 *JNH*, July 9, 1931.

22 *JG*, Nov. 11, 1931; *SLPD*, Nov. 10, 1931.

23 *JG*, Nov. 11, 1931; *SLPD*, Nov. 10, 1931.

24 *Racine (WI) Journal-News*, Nov. 17, 1931; *Jefferson City Post-Tribune*, Nov. 11, 1931.

25 "State v. McCann"; *JG*, May 20, 22, 1932.

26 *Sedalia Democrat*, Dec. 13, 1932.

27 *Chicago Tribune*, Jan. 16, 1934; *San Francisco Chronicle*, Apr. 8, 1934.

28 *Jefferson City Post-Tribune*, Jan. 17, 1934; *Jeff City Daily Capital News*, Jan. 18, 1936; Iowa Death Records.

29 *Carthage Press*, Dec. 23, 1954; *Los Angeles Times*, Nov. 15, 1958; Jo Ellis, "New Book Recalls Crime Drama from Area's Past," *JG*, Oct. 11, 2015; Find A Grave, Memorial #85912810.

Chapter 27
The Killing of Coyne Hatten

1 *JG*, May 17, 1931.

2 *JG*, May 17, 21, 1931.

3 "State v. Creighton."

4 *JG*, May 17, 1931.

5 *SLPD*, May 18, 1931; *Sedalia Democrat*, May 19, 1931; *JG*, May 20, 1931.

6 *Sedalia Democrat*, May 19, 1931; *Chillicothe Constitution-Tribune*, May 19, 1931; *JG*, May 20, 1931.

7 *JG*, May 20, 1931.

8 *Ibid.*

9 *JG*, May 21, 1931; *Lincoln (NE) Star*, Feb. 26, 1931; MSPRD.

10 *JG*, May 21, 1931.

11 *Ibid.*

12 *JG*, May 22, 1931.

13 *Ibid.*

14 *JG*, June 25, 26, 1931.

15 *JG*, June 27, 1931.

16 *Chillicothe Constitution-Tribune*, July 10, 1931; *Macon (MO) Chronicle-Herald*, July 24, 1931.

17 *Chillicothe Constitution-Tribune*, Aug 30, 1932.

18 *Maryville Daily Forum*, Jan. 17, 1933.

19 *Chillicothe Constitution-Tribune*, Feb. 22, 1934; *JG*, Dec. 30, 1934; *JNH*, Sep. 4, 1941.

20 MSPRD.

21 *JNH*, Sep. 23, 1954, July 19, 1955; *Macon Chronicle-Herald*, Jan. 25, 1955; *SLPD*, Jan. 30, 1956.

Chapter 28
Typical Ozarks Hillbillies

1 *JG*, Nov. 17, 27, 1931; US Census, 1930; "State v. Worden." A very similar version of this chapter was first published in *Yanked Into Eternity*, one of the author's previous books.

2 *JG*, Nov. 17, 27, 1931; "State v. Worden."

3 *JG*, Jan. 30, 31, 1932; "State v. Worden."

4 *JG*, Nov. 17, 27, 1931.

5 *JG*, Nov. 17, 27, 1931

6 *JG*, Nov. 18, 27, 1931, Feb. 10, 1933.

7 *JG*, Nov. 27, Dec. 13, 1931, Mar. 4, 1932.

8 *JG*, Nov. 27, 28, 1931.

9 *JG*, Nov. 27, 28, 29, 1931.

[10] *JG*, Dec. 9, 1931.

[11] *Ibid.*

[12] *JG*, Jan. 28, 1932.

[13] *JG*, Jan. 29, 30, 1932.

[14] *JG*, Jan. 30, 1932.

[15] *JG*, Jan. 31, 1932.

[16] *JG*, Jan. 31, 1932; *JNH*, Feb. 1, 6, 1932.

[17] *JG*, Feb. 19, 1932.

[18] *JNH*, Feb. 23, 1932.

[19] *JNH*, Feb. 23, 1932; *JG*, Mar. 1, 3 1932.

[20] *JNH*, Mar. 3, 1932.

[21] *Ibid.*

[22] *JG*, Apr. 19, May 24, 1932.

[23] *JG*, Dec. 15, 28, 1932, Jan 17, 19, 1933.

[24] *JG*, Feb. 7, 9, 10, 1933

[25] *JG*, Feb. 11, 1933.

[26] *JG*, Feb. 14, 1933; Missouri Death Certificates.

[27] *Van Buren Current Local*, Feb. 16, 1933; Missouri Death Certificates; Worden newspaper clippings, Jasper County Records Center; *JG*, Feb. 11, 1933.

Chapter 29
Bonnie and Clyde

[1] Milner, *The Lives and Times of Bonnie and Clyde*, 51.

[2] Milner, 52; *JG*, Dec. 1, 1932.

[3] *JG*, Dec. 1, 1932.

[4] *Ibid.*

[5] *Ibid.*

[6] *Ibid.*

[7] *Ibid.*

[8] *Ibid.*

[9] *Ibid.*

[10] *JG*, Dec. 1, 1932; Milner, 52.

[11] *Springfield Leader and Press*, Apr. 23, 1968; *Springfield Press*, Jan. 27, 1933.

[12] *Springfield Leader and Press*, Apr. 23, 1968; *Springfield Press*, Jan. 27, 1933.

[13] *Springfield Press*, Jan. 27, 1933; *Springfield Leader and*

Press, Apr. 23, 1968.
[14] *Springfield Press*, Jan. 27, 1933.
[15] *Ibid.*
[16] *Ibid.*
[17] *Ibid.*
[18] *Ibid.*
[19] *Ibid.*
[20] *Ibid.*
[21] *JNH,* Feb. 1, 1933.
[22] Wood, *Gunfights*, 209-215.

Chapter 30
A Robbery Gone Bad

[1] *JNH*, Mar. 5, 1934.
[2] *Ibid.*
[3] *JNH*, Mar. 5, 6, 1934.
[4] *JNH*, Mar. 5, 1934.
[5] *JNH*, Mar. 6, 1934
[6] *Ibid.*
[7] *JG*, Mar. 7, 1934.
[8] *JNH*, Mar. 8, 1934.
[9] *JNH*, Mar. 17, 26, 27, 1934; *JG*, June 12, 21, 1934.
[10] *JNH*, Mar. 27, 28, 1934; *JG*, Mar. 29, 1935.
[11] *JG*, Apr. 17, 19, 20, May 4, 1934.
[12] *JG*, June 9, 12, 21, 22, 1934.
[13] *JG*, June 29, 30, July 18, 1934.
[14] *JG*, Aug. 5, Sep. 13, 1934.
[15] *JG*, Mar. 29, June 11, 1935.
[16] *JG*, Sep. 12, 13, 1935.
[17] *JG*, Nov. 6, 1935, Mar. 8, 15, 1936.
[18] *JNH*, June 30, 1936.
[19] *JNH*, Feb. 19, 1937.

Chapter 31
Jealousy and a Quarrel

[1] *JNH*, Aug. 4, 1938; *JG*, Aug. 6, 1938.

2 US Census, 1930, 1940; *JG*, June 21, 1938; *JNH*, Aug. 4, 1938.

3 *JNH*, Aug. 4, 1938.

4 *JNH*, Aug. 4, 1938; *JG*, Aug. 6, 11, 1938.

5 *JG*, Sep. 27, 1938.

6 *JG*, Sep. 28, 1938.

7 *Ibid.*

8 *Ibid.*

9 *JG*, Sep. 28, 1938; *Jefferson City Post-Tribune*, Nov. 14, 1938.

10 *JG*, July 11, 1939; "State v. Jackson."

11 *JG*, Oct. 8, 15, 24, Dec. 7, 1939.

12 *JG*, Dec. 6, 7, 1939.

13 *Jefferson City Post-Tribune*, July 3, 1940; *Jefferson City Daily Capitol News*, Aug. 14, 1940.

14 *JNH*, Sep. 20, 1940; *Jefferson City Daily Capitol News*, Sep. 20, 1940.

Chapter 32
Slain at a Nightclub on West Seventh

1 *JG*, Feb. 23, 1940; *JNH*, May 13, 1940.

2 *JG*, Feb. 23, Mar. 1, 1940.

3 *JG*, Feb. 23, 1940.

4 *Ibid.*

5 *Ibid.*

6 *Ibid.*

7 *Ibid.*

8 *Ibid.*

9 *Ibid.*

10 *Ibid.*

11 *Ibid.*

12 *Ibid.*

13 *JG*, Feb. 24, 1940.

14 *JG*, Feb. 27, 1940.

15 *JG*, Feb. 29, 1940.

16 *JG*, Mar. 14, 1940.

17 *JG*, Apr. 9, 1940; *JDH*, May 9, 13, 1940.

[18] *JG*, May 15, 1940.

[19] *JNH*, May 15, 1940.

[20] *JG*, May 16, 1940.

[21] *JDH*, May 16, 1940.

[22] *Ibid.*

[23] *JDH*, May 17, 1940.

[24] *JG*, May 18, 21, Oct. 11, 1940.

[25] *JG*, Nov. 4, 1940, Jan. 7, 12, 28, Mar. 29, 1941.

[26] *JG*, Apr. 2, 15, 1941.

[27] *JNH*, Sep. 23-27, 1941; *JG*, Sep. 28, 1941.

[28] *JG*, May 9, 1944, Feb. 1, 1949.

Chapter 33
Badman Bill Cook

[1] *JG*, Jan. 5, 20, 1951.

[2] *JG*, Jan. 20, 1951.

[3] US Census, 1930, 1940; *SLPD*, Jan. 21, 1951; Criminal Identification Record, Intermediate Reform for Young Men, Missouri State Archives, Jefferson City, Missouri.

[4] Missouri Death Certificates database; *SLPD*, Jan. 21, 1951; *JG*, Jan. 16, 1951.

[5] *JG*, Jan. 16, 1951.

[6] *Ibid.*

[7] *JG*, Jan. 16, 1951; *SLPD*, Jan. 21, 1951; MSPRD.

[8] *JG*, Jan. 16, 1951; *SLPD*, Jan. 21, 1951.

[9] *JG*, Jan. 16, 1951; *SLPD*, Jan. 21, 1951.

[10] *JG*, Jan. 20, 1951, Nov. 29, 1951; US Census, 1930.

[11] *JG*, Jan. 20, 1951.

[12] *JG*, Jan. 16, 1951.

[13] *JG*, Jan. 16, 20, 1951.

[14] JG, Nov. 29, 1951; *Long Beach (CA) Independent*, Jan. 7, 1951.

[15] *JG*, Jan. 4, 5, 6, 1951.

[16] *Long Beach Independent*, Jan. 7, 1951.

[17] *JG*, Jan. 16, 1951.

[18] *JG*, Jan. 20, 1951.

[19] *Oklahoma City Daily Oklahoman*, June 2, 1951; *JG*, Dec. 13, 1952.

[20] *JG*, Dec. 13, 1952; *JNH*, Dec. 17, 1952.

Chapter 34
The Brutal Assault on Lisa Schuh

[1] *JNH*, July 24, 1961.

[2] *Ibid.*

[3] *Ibid.*

[4] *Ibid.*

[5] *JNH*, July 24, 1961; *JG*, July 25, 1961; *Springfield Leader-Press*, Sep. 22, 1961.

[6] *JNH*, July 24, 1961.

[7] *JNH*, July 24, 1961; *JG*, July 25, 1961.

[8] *JG*, July 27, 28, 1961.

[9] *Springfield Leader-Press*, Sep. 22, 1961.

[10] *Springfield Daily News*, Sep. 14, 1961; *Springfield Leader and Press*, Sep. 15, 26, Oct. 17, 1961.

[11] *Springfield Daily News*, Nov. 6, 8, 9, 1961; *Springfield Leader and Press*, Nov.10, 1961; *JNH*, Nov. 9, 1961.

[12] *JNH*, Dec. 28, 1961, Jan. 3, 4, 1962; *JG*, July 9, 1963.

[13] *JG*, Aug. 20, 21, 1963.

[14] *JG*, Feb. 11, 14, 21, 28, 1964.

[15] *Jefferson City Post-Tribune*, Mar. 6, 1964.

[16] *JG*, Feb. 18, 1965; *JNH*, Apr. 30, 1965.

[17] *JG*, Dec. 4, 1994.

Chapter 35
Murder at the Cold Spot

[1] *JNH*, Mar. 3, 1967.

[2] *JG*, Mar. 7, 1967; *JNH*, Apr. 14, 1967.

[3] *JNH*, Mar. 31, Apr. 14, 24, 1967.

[4] *JG*, May 5, 18, 1967; *JNH*, June 14, 1967.

[5] *JG*, Feb. 14, 17, 1968.

[6] *JNH*, Feb. 21, June 3, 1968; *JG*, Apr. 16, 17, 1968.

[7] *JG*, June 17, Aug. 24, 1968; *JNH*, Sep. 30, Nov. 21, 1968, Jan. 10, 1969.

[8] *JNH*, Mar. 11, 13, 14, 1969; *JG*, Mar. 15, 20, 1969.

[9] *JNH*, Apr. 10, 18, 1969, June 8, 1970; *JG*, Apr. 29, 1969; "State v. Sinderson."

[10] Sinderson Commutation Papers.

Chapter 36
The Beating Death of Steven Newberry

[1] *JG*, Dec. 9, 1987.

[2] Jones, "Satanists' Trail."

[3] *Ibid.*

[4] *Ibid.*

[5] *Ibid.*

[6] Jones, "Satanists' Trail"; *JG*, Dec. 10, 1987.

[7] Jones, "Satanists' Trail"; *JG*, Dec. 9, 1987.

[8] *JG*, Dec. 9, 12, 1987.

[9] Jones, "Satanists' Trail"; *JG*, Dec. 24, 1987.

[10] *JG*, Dec. 24, 1987; Jones, "Satanists' Trail."

[11] *JG*, Dec. 24, 1987; Jones, "Satanists' Trail."

[12] *JG*, Apr. 27, May 3, 1988.

[13] *JG*, May 4, 1988.

[14] *Ibid.*

[15] *JG*, May 4, 5, 1988.

[16] *JG*, May 5, 1988; *Springfield News-Leader*, May 6, 1988.

[17] *JG*, June 17, 18, 1988; *Springfield News-Leader*, June 17, 1988.

[18] *JG*, June 19, July 12, 1988.

[19] State of Missouri v. Theron Reed Roland; *Springfield News-Leader*, Mar. 14, 1991.

[20] *JG*, Oct. 23, 2018.

Bibliography

Criminal Identification Record, Intermediate Reformatory for Young Men, Algoa, Missouri. Missouri State Archives. Jefferson City, Missouri.

Find A Grave. https://www.findagrave.com.

Harper, Kimberly. *White Man's Heaven: The Lynching and Expulsion of Blacks in the Southern Ozarks, 1894-1909.* Fayetteville: University of Arkansas Press, 2010.

History of Newton, Lawrence, Barry and McDonald Counties, Missouri. Chicago: Goodspeed Publishing Co., 1888.

An Illustrated Historical Atlas Map of Jasper County, Mo. n.p. Brink, McDonough & Co., 1876.

Iowa Death Records, FamilySearch.org.

Jasper County Circuit Court Records. Jasper County Records Center. Carthage, Missouri.

Jones, Tamara. "Satanists' Trail: Dead Pets to a Human Sacrifice." *Los Angeles Times*, October 19, 1988.

Kansas State Penitentiary at Lansing Records. Kansas State Historical Society. https://www.kshs.org/p/kansas-state-penitentiary-at-lansing-records/17871.

"Kimes-Terrill Gang." *Wikipedia*. https://en.wikipedia.org/ /wiki/Kimes-Terrill_Gang.

Milner, E. R. *The Lives and Times of Bonnie and Clyde.* Carbondale: Southern Illinois University Press, 2003.

Missouri Death Certificates database. Missouri State Archives. https://s1.sos.mo.gov/records/Archives/ArchivesMvc/ DeathCertificates#searchDB.

Missouri's Judicial Records database. Missouri State Archives. https://s1.sos.mo. gov/Records/Archives/ArchivesDb/ JudicialRecords.

Missouri State Penitentiary Records database. Missouri State Archives. https://s1.sos.mo.gov/records/archives/

archivesdb/msp/.

Missouri State Penitentiary Register. Missouri State Archives. Jefferson City, Missouri.

Montana State Prison Records. Montana Historical Society. Helena, Montana.

Oklahoma State Penitentiary Records. Oklahoma Historical Society. https://www.okhistory.org/research/prison search.

"Patrolman Claude Brice." Officer Down Memorial Page. https://www.odmp.org/officer/2243-patrolman-claude-brice.

Reports of Cases Determined in the Supreme Court of the State of Missouri Between April 15 and May 21, 1901, vol. 162. Perry S. Rader, Reporter. Columbia, MO: E. W. Stephens, 1901.

Reports of Cases Determined in the Supreme Court of the State of Missouri, vol. 223. Perry S. Rader, Reporter. Columbia: MO: E. W. Stephens, 1910.

Robert Eugene Sinderson Commutation Papers. Missouri State Archives. Jefferson City, Missouri.

Soldiers Records: War of 1812-World War I. Missouri Sate Archives. Jefferson City. https://s1.sos.mo.gov/records/archives/archivesdb/soldiers/.

"State of Missouri v. Theron Reed Roland." *FindaCase.com.* http://mo.findacase.com/research/wfrmDocViewer.as px/xq/fac.19910312_0024.MO.htm/qx.

"State v. Creighton, 52 S.W.2d 556 (Mo. 1932)." *Supreme Court of Missouri.* https://www.courtlistener.com/opinion/3549651/state-v-creighton/.

"State v. Jackson, 344 Mo. 1055." *Casetext.* Supreme Court of Division Two, July 7, 1939. http://casetext.com/case/state-v-Jackson-1110.

"State v. McCann." Supreme Court of Missouri, Div. 2, Feb. 17, 1932. *Casetext.* https://casetext.com/case/state-v-mccann-24.

"State v. Sinderson." *Justia US Law.* https://law.justia.com/cases/missouri/supreme-court/1970/54691-0.html.

"State v. Worden, 56 S.W.2d 595 (Mo. 1932)." Supreme Court of Missouri. *Court Listener.* courtlistener.com/opinion/

3552390/state-v-worden/.

Sturges, J. A. ed. *Illustrated History of McDonald County, Missouri.* Pineville, MO: n.p., 1897.

US Census. FamilySearch. https://www.familysearch.org/en/.

"Wilbur Underhill: He Was Known as the 'Tri-StateTerror.'" https://major-olinski.com/OUTLAWS/UNDERHILL. html.

Wood, Larry. *Desperadoes of the Ozarks.* Gretna, LA: Pelican Publishing Co., 2011.

Wood, Larry. *Ozarks Gunfights and Other Notorious Incidents.* Gretna, LA: Pelican Publishing Co., 2010.

Underhill, Robert. *Criminals and Folk Heroes.* New York: Algora Publishing, 2015.

Index

About the Author

Larry Wood is a retired public school teacher and a freelance writer specializing in local and regional history. He has published two historical novels, eighteen nonfiction history books, and approximately 500 magazine stories and articles. He has also contributed short stories to several anthologies, including the popular *Mysteries of the Ozarks* series.

Wood has won numerous writing awards from organizations like the Missouri Writers Guild and the Ozarks Writers League. In 2011, he received the Walter Williams Award, given by the Missouri Writers Guild for best major work, and he has won the same organization's Show-Me Award for best book about Missouri four times. In 2016, he was named an honorary lifetime member of the Missouri Writers Guild. Wood maintains a blog on Missouri and Ozarks history at www.ozarks-history.blogspot.com.

Made in the USA
Columbia, SC
14 March 2020